Tibetan Journey

Tibetan Journey

ALEXANDRA DAVID-NEEL

BOOK FAITH INDIA

Published by
BOOK FAITH INDIA
416, Express Tower
Azadpur Commercial Complex
Delhi-110033
(INDIA)
First Indian Edition 1992
© Publisher
ISBN 81-7303- 004-9
Rs. 350

Printed at
Ram Printograph
Delhi-110051

Author's Note

FOR the sake of simplicity all Tibetan words in this book have been transliterated phonetically without regard to the real Tibetan spelling, which is very misleading to the uninitiated. For instance: *cha,* bird, is written *bya*; *tulku,* an incarnated lama, is written *sprulsku*; *gyenpa,* to adorn, to decorate, is written *brgyanpa*; and so on. The phonetic transliteration will enable readers to know—approximately, at least—how the Tibetans themselves pronounce the Tibetan words that appear in the narrative.

I wish to express my deep gratitude to Miss Violet Sydney for the most valuable help she has so ungrudgingly given me in the preparation of this English account of my journey.

Contents

Contents

Illustrations

ix

ILLUSTRATIONS

x

Tibetan Journey

THE ROAD TO LABRANG TASHIKYIL

APEERLESS sun shines in the blue sky. The yellow frozen earth glitters in the light of morning.

It is early February. Snow still covers the surrounding summits and lies heaped along the narrow alleys of the great Kum-Bum monastery, but the roads are transfigured in the gay light of Spring. Through every pebble, every blade of grass, they sing, as only roads can sing, the joyous enticing songs of travel.

The luggage-laden mules, decorated with red pompoms, impatiently shake their neck bells. I am ready to embark upon a journey which promises many difficulties. It consists in following the long track of borderland that lies between China proper and Tibet, which is inhabited by various more or less independent tribes, some of Tibetan and others of mixed and unknown origin, who resist with equal obstinacy the authority of both the Tibetan and Chinese governments.

I mean to cross that country incognito, under the guise of a lamaist nun of rank, accompanied by a steward and a few men servants. My adopted son, who is an authentic Tibetan lama, is to act the part of steward, while all the servants actually belong to the inferior lamaist clergy. In anticipation I taste the joyous excitement of such an adventure; yet some regrets cast a melancholy shadow over my departure.

I would willingly have spent the rest of my days in the lulling calm of the monastic citadel where I have lived for the past two years and eight months. My small house with its amusing frescoes was so peaceful, tucked away in the corner of a tiny cloister in the princely palace of Pegyai Tulku. From my balcony I had grown accustomed to contemplate the golden roofs of the temples and, beyond them, the grassy slopes where grazed the shaggy yaks and the stately camels of the Mongolian caravans. Seated there, in the evenings, I liked to listen to the grave harmonies of the sacred music, when the lamas serenaded the gods from the high terraces of the great hall. But still more I valued the serenity of the hours passed in following the thoughts of ancient Buddhist sages, in the books that had been taken for me from the sealed bookcases, where they lay in wrappings of iridescent yellow brocade. It was delightful to study and meditate in such surroundings; the mind experienced, to the point of intoxication, the subtle voluptuousness of solitude and silence.

And yet, I am leaving Kum-Bum. To have definitely established myself there, I should have to become a member of the monastery, and my sex debarred me from this right.

Tibetan custom requires that at the departure of a distinguished guest, he must be accompanied for some considerable distance on his road by those with whom he has stayed. The steward and *trapas*[1] of Lama Pegyai wished to conform to this practice and to escort me for several miles, but I insisted that they should save themselves such useless fatigue, and I dismissed them near a little bridge that marked the boundary of the monastic city. There, we exchanged good wishes and the usual complimentary scarves,[2] and my little caravan went its way.

---

[1] All the lamaist monks of the lower clergy are called *trapas* (pupils). Ecclesiastical dignitaries alone have the right to the title of *lama* (written blama—superior). However, by courtesy, a distinguished, learned, or aged monk, is often called *lama*. I have followed this custom in the present book by giving the title of "lama" to all those to whom I would give it were I speaking to them.

[2] *Kadas* (kha btags): scarves that are presented and received on all occasions as tokens of respect, of politeness, of welcome, etc.

THE LAMA YONGDEN IN TRAVELLING DRESS :
TOBGYAL HOLDING THE BRIDLE

MY SMALL PARTY LEAVING KUM-BUM
MONASTERY

My son[1] and I continued on foot as far as the top of the last hill from where the monastery could be seen. There, in the snow, among the stones, we lighted our incense sticks in honour of the Founder of the Gelugspa sect, Tsong Khapa, who was born at the spot where Kum-Bum has since been built to glorify his memory.

While the thin threads of perfumed smoke rose in front of us, I gazed for the last time upon the radiant picture of the great monastery with its many white buildings, its red palaces, and its golden roofed "houses of the gods."[2] Reverently my servants prostrated themselves, Yongden uncovered, and I bowed. Silent, motionless, we listened to the voices of the hopes and fears that surged within us. Joyous confidence and painful misgiving mingled and fought, for different reasons, in each of us. To start on a long journey, in this part of Asia, is always a step into the unknown.

At length, I turned away, breaking the charm that held us. The others followed me down the path that lay on the other side of the mountain. A few paces, and Kum-Bum was out of sight.

Temperamentally there is nothing of the Don Quixote about me, but although I do not seek adventures, they are never long in coming. The very day of our departure, we nearly had a fight with the leaders of a Mongolian caravan. Between Lusart and Sining, on one of those unspeakable Chinese roads bedded between steep earth walls, twelve to fifteen feet high, that are just wide enough to admit the passing of a cart, we ran against a caravan of camels.

It had been agreed that, by turns, one of the servants

---

[1] Lama Yongden, well known to the readers of *My Journey to Lhasa* and *With Mystics and Magicians in Tibet*, is a young Tibetan scholar who has accompanied me on my travels and who has become my adopted son.

[2] *Lha Khang* (habitation of a god) is the name given to temples by Tibetans.

should follow the luggage mules on foot. Thus, only five of us—including myself—were provided with mounts. In order, however, not to subject any of the men to the humiliation, to which a Tibetan is particularly sensitive, of leaving the monastery on foot while his companions were mounted, I had lent Sönam my big black mule. In the meantime I travelled in a Chinese carriage, one of those old-fashioned springless carts of northern China, which for lack of roads, cannot be used beyond Sining and Kum-Bum, where the great Tibetan solitudes begin.

It was this vehicle that obstructed the road in face of a hundred camels laden with merchandise. Arrested in their progress, pushed by those that continued their mechanical march at the tail of the procession, the great beasts cried out as they jostled one another in the narrow passage.

At the moment, I happened to be stretching my cramped limbs, by walking on the top of one of the walls bordering the road. From this vantage ground the situation was clearly visible. For them to pass one another was an impossibility, either the camels or the cart would have to go back, and it was a case of backing in one direction or the other for about a mile.

Custom requires that before entering a cutting of this kind, the driver of a beast or cart must call out so as to warn others who may be coming in at the opposite end. We had not heard the Mongolians' hail, and as to my men, I think they had likewise omitted to herald their presence. Doubtless, the fault lay with both parties, but in the East it is just this fact that matters the least. What must be safe-guarded before all else is one's prestige. Let anything happen rather than "lose face" think the Chinese and Tibetans. My boys shared this conviction, and, lest I should forfeit their esteem, which would be a serious matter during a hazardous journey such as ours I felt obliged to conform to their opinion. In the present

4

case, the " face " demanded the retreat of the camels and the triumphant advance of my cart.

"Go back! " said Yongden to the Mongolian who walked at the head of the caravan and who, at the moment, was flattened between my horsemen and his hustling beasts.

"Go back! " echoed my servants.

Two of the other drivers ran up to the ridge that overlooked the passage.

"Impossible! " one of them exclaimed, " we have more than a hundred animals and you have only a single cart. As to your mules, it is easy for them to turn round."

I continued to watch the proceedings from above. Obviously, the good man was right. Logic, commonsense, judgment were in accord : it was for our cart to back. . . . But there was the " face ", and compared with it, logic, commonsense and judgment are paltry considerations, in that country. Were I to give way, I should pay a heavy penalty for my weakness, when, one day, real danger threatened and I should need my men to stand firm and put their whole trust in me. But what possible connection could all this have with the backing of a cart in a road cutting? None, but I could not change the mentality of my travelling companions.

"Go back! " said Yongden in answer to the Mongol's objection.

"Go back! " re-echoed the others.

The argument grew heated, insults were exchanged, threats, and, adding to the uproar, came the camels' discordant cries. Our frightened mules tried to rear, but on being unable to, for lack of space, they turned and bit one another. There was a chaotic scene at the bottom of the ravine.

A Mongol lifted his gun. Matters were becoming serious. That armed challenge now made it impossible for me to give way, even had I wished to.

"We, too, have our guns," retorted my men, who

5

were accustomed to live in the *chang thangs*[1] where skir-
mishes are frequent, and they unslung their rifles.

Were they going to kill one another? . . .

The Mongols probably thought that people with such
determination must occupy a peculiarly high rung of the
social ladder, and that to wound or kill one of us would
bring serious consequences to the murderer. They
decided to withdraw.

The camels, which were attached to one another by
their noses and tails in long strings of eight to ten beasts.
were, owing to their bulk and slowness, ill-suited for such
a manœuvre. While the drivers were busy with them,
I quietly slipped from my post of observation, re-entered
the cart, cause of all the trouble, and, on the passage
becoming free, travelled with great dignity to the end of
it. The "face was saved".

All the same, I was not mandarin enough at heart to
rejoice at my victory. Catching the attention of the
camelmen, who were following me with their eyes, I
signed to them and held up two Chinese dollars, then,
passing my hand under the curtains that surrounded my
carriage, I dropped the two large pieces of money. The
Mongols understood my gesture; they would pick up the
money after I had gone by and praise me for my charity.
My people had not seen anything . . . the "face"
remained "saved".

The very beginning of my journey was spoilt by the
death of two fine young dogs that had been born in
my house in Kum-Bum. I had taken them with me as
travelling companions and guardians of the camp at
night.

Soon after leaving Sining, one of them, a Mongolian
griffon, suddenly developed disquieting symptoms of
rabies. He tried to run away, could no longer swallow,

[1] The solitudes of Northern Tibet inhabited only by herdsmen living
under tents.

seemed afraid of his food, shook his head, and barked in a curious way.

I wonder whether a novelist has ever tried to describe the feelings of a person who is travelling with a mad animal. I doubt it; such a thing would appear too improbable. In the West, the fate of such a dog is quickly settled.

But we were in Asia. I was with Buddhists and monks, and not one of them would have killed the poor beast; and, as to me, I should never have ordered it. The only thing to do was to take precautions.

The little griffon was put into a basket, which was strapped on to a mule, and we continued our way.

When we reached Lanchow, the dog died after much suffering. Then his brother fell ill. His death was still more heart-rending. For two days he remained crouched against me, refusing to leave me. He stood up on his hind legs, with his front paws on my knees, and looked intently into my eyes. Sometimes he laid his little black nose upon my cheek.

What was it that he wished to say to me? . . . "I must go" or " I want to stay, keep me! "

Did he realize my powerlessness; did he seek help elsewhere? He went to the stables, and stopping by each of the mules, seemed to implore their aid. The kindly beasts, knowing him for a comrade, lowered their heads to sniff at him and moved with care, lest they should hit the tiny sufferer that staggered feebly, in the straw, among their great legs.

It was the end. I could not keep him, any more than I had been able to keep his brother.

One evening, when the moon was veiled in mist, we silently buried him at the foot of a hillock, at the edge of a Chinese cemetery. The respect in which such ground is held would ensure to the poor little fellow a peaceful dissolution, and protect him from the knife of the native "furrier" who sells dog skins.

7

Some may think: What ridiculous sentimentality. They were only animals. But this would be a very superficial view to take. What matter whether, according to our human estimation, the value of a being that disappears be great or small? The cruel enigma of its disappearance still remains. Death had come: it had immobilized a joyous activity, extinguished a flame of intelligence, transformed into an inert thing—which decomposition would soon dissolve—a being that had thought, felt, loved. Its terrible mystery forced itself on to me and cast a melancholy shadow over my journey.

I did not linger in Lanchow, as I knew the town well. Built on the banks of the Yellow River, the capital of Kansu is the most important city in North-West China. To find its equal it would be necessary to go to far distant Tih-wa-fu (Urumchi) in Sinkiang (Chinese Turkestan), and this region of Turkish Moslems is, correctly speaking, no longer China. Many other Chinese towns are richer in monuments than Lanchow, which is noticeably wanting in this respect, but its open aspect, its large and airy streets, please the Westerner. He feels more at home there, less in China perhaps, than in Chengtu, the opulent capital of Szechwan, or in some of the other cities of the "Middle Republic".

The people of Kansu are also very different from those of the coast or the Southern provinces. They do not in any way resemble the little rice-eating Chinamen, whom many foreigners take as representing the uniform type of China's inhabitants. The men of Kansu are usually tall, well-made, white-skinned rather than yellow, and often handsome. Their chief food consists of bread and a kind of macaroni; rice is only an accessory. In Kansu, life in general is more free, less limited by rite and custom than in the Central provinces; the influence of alien races is clearly visible there. The pure Chinese, who are well aware of this fact, often show a certain

8

A BRIDGE IN LANCHOW

contempt of their compatriots of the borders, in whom they do not recognize their blood, and whom they sometimes call "barbarians"—an unjustifiable attitude.

Situated at about 1,800 miles from Pekin, and not served by any railway, Lanchow[1] easily escapes Central Government control. It has probably always been thus, and it is doubtful whether the Administrative Board that has its seat at present in Nankin will be more successful than its predecessors in forcing obedience upon far-off Kansu. Be that as it may, the notables of Lanchow have succeeded more than once in demonstrating their independence of the Chinese Government.

To go to Labrang Tashikyil I had the choice of several routes, but as at that time the Mohammedans were again occupying public attention to a marked degree, I was curious about them, and took the route by Hojo, the stronghold of Islamism in Kansu.

In order not to attract too much attention, and also to save money, I had decided to travel as modestly as possible. To this end I had bought a horse and seven mules, intending to hire during the course of the journey any other beasts that might be needed to carry our luggage. Besides, I had so calculated the weight of this luggage that, by my servants going on foot, the six mules would be able to carry it all. If we were forced by circumstances to take with us a greater supply of food than usual, we would be able to do so by using for this purpose the horse Yongden rode as well as the big black mule I had reserved for myself. As we were all good walkers this prospect did not alarm us very much.

[1] A Railway had been planned long before the Great War, but the work was stopped near Honan, and had not been resumed at the time of my journey. The portion of the way from the end of the line to Lanchow, which had to be done by cart, took usually about 28 days to travel over. Since then, the railway line has been extended, and from its end, motor-cars reach Lanchow in six days.

At Lanchow I had occasion to congratulate myself on my foresight. All the muleteers refused to go to Hojo, fearing to have their beasts stolen or to be themselves maltreated by the Mohammedans. The journey there was represented as being highly dangerous, and the people begged me to take another route. However, I seldom allow myself to be dissuaded from doing what I have planned, and at last I found a man willing to hire me three mules and accompany us as far as the dread city.

The way was not without interest. We ferried across the Tao and then entered a region of arid mountains, where the reflection from the chalk white soil was almost blinding.

Misfortune still continued to dog our steps. Shortly after crossing the river, Yongden was taken ill with a violent attack of fever. I gave him quinine, but it had little affect. Nevertheless he insisted on our continuing the journey, and, although he had passed a bad night, we resumed our march early next morning. After valiantly fighting a growing weakness until nearly evening, he suddenly fainted. Our boys had hardly time to prevent him from falling from his horse, and he collapsed at the side of the road.

We were not far from a village, but there was no inn. Realizing our difficulty, the old " akon "[1] of the local mosque offered us hospitality. His tiny dwelling consisted of one room, a kitchen, and a stable that gave on to a court, bordered on the far side by the wall of the little mosque.

The good man and his wife gave up their room to the invalid and retired into the kitchen. Yongden was delirious and only half conscious; his incoherent muttering showed that his mind was filled with thoughts about his own country.

[1] It is the title that the Mohammedans of Kansu give to the one who directs the prayers and fulfils other religious duties.

The one among my servants who acted as cook lit a fire in the corner of the yard and prepared supper. This was done so as to avoid contaminating our host's kitchen, by bringing into it the flesh of an animal that had not been killed according to the Mohammedan rite. I had already carefully assured them that I had no pork among my provisions. When the soup was ready, I too sat down in the yard to eat.

Around me everything was whitewashed: the tiny house, the walls of the enclosure, the mosque and its minaret. No magical figure, printed on red or yellow paper, decorated the door; no ancestral altar, no statue of a deity was to be seen in the interior. A very different atmosphere from that which pervades the Chinese towns emanated from all things. The sun was setting. Very dignified in his long black robe, our aged host ascended the humble minaret and, in an attenuated but firm voice, proclaimed the oneness of Allah and convoked the faithful to prayer. Then, in the clear sky, a thin crescent moon rose above a tall cypress and Islam reigned supreme.

The next day Yongden again insisted on our continuing our journey. He declared that nothing would contribute more effectively to his recovery than to leave the district where he had got the fever. There might be something in what he said; and, anyway, it was impossible for us to take unfair advantage of the old couple's hospitality.

Our way continued through parched country, where the inhabitants depend entirely on what water they collect in cisterns during the rainy season. This dirty stagnant liquid, which we were obliged to use for our tea and for cooking, was hardly suitable for a feverish patient. Nevertheless, Yongden's condition became no worse; he recovered as suddenly as he had fallen ill.

We are already far from Lanchow, and the vague

security that is felt in the immediate vicinity of the
Chinese authorities does not extend as far as the region
we are now entering. It has a very bad reputation. We
had been specially warned against certain gorges as places
where travellers are often robbed, and sometimes, even,
honeycombed with sword-thrusts. We are well aware
that we will often run the risk of such dangers on the
journey we have undertaken, therefore the news does not
disturb us. In the present case it is probably only a
question of three or four thieves who have joined
together, not of a real band. The route is not used by
caravans, therefore thoroughbred brigands would find no
business there.

All the same, in anticipation of the robbers who may
fall suddenly upon us, I order my people to put on their
"war-kit." For them, this consists in taking off their
long Mongolian robes, keeping on only their trousers and
a short vest made of black ticking, and in slinging a
loaded rifle over the shoulder. This costume is very
similar to the one adopted by many of the frontier
soldiers, and is liable, for this reason, to mislead the
robbers and inspire them with a certain apprehension.
They are well aware that if they rob or molest "braves"[1]
they will be followed and severely punished, whereas in
attacking civilian travellers they have little to fear.
Before entering the province of Amdo, I had never
carried arms while travelling. I only departed from my
customary habit in order to conform to that of the
country and, above all, to satisfy my men's pride, who
would have felt themselves humiliated had they not had
guns on their backs and swords at their belts. As for
myself, with or without reason, I believe in my lucky star.
I cannot imagine any danger that I could not successfully
circumvent by my wits alone. Up to now this belief has
been justified.

As always under such circumstances, I act as scout.

[1] The name that Chinese soldiers give to themselves.

Getting down from my mule, I hobble slowly forward. Upon this occasion I am dressed in an old Chinese robe, and exactly resemble a peasant woman on her way to a neighbouring village. Such a one would hardly be likely to attract the attention of thieves.

If I come across anything suspicious I have arranged to intone a pious chant. In the case of pressing danger, I shall blow the whistle that I always carry hanging from my neck, for the purpose of calling us together again when we have separated to reconnoitre the route. But all is well. In vain I peer down into the ravines and crevices that cut the steep sides of the defile, not even the shadow of a human being is to be seen. On nearing the end of the gorge and finding we have all come happily through it, I express my satisfaction by a joke that I have repeated on many similar occasions.

"Tobgyal, had you prepared the bottle of tea?"

All three men burst out laughing, the one who has been questioned as heartily as his two companions, although the joke is at his expense.

I am referring to a comic incident that had occurred some years before. I was then on my way to the monastery of Detza, which is situated at about a day's journey from the bank of the Yellow River. The region I had to pass through is almost completely uninhabited and is the hunting ground of daring Tibetan brigands, who are much more formidable than their Chinese confreres.

Two years previously the steward of a lama, who was then my neighbour, had been seized by them while returning with a big sum of money, which he carried in his saddle-bags. Not only did the thieves steal the money, but also his rich silk robe and all his other clothes. When he was quite naked, they tied his hands behind his back and, using his long sash as a cord, fastened him to a tree. They then left him, taking his horse with them. The unfortunate steward passed the long winter's

·night in this position. By dint of repeated efforts, he succeeded in freeing himself at dawn, and, half frozen, dragged himself as far as a farm, where he received help.

But there is no need to go so far back for an example. Only the week before I reached that place, bandits had riddled with bullets a wretched farmer whom they thought had money on him. The man managed to escape, owing to the swiftness of his horse, but he reached his home only to die there two hours later.

Events of this kind are not uncommon in those regions. If people paid too much attention to them, they would never go beyond the limits of their town or village and would shut themselves up indoors every evening before sunset.

Now it happened that late in the afternoon we found ourselves in a valley which was covered with thickets. In order to relax our muscles after a long ride, we had dismounted from our beasts and were walking beside them. My adoptive son and I had outpaced the rest and, on arriving at a clearing, I seated myself on a rock, with the intention of making the servants also stop there for a few moments' rest; but, when they reached me, the one whom we called Sotar[1] said to me in a low voice:

"Robbers are watching us, I saw them hiding behind the trees."

There was nothing astonishing in this. Without showing the least haste, I got up to continue my way. It was evidently not the moment for a halt. We would do better to hasten towards some inhabited spot; at the same time it would be prudent not to show fear or even to appear to have seen the robbers.

After having gone a few steps, I too saw three men with guns lurking in the bushes.

[1] Sotar is a Hindi word that means something like overseer, surveyor, little chief in charge of porters etc. . . . The man whom we called by this name was a Tibetan who had been with an English officer of the cartographic service at the Tibetan frontier. He spoke Hindi perfectly.

" Get my revolver from my saddle-bag and bring it to me without their seeing you do so," I said to Tobgyal.

He was a *trapa* from Kum-Bum, and an excellent boy, but one who was not conspicuous for his bravery. To tell the truth he was a bit of a coward. The knowledge that armed robbers were close to us disturbed his mind. He opened the saddle-bag, took something out and brought it cautiously to me; however, when he drew the object from under his robe, where he had hidden it on his chest, it was found to be not the revolver, but a thermos flask full of tea, which I was in the habit of carrying with me.

Regardless of the situation, I burst out laughing at this unexpected apparition.

" Go," I said to the fool, " go and bring the biscuit tin too, we will offer them tea."

My son and the three servants joined in the laughter. The thieves must have wondered what was happening, and our mirth may have saved us from being attacked. We sprang into saddle and rode quickly away. Were the wretches without horses or did they not dare to follow us? The fact remains we were not attacked.

From that day forward, however, poor Tobgyal had never ceased to be teased about his mistake by his companions, and, I must confess, by me too, although this was not very charitable on my part. Nevertheless, he ended by becoming accustomed to it and laughed with the others.

That night our resting place was an isolated farmstead, which stood in the midst of a magnificent chaos of fallen rocks, overlooked by high red mountains. The moon soon came to light up this fantastic scene, but her rays were too feeble to reveal the whole of the plain or valley that stretched in front of us, and the mass of gigantic boulders mysteriously lost itself in a blue mist.

As soon as I had finished my meal, I wanted to go out.

15

When my hosts saw that I intended to leave the house, they earnestly begged me not to. They feared, they said, that I might meet evilly disposed wanderers: human beings or beasts of prey, which haunted the region. A young Chinese girl was particularly vehement in her efforts at dissuading me. I was touched by her solicitude, but all the same I went out. Perhaps, absorbed in my thoughts, I went farther than I meant to, and, also, I probably remained a long time seated on a stone between two big rocks, which formed a sort of sentry box and sheltered me from the wind. It would have been difficult for me to say how long I had been out when I heard footsteps approaching. They certainly were not those of an animal; the regular tread could only be that of a human being, and as the walker was coming from the opposite direction to the farm, it could not be anyone sent by the farmers to look for me. I drew back as far as possible between the two rocks. It was unlikely that anyone could see me in my hiding place. In fact, a man did pass quite close to me without stopping, walking straight on in front of him, unhesitatingly, as does a person who is perfectly acquainted with his destination.

It could not be one of the people belonging to the farm, for had I not been told and retold, as argument against my taking a nocturnal stroll, that everyone was indoors at that hour and dared not venture out again. Yet in the direction in which the man was going, there was only the farm and, beyond it, the rocky gorge of ill-repute that we had just passed through. Whoever he might be, it was useless to let myself be seen by him. I therefore waited some time before leaving my refuge, which had now lost all its charm for me. My thoughts had been interrupted, I began to feel cold, and the moon's rapid descent towards the summits, behind which she would soon disappear, made me feel that I might not be able to find my way back in the sudden darkness. However I reached the farm without difficulty, but just as I was about to turn

16

LANCHOW, CAPITAL OF THE KANSU PROVINCE,
ON THE BANK OF THE YELLOW RIVER

MAIN STREET OF HOJO

the corner of the building, I heard someone whispering. What did it mean?

Whilst I remained undecided, hesitating to go forward, one of the two watch-dogs, which had been tied up in order to allow me to re-enter the house without being attacked by them, scented me and began to bark, echoed by his companion. At the sound, a man fled precipitately. Was he a thief? I ran quickly to the door.

At the open door I found the young Chinese girl who had so particularly urged me not to go out. She had not had time to go back into the house. The mystery was solved. The wanderer was her lover, who was doubtless well known to the dogs, for they did not bark at him. Juliette exhibited astonishing composure, declaring that she had been so anxious, so very anxious, at knowing me to be out alone in the night, that she had been unable to sleep and had come down to await my return.

"It is I who am returning," I called in a loud voice to the masters of the house, whom the barking might have awakened. And, in order to divert their attention and to help the young girl to regain her couch in safety, I noisily bolted the door and quickly carried away the lamp that had been left burning for me. But the little sweetheart had already disappeared, more swiftly, more silently, than do the "spirits" that are spoken of in her country's tales.

On leaving that arid region, Hojo suddenly appeared to us as we gained the summit of a pass. The town, surrounded by walls, rises in a vast green plain, across which flows a sparkling river. This oasis in the middle of a parched country forms a surprising and charming contrast, and it can be easily understood why the Mohammedans of Kansu are so attached to this cool citadel: earthly replica of the flower gardens in Allah's paradise.

My stay in Hojo was far from agreeable. I was taken

ill with fever, just as my son had been, some days before. One of the mules began to swell and nearly died. Snow fell, and the North wind blew, icily. We were stranded for many days in an inn, waiting for the beast to recover.

II

THE PEOPLE OF THE SOLITUDES

OUR route takes us along narrow valleys where wind emerald rivers. At a period, not long distant, the country must have been covered with forests, but the natives have ruthlessly cut down the trees. Many of the mountains are entirely stripped, and landslides occur that threaten to obstruct the valleys, while torrents, bounding down among the enormous boulders, wear away the arid mountain slopes and hasten the devastation.

Since the timber cannot be floated down these shallow rivers it is the demand for charcoal that has caused the wholesale felling of the trees. From the giant firs, the woodcutters unskilfully produce an inferior charcoal, the greater part of which crumbles to powder and remains on the ground. They deliver what is transportable to Chinese intermediaries, or, less often, they themselves take it by mule to the towns, where it finds a ready market.

From Hojo, by going further into the mountains, we regained the wild country of Amdo.[1] Amdo is characteristically Tibetan, although it does not form part of the territory subject to the rule of the Dalai Lama. The Chinese authorities exercise a vague control over it and impose a few taxes, but only in exceptional cases do they interfere in its home affairs. At ordinary times the population is governed by local chiefs, who are not associated one with the other.

The Tibetans of Amdo consist of herdsmen (*dokpas*),[2]

---

[1] The province we had left on quitting Kum-Bum.
[2] Written *hbrogpa*: literally " people of the solitudes ".

who live in tents at the north-east border of the great grassy deserts (the *chang thangs*), and of *yudogs*,[1] that is to say, village-herdsmen. The latter live in hamlets and cultivate the soil during part of the year, but when summer comes, they entrust the care of their rustic dwellings and the duties of harvesting the crops to a few among them—often the women—, and the majority of the population go away with the herds to the high grazing-lands.

As we go forward, our nightly lodgings become more and more wretched. We hesitate, however, to camp out, as much on account of our animals, which, in this season, require to pass the night in a stable, as on account of possible robbers. If it is to be believed what well-informed people say: In every peasant of this country is hidden a thief, who is ever on the watch.

Still, these rascals are not wanting in prudence. To rob the guest who sleeps in their house seems to them a dangerous proceeding.

The despoiled traveller, particularly if he be a man of some importance, may complain to the local chiefs, or, even, to the Chinese authorities—if he disregards the costs of justice. Sometimes, soldiers passing through the country will act for him as judges and carriers out of the sentence, and the peasant will feel the heavy burden of this intervention, which is anything but gratuitously given. A pound of sugar stolen from a traveller may cost him a horse.

In camping in the open you lose the benefit of the salutary fear that this minimum of justice inspires. For against whom is the complaint to be brought, if, during the night, one or two mules have disappeared? The natives will swear that they have seen nothing, heard nothing, that the thief is certainly not one of them, that no one has left the village. How can a stranger prove that

[1] Written *yul hbrog* (*de yul* = country and by extension village, and *hbrog* = solitude).

20

they lie? He is at liberty to storm and rage as he pleases; his property is being driven far away over the mountain and he will never see it again.

To administer justice oneself, outside of established customs, is not permitted by the Tibetans. Extortions of every kind are permissible in this blest country, above all in the border regions, but there is the "way" to be observed. To go wide of accepted tradition in this matter is to make trouble, in the course of which guns have their say and the imprudent traveller may perhaps be removed.

In spite of this I have often disregarded the wise precautions that I have been recommended to take and that current facts have fully justified. I owe it to my Tibetan and Chinese friends to say that nothing really unpleasant has ever resulted from my imprudence. There is little to mention on this subject, but the stealing of a Chinese robe from Yongden. It was taken in broad daylight from his room in an inn, while he was having tea with me in the adjoining room.

In the region through which we are now passing, each village consists of a few houses only: ten at most, more often just four or five. Naturally there are no inns; a fact that is common to nearly every part of Tibet except Lhasa, Shigatse, Chiamdo, and a few other important towns. Each evening, it is necessary to go a-begging for permission to pass the night under a peasant's roof. Such hospitality is not gratuitous, but there is no fixed charge. On leaving their hosts, travellers give them a certain sum of money or some useful provisions—tea or salt. . . . From them they also buy straw, fodder for their beasts, and sometimes supplies of butter, *tsampa*,[1] or meat. In this way, a farmer always finds some profit in giving shelter.

Nevertheless,. it occasionally happens that lodging is refused you, either because you inspire distrust or for

[1] Flour made from roasted barley. It is the Tibetan's principal food

other reasons.[1]   Since I have shown up the villagers' tendency to rob the passer-by, I must in fairness say that some travellers prove themselves scarcely more honest in their dealings than do their hosts.   For them, it can only be a question of petty larceny, but even this is a serious loss for the poor country people.   Sometimes the visitors will appropriate a few large balls of spun wool that is ready for weaving, sometimes a big piece of dried meat. They likewise gladly increase their stock of butter and *tsampa* at their hosts' expense, and the more daring among them take away a pair of boots, a blanket, or a dress.

The theft is usually artfully carried out, during the night, and as travellers are in the habit of leaving before sunrise, those who have sheltered them are often still asleep.   In this way it is easy for the departing guests to hide their ill-gotten goods in their luggage.

A young tramp, whom I picked up on the road and whom I fed in exchange for various small services, stole a sheepskin robe in this manner from a farm in which we had passed the night.   I only saw the stolen object a week after the theft had been committed, when the rogue put it on.   As we had travelled a considerable distance since leaving the farm, I could not retrace my steps just for the purpose of restoring the robe, which was moreover fairly worn and dirty.   It would have been of no avail to abandon the culprit and order him to go back, he would not have obeyed me.

"They are rich people," he said in answer to my reproaches.   "They have a comfortable home.   In the corner where I found this robe, there were five or six others in a heap, covered with dust, unwearable.   I am going far, I often sleep outdoors, my clothes are in rags. . . . I suffer from cold . . ."

[1] The fear that a demon may have during the journey become attached to the traveller and that it may enter with him into the house is one of these reasons.   For further particulars see Chap. IV of present book and also *My Journey to Lhasa*.

22

These arguments appeared convincing to him and fully to justify his act. It would have been quite useless for me to have sought to persuade him that according to a certain moral code he should have continued to suffer.

This daily search at sunset for lodgings at times leads to strange adventures, in strange places, and among no less strange people.

One evening, we have a mean little house pointed out to us as a place where perhaps we could pass the night. Its proprietors are Chinese. A little old man receives us. He refuses, even for good payment, to give me the fairly clean room that he himself occupies, and insists on assigning to me as night quarters a kind of alcove in the room where all the women and children sleep. The thought of such promiscuity appals me. Notwithstanding our fatigue, we retrace our steps to another hamlet and ask a Mohammedan for shelter.

We are given a kindly welcome. The master of the house offers me his room and immediately carries away his blankets, with the intention of passing the night elsewhere. My son will sleep on the floor in a corner of my room, and the servants will be put up by a neighbour. It is seldom that we separate in this way. Prudence forbids it; but in the region we are crossing, it is usually possible to trust the Mohammedans, if not always in regard to business matters, at least in that which concerns personal safety.

My host's house suggests easy circumstances. The room I occupy contains several fine chests, and its walls are ornamented with primitive prints on yellow paper, such as are to be seen in any Chinese room; but instead of Taoist deities seated on clouds, the artist has sketched quaint views of Mecca and amusing crowds of faithful bowed in prayer.

When night arrives my host comes in to light a little Tibetan lamp and some incense sticks before the image of the Kaaba, which stands at the head of my bed, and I go to sleep thinking of distant Arabia.

The next day I learn that if I had accepted the old Chinaman's hospitality, I should have slept in a little recess where a leper had lain for a long time and on the very *kang* upon which he had died four days before. Perhaps no ill would have come to me had I done so; all the same, I congratulate myself on having found another lodging. I am certain, however, that the man who offered me this infected alcove harboured no evil thought. His people will certainly have slept there. The fear of contagion is little felt among the natives.

It is necessary for me to explain the word *kang*, which I have just used. Both the Chinese of Kansu and the Tibetans of the frontier who live in the Chinese fashion, do not use beds. In the rooms they build stone and earth platforms of varying dimensions: some not more than four feet wide and eight feet long, while others may be ten feet by fourteen or even larger. The underneath of the platform forms an oven, in which a fire is lighted during the winter; thus the top of the *kang* becomes a kind of stove for heating the room. However, this is only its secondary use. The platform serves principally for bed at night and, during the day, as the place where you sit in the warm, cross-legged, tailor fashion, to eat, read, write, or talk with visitors.

For my part, I hardly know of a more disagreeable sensation than that of lying stretched on this surface, which sometimes becomes heated to the point of scorching or even burning holes in the blankets that you have placed there as bedding and as a protection against burns. With an outside temperature of 25° Centigrade below zero, with the wind whistling through the badly jointed doors and the always more or less perforated paper of the paneless windows, you feel frozen in that part of you which is turned away from the *kang* and roasted in that which is touching it. You pass your nights in turning

24

from side to side, cooking yourself first on the one side and then on the other, as it is related that St. Laurence did on the Roman torturers' grid. So it happens that young children, left asleep on these overheated platforms, are sometimes cooked alive. A number of babies perish in this way each year, to the despair of their parents, but their experience is of little avail to other mothers, and besides there is no other way of preserving the children from the cold.

A well-made *kang* has two openings, both on the out-side of the house. Through the one, the fuel is intro-duced: generally a very dry mixture of straw and cattle dung; through the other, the smoke escapes. This kind of oven is hermetically closed on the room side, so that neither smoke nor fumes can penetrate into the apartment. However, one comes across few *kangs* as well built as this. Most of them show cracks on the room side. Some, too, have only one opening, so that there is no possibility of producing the necessary draught. Others again can be fed only through a doorless hole that gives into the room, filling it with evil smelling fumes.

I have also seen some *kangs* that had only unjointed planks for covering over the ash-packed fire. In places, near collieries, the natives even burn coal in these contrap-tions, and it was on one of these, in a farm where I had gone to visit a sick woman, that my son and I very nearly died of asphyxia. This also happened in Amdo, but many months before I undertook the journey that I am recounting here, and in another part of the country.

The parents of the invalid had begged me to remain until the next day in order that I might see the effect of the medicines I had administered. For this reason and also because the roads were anything but safe after dark, I had consented to spend the night at the farm.

My hosts had given me the best room in the house, and, as is the custom of the country, I was expected to share it with my son. We were provided with an

25

excellent meal, which was served on low tables on the top of the *kang*. Then, on being left alone, it was not long before we went to sleep, fully dressed—as is also the custom of the country—, lying on cushions that had been arranged on the warm *kang*.

In the middle of the night I awoke with a heavy head and a body quite incapable of movement. However, I had sense enough left to realize what was the matter, and I made a violent effort to call Yongden. It was very difficult to make him hear; he was already semi-conscious.

"Quick, quick!" I cried. "Get up and carry me out of here. We are going to die."

In a few minutes he managed to move and to drag himself in my direction. The *kang* was large; the lama had been lying near the wall, whereas I was at the opposite end, near the window. The shutters were closed. The room was almost in total darkness. In crawling across the space that separated us, Yongden overturned the tables on which still lay the remains of our supper, then feeling my head under his hand, he gripped it tight—and pulled. He hardly knew what he was doing. In his torpor, he had only understood that he must get me out of the room. Dragged by him, my body reached the edge of the platform and fell heavily to the floor. Yongden, who had managed to slip down from the *kang*, and was now in a more or less upright position, did not let go of me, but tightened his grip. I felt his fingers bury themselves in my eyes, in my throat, and he never ceased to pull and pull. . . .

Somehow he succeeded in opening the door giving on to the yard; but, there, his strength gave way; just as we passed through it, he collapsed. It was the 25th of December, a perfect moonlight night, and terribly cold. After having been nearly asphyxiated, we then ran the risk of being frozen. Fortunately, someone had heard the noise we had made in overturning the tables laden with crockery and in opening the door. Help came. I

26

remember how, when we had regained consciousness, we were offered by way of remedy, a decoction of coal in water. We energetically refused to take it.

The Chinese, as well as the Japanese, appear to be very little affected by the fumes of carbonic acid gas; all the same, from time to time, one hears of deaths that have been caused by *kangs* or braziers. A Tibetan lama and two men of his suite died at Kum-Bum in this way, while on a visit to the monastery. It is astonishing that a people who are so perfectly civilized in a number of other points do not make use of chimneys.

On penetrating farther into Amdo we rarely meet any Chinese; occasionally one or two merchants on the road, or one who is established at the head of an isolated branch of his firm. Apart from these few exceptions, the rest of the population is Tibetan.

The Tibetans of Amdo are quite different from those of the central provinces round Lhasa and Shigatse. These last hold their countrymen of this distant North in contempt and scornfully speak of them as *thapas*,[1] that is, "people of the extremities", people of the frontiers; a term that, in Tibetan, has the sense of uncivilized.

Indeed, when you look closely at a native of Amdo, whose only covering is a dirty sheepskin robe, he has the appearance of a barbarian. Still, if he is looked at from the distance, his aspect changes. The grease that spreads over the skin of this one garment—worn with the wool on the inside—gives it a surface that exactly resembles olive or dark green velvet. Then, when a sword in a silver and coral ornamented scabbard is passed through his belt, a gun is slung over his shoulder, and he seated tall and impressive on his horse, this rustic becomes transformed into a stately knight.

The effect on the women is even more surprising. On their very long, almost trailing robes, which are as

[1] Written *mthahpa*.

27

"patinated" as the men's, the coquettes sew for orna-
mentation some bands of highly coloured cotton material:
red, green and crude blue; and from their belts, which are
often in chased silver or at least decorated with silver
ornaments, they hang scarves in the same vivid colouring.
Indoors as well as outdoors, they all wear picturesque
hats: some pointed like those of our pierrots, others
round, made of fox skin or of felt edged with white
astrakhan.

Dressed in this way in the fields, they look like so
many mediaeval ladies incongruously harnessed to primitive ploughs, or hoeing the ground in preparation for
the next sowing. Such a picture recalls the old chivalric
romances in which wicked magicians imprison poor enchanted princesses. Under the spell of remembrance,
one scans the horizon for the paladin on his way to
deliver them. But he never appears. Even of ordinary
men there are few in that landscape; just one or two at
work, here and there. It is not that laziness keeps them
at home. No, indeed! They belong to a valiant race,
and prove it by choosing, for their part, a work that they
deem more virile than that of farming. In plain language,
the proud husbands of the ladies in fur hats and silver
belts scour the country in quest of travellers to rob. Thus,
while the husband undertakes to increase the common
budget with booty, the wife farms the family's land. A
fair "division of labour"!

It was not far from Sasoma. The tired mules had
walked slowly all day, and when evening came there was
still no sign of a village. At last, in the distance, we
descried an isolated farm, and, turning towards it, went
to ask for a night's shelter.

Our arrival was heralded by the ferocious barking of
five dogs, three on the chain and two free, which were
with difficulty restrained by the farm women who ran out
on hearing them.

AMDO FASHION :
DRESS MADE OF SHEEP SKIN

FASHIONABLE LADIES OF AMDO
WEARING POINTED, FUR-TRIMMED FELT HATS

The three women, one old and two young, appeared to be the sole occupants of the house. They received us coldly. We felt that they would willingly have closed their doors to us, but our monastic robes prevented them from doing so. There are few Tibetans who would dare to refuse hospitality to a lama of high rank, and Yongden had not failed to announce me as a *Khadoma*[1] from the Koko Nor.

The *Khadomas* are feminine genii, who, according to the Tibetans, incarnate sometimes in our world. Some Tibetan nuns of distinctive personality, or those who occupy important positions as monastic dignitaries, are held to be incarnated *Khadomas*. For a few years, rumours, at first vague, then becoming more consistent, and finally confirmed by several lamas, had ascribed to me this flattering origin. I did not object. The position it gave me had many advantages: it drew towards me the respect and sympathy of the natives, facilitated my investigations, and, withal, was in no way disagreeable. Moreover, if nothing absolutely proved that I was a *Khadoma*, nothing, on the other hand, definitely proved that I was not. To slight those who had acknowledged me as such would have been ingratitude. I therefore remained a *Khadoma*, and now I am not at all sure that I am not one.

The women showed us into a large room, which was used by the owners of the house as kitchen and bedroom in one. Our guides hardly spoke and, contrary to habit, they asked us no questions concerning the object of our journey. They silently arranged some cushions near the hearth for me to sit on and then placed a low table in front of me.

My servants unpacked the provisions and I began supper.

The absence of men about the place puzzled me,

---

[1] Written *mkah hgroma*, literally: "one who goes in the sky", "a walker in the sky or in the space".

and, knowing what was said about the customs of the country, I casually asked, while still continuing to eat:

"Are you not married? Where then are your husbands?"

"Mine is dead," gravely answered the old woman. "These two women here are the wives of my sons."

"Are they not at home?" I insisted.

"My husband has gone away 'to trade'," said one of the two women. Then, pointing to her sister-in-law, she added: "Hers has gone to see a relation who has had an accident."

I was sufficiently acquainted with the phraseology of the country to understand. The euphemistic expression "gone to trade" or the more picturesque one of other regions "gone to pick medicinal herbs on the mountains" signifies to join a party of brigands.

Did the women think I would not understand them, or rather, did they believe that they could not hide anything from a *Khadoma* and that, in questioning them, I was only testing their truthfulness, having in reality full knowledge of that of which I pretended to be ignorant. The latter hypothesis is more in keeping with the Tibetan mentality.

I did not question them further, but absorbed myself in the recitation of the evening office, as is the habit of distinguished lamas. Withdrawn into a corner of the room the women kept a pious silence. All of a sudden the sound of a horse's quick trot came from outside, and the dogs began to bark, but this time, joyously, as if welcoming the master's return.

As is usual, one of the women rushed to hold the horse's bridle and to lead it to the stables. No sooner had she drawn back the bolt, than a tall young man came quickly in and, without seeing me, said abruptly:

"He is dead, the bullet penetrated his chest."

Mutely the old woman nodded in my direction. The

30

man turned towards me, looked for a moment at my lamaic robes, then coming to me said:

"My maternal uncle (ajan) has just died. His friends have sent for his *lama*[1] to do the *powa*.[2] But if you have the power of celebrating this rite, will you not do it also, so that my uncle may have a happy rebirth in the Paradise of the Great Beatitude."

"Since your uncle's body is not here, it is necessary, for the *powa* to be effective, that the rite should be performed over an object he habitually carried on him: one of his robes, or something else," I answered.

Such, indeed, is the rule. By bringing this fact to my host's notice, I hoped to be dispensed from having to recite the office for the dead, a duty that no lama who has received the required initiation can refuse; for charity demands that he should lend his aid to the deceased's spirit.

"He was my brother, Jetsun Kushog,"[3] the old woman said in her turn. "If you can, help him."

Tears fell down her wrinkled cheeks.

"I have the sword he always carried at his belt," quietly continued the young master of the house. "My uncle had it on him when he was wounded. His son is dead; it is I who inherit his weapons."

He went out and returned a moment later carrying a gun and a sword that was sheathed in a scabbard orna-

---

[1] By using the expression *his* lama, the man referred either to the deceased's spiritual adviser or to the head of the monastery to which the deceased was in some way attached—as benefactor or otherwise. This lama, alone, is fully qualified to celebrate the religious rites for the benefit of the dead person and to guide his spirit in the Beyond. Nevertheless, great lamas or anchorite lamas can supplement or help his efforts by their superior powers.

[2] A rite that consists of making the spirit escape from the body and in guiding it away from the *Bardo* (where it wanders after the death of the body), into a happy dwelling place. For explanations on the subject of *powa* (written phowa) and the *bardo* see those given in *With Mystics and Magicians in Tibet*, or in the *Tibetan Book of the Dead* by Evan-Wentz.

[3] Very polite mode of address when speaking to a nun of high rank. Less respectfully the nuns are called *ane* or *jomo*.

mented with silver and coral. He placed the latter on the low table before me.

I felt that in spite of their apparent calm my hosts were deeply distressed and, above all, anxious to ensure the happiness of their relation in another world. The best thing was to give them the consolation for which they begged.

"Very well," I said, putting my hand on the deceased bandit's weapon, " this will do. Leave me."

The young man went away, and the women at once joined him outside. The confused sounds of an animated conversation reached me. Some words, more loudly and more insistently uttered than the rest, became audible. . . . " He said you were to join them at once. . . ." " . . . Your brother left yesterday. . . ." Then my host re-entered the room, approached me, and prostrating himself, said :

" I must leave again at once. Give me your blessing, Jetsun Kushog, and a *sungdu*[1] to protect me."

No explanation was necessary. I understood that the man was going to join his brother and that an expedition was in preparation, during which he would run the risk of meeting the same fate as the uncle whose spirit he asked me to send to the Paradise of the Great Beatitude.

To attempt to argue with him, to keep him back, would have been useless. Such an idea did not occur either to his mother or to his wife; he was merely obeying a time-honoured custom, which appeared to them as ineluctable and natural as the course of the stars.

I tore a strip off the end of a silk scarf, and while knotting it, silently gave out the wish that the man would escape danger, cause none to anyone, and might acquire more enlightened views than those that were dictating

---

[1] A thin ribbon that is torn from a piece of material, usually silk, in the middle of which a lama makes a knot. To this knot the lama communicates protective virtues by reciting certain mystic words, mentally forming a strong wish for the well being of the one who will wear the ribbon, and, finally, blowing on it.

his present conduct. After which, having blown ritual-istically upon the knot, I handed it to my host, who tied it round his neck.

He thanked me. Then prompted, perhaps, by an unconscious desire to justify himself before me, or im-pressed in spite of himself by the recent death of his uncle, he spontaneously added:

"Jetsun Kushog, I have always been charitable to the poor, and in my house monks and pilgrims are always well received. I have only killed one man, and I did it in fair fight. Look, it was very nearly I who was the victim." As he spoke he let fall his fur robe and on his chest I saw the scar of a large wound.

While the young women prepared provisions for the road, he drank the bowl of spirits that his mother handed him and ate a few mouthfuls of dried meat and a ball of *tsampa*, then went out into the night. The sound of his horse's hoofs died away in the distance, and, again, there was silence.

Seated together, in the corner of the room, the women told their beads, reciting "mani".[1] Their faces reflected a calm melancholy, a kind of serene passivity that accepted, without despair, without revolt, an inevitable destiny. They reminded me of fishermen's wives, during a storm, when their husbands are at sea.

With the *jagpa's*[2] sword lying in front of me, I began the office for the dead man and, following the sacred rite, called to the spirit of the deceased, adjuring it to let itself be guided to the blissful abode. Did he hear me, this hardened brigand who had fallen in the field where "mighty-hearted braves" face one another?

In their dark corner, the women continued their weary and monotonous drone:

Aum mani padme hum!

[1] Current expression for the sacred formula "Aum mani padme hum!"
[2] Highwayman, one of a gang of brigands.

33

The next morning I asked permission to remain at the farm until the following day, so that my animals might have a twenty-four hours rest. Apart from this reason, I was especially eager to take advantage of the occasion that presented itself to question my hostesses about the local customs regarding brigandage. Because I had officiated for the *post mortem* welfare of their relation and also because it was known that I was aware of the kind of "trade" practised by the master of the house, I had every reason to hope they would answer me with frankness. I was not wrong in my supposition; the women told me all there was to know on the subject. Of what they said, one curious thing was worth remembering. In the region there existed a sort of secret "compulsory service", which obliged all fit men to take part in the "trading" expeditions that were decided upon by a council of chiefs; these chiefs also presided over the distribution of the conquered booty.

This "service" explained the meaning of the phrases I had overheard the night before: "He said you were to join them at once. . . ." "Your brother left yesterday. . . ."

III

PRIMITIVE COMMUNISM IN TIBET

DURING the course of my travels I have found the "trading" customs of Amdo in the country of the Ngologs, in that of the Popas, and in the mountains that surround the valley of the Upper Salwen. But up to that moment, the various practices of a "Socialistic" nature that I had noticed in the different Tibetan communities had been directed towards more pacific ends. It goes without saying that these good people were totally ignorant of what is meant by socialism in the West. Their decidedly odd social systems were simply the outcome of their own ideas concerning the obligation incumbent upon everyone to co-operate in certain works and the general application of the principle of equality.

Of the amusing recollections I have on the subject, the most striking are those that are connected with a village in the Himalayas, at an altitude of about 8,000 feet, not far from Kampa Dzong, a little fortress on the southern border of Tibet. The village is called Lachen. Although it lies a few miles outside the official boundary of Tibet, its inhabitants are all Tibetans, probably descendants of herdsmen who have emigrated from Ha. Ha is a region that now forms part of the Tibetan state that is called Bhutan, on the maps, and Dugyul—land of the thunderbolt—, by the natives.

At Lachen, about eighty families are serving their apprenticeship as agriculturists, by cultivating barley and potatoes. All the same, they have not entirely given up the pastoral habits of their ancestors. In summer they leave their cottages to go camping on the adjacent high table-lands,[1] to pasture their herds of yaks there. Then, towards the end of September, when the snow becomes too deep, some of them take their animals to the other side of the frontier, into Tibet, where the climate, though very cold, is drier and the grass-lands generally free from snow. The other Lachenpas return to their village and remain there until the next year.

I lived for a long time in that remote region, either in the monastery that overlooks the village or in the neighbourhood.[2] It was in this way that I came to witness the workings of the most absurd caricature of a socialist government imaginable.

The chiefs of the commune, three in number, were elected for a year, and together with this triumvirate operated a council of about ten members. Chiefs as well as councillors regulated current affairs and acted as judges. When a more important decision had to be arrived at, all the men in the village were convoked to discuss the matter and a vote was taken at the end of the debate.

In principle, each villager had to contribute to the expense and work of all that concerned public interest and to share in any profits that might fall to the community. This constitution in itself was wholly praiseworthy. However, the value of even the best of programmes lies in the way it is understood and applied, and it was precisely in this that the droll interpretation conceived in the minds of the Lachenpas intervened.

It has been said that the three chiefs had to be elected, and in truth they were, but it must not be thought that all the villagers were eligible. According to a tacit agreement, the triumvirate had to be chosen from among the " rich ", and this custom was supported by the " poor " with even greater determination than by their more for-

---

[1] At an altitude of about 12,000 feet.
[2] See the account of my stay in *With Mystics and Magicians in Tibet*.

tunate fellow-citizens. "Whoever," they declared, "would think of obeying a man who possessed neither cattle nor property. A *piukpo*,[1] a man of substance, alone can inspire respect."

Therefore, chiefs and councillors invariably belonged to the more or less ragged plutocracy of the hamlet. In their mode of meting out justice they strictly conformed to the methods prevailing in Tibet, and, it must be said, in many other Eastern countries.

Both plaintiffs and defendants prefaced their appearance in court with presents. They repeated these tangible proofs of their respect when they came in person before the arbiters of their dispute. Upon the worth of the gifts depended the opinion of the good judges, therefore the most important question for a pleader was to know exactly what his adversary was going to offer, so as to be able to surpass it in munificence. In this way all need for tedious and useless oratorical efforts during the proceedings was avoided.

In Lachen, as elsewhere in Tibet, everything was settled by the imposition of fines: theft, assault, even manslaughter and murder.

The magistrates began by appropriating to themselves a portion of the fine paid by the guilty party. With the remainder they offered a banquet to all the men of the village—triumvirs and councillors assisting of course.

To eat was the predominant thought of everyone. As soon as profit of any kind accrued to the community, it was converted into food. This the men ate seated in a circle in the rustic village forum: a bare piece of ground that was reserved for public meetings, and to where, on such days, they brought the municipal cauldrons. These cauldrons were looked upon as common property, but alas! their contents were far from being so. When

---

[1] Written *phyugpo* = rich. Tibetans from Lhasa pronounce: *chugpo*.

portions of a yak[1] or a few sheep were boiled in them,
the choice pieces, the juicy parts of the meat, went to
the magisterial officials, who sat on carpets at one end
of the assembly, while the " poor " had to content themselves with gnawing a few bones.

If the sum to be spent was a small one, the community
was invited to a "tea". At this, also, the officials and
other *piukpos* were served first and received all the butter
that floated on the beverage,[2] while their possessionless
fellow-citizens took their share of the common benefit in
the form of some bowls of thin, blackish water.

One day, a prince of Sikkim had conceived the idea
of founding a school in Lachen in order to raise the
intellectual level of its inhabitants. A laudable enter-
prise, but less happy had been the choice of schoolmaster.
He was a Tibetan, an inveterate drunkard, who, having
killed a man in a brawl, had passed over the frontier to
escape the consequences of his act.

With the triumvirate lay the right to designate the
boys who were to be admitted to the benefit of school
attendance. It would be a mistake to imagine that this
privilege was a source of competition. Quite the reverse.
If, with the customary presents, parents went to beg for the
goodwill of the chiefs, it was with the sole intention of
getting their sons exempted from the obligation of having to learn to read. The boys, they thought, were much

---

[1] *Yak*: the long-haired grunting ox, native of Tibet.

[2] In Tibet, tea is prepared in the following manner: the tea, which is
bought in compressed bricks, is broken into small pieces and boiled for
a long time. It is then poured into a churn. Into this is thrown some
salt, a little soda, and a more or less large quantity of butter, according to
a person's means. After the mixture has been well churned, it is passed
through a sieve so as to remove any remaining tea leaves. The strained
liquid is poured into big metal (copper or silver) tea-pots—the poor use
earthenware ones—, which are put on the side of the fire to heat. At
the moment of serving the tea the pot is gently shaken in order to mix
the butter well in. But notwithstanding this last manœuvre those who are
served first always get their tea more buttered than those who receive
the dregs. When a large number of people are to be given tea, it is
brought in in wooden tubs and served out in wooden ladles. It is especially
then that the last to be helped gets a butterless liquid.

more useful to them as guardians of the yaks on the mountains. Chiefs and councillors shared this view and, accepting the *piukpos'* gifts, willingly granted them the favour they craved.

Nevertheless, as the princely founder of the school wished to see pupils in it and had the power of penalizing the recalcitrant commune, education was forced upon the children of parents who were too poor to win the chiefs over with gifts, the very ones who, for lack of servants, had absolute need of their sons to guard their cattle and cultivate their fields. To these unfortunate youths the authorities gladly added the " good-for-nothings ", boys who were considered mentally deficient; for, as one of the councillors quite seriously remarked to me: " Since they are incapable of doing anything whatsoever, nobody will be a loser by their not working."

I have said that a monastery overlooked the village. Now a monastery requires the presence of monks. But the reasons for which the parents endeavoured to keep their sons from going to school became even more imperative when it was a question of depriving themselves for ever of their childrens' work, and, in addition, of having to provide for them when they became *trapas* (monks). Only the well-to-do could be tempted by the honour that is attached to having a member of the clergy as a near relation, and these families were not sufficiently numerous in Lachen to fill the small local lamasery, tiny as it was, with novices.

And, here, state considerations intervened once again. The Powers agreed that *trapas* were necessary, even indispensable. " The *trapas*," they declared, " drive away the demons, who, without them, would ravage the herds and kill men. They cause rain to fall when the crops require it and keep away the hail. They guide the spirits of the dead to agreeable paradises. They foretell the future, exorcise those who are tormented by evil spirits and, by celebrating beneficent rites, cure the sick. . . .

39

What do they not do? It is quite impossible to do without them. . . ."

The triumvirs therefore devised vocations, and, if they sometimes made a mistake, it couldn't be helped! The boys who were chosen by them put on the monastic habit, learned to blow the conches and *ragdungs*,[1] to make the large bronze cymbals vibrate, and to chant the ritual harmoniously. Whether or not these youngsters liked their role, they at any rate rendered themselves useful to their fellow-citizens.

However, their condition was not devoid of advantages. As the monastery of Lachen belonged to one of the "Red Hat" sects, its *trapas* were allowed to marry; they could own a house in the village, live there with their family, till their fields, and look after their cattle. But, over and above these ordinary facilities of life, which they had in common with the other villagers, they enjoyed the special privilege of being exempt from taxation and corvée as well as of being independent of the chiefs and council, whose authority extended only over laymen.

In the Spring, triumvirs, councillors and people assembled in the forum. A plenteous banquet preceded a discussion that had for subject the date upon which the potatoes were to be planted and the barley sown, first in Lachen, then later, in a summer resort, a dependency of the village, which was situated at a higher altitude.

After having consumed many pots of beer, the assembly fixed these dates, and on these days, in each place, all the barley had to be sown and all the potatoes planted. But mark carefully: all in a single day and by everyone the same day.

"If," they said, "the people sow on different dates, they will also harvest on different dates. The first of them who will have potatoes for exportation into Tibet

[1] Long Theban trumpets.

or into Sikkim will obtain for these early ones a better price than the others will get for theirs that come later into the market. Such competition is bad, all must have equal advantages."

The date for the harvest and that for the digging up of the potatoes were decided at a similar meeting. Apart from all commercial questions, it was likewise forbidden to dig up a single potatoe in one's own field for home consumption before the stated date. "No one must regale himself selfishly, alone," admonished the quaint wisdom of the Lachen natives. "Everyone must wait until all can do it together."

It would have been quite useless to argue that, from one end of the year to the other, the *piukpos* regaled themselves without inviting their poorer fellow-citizens to share their meals; neither the " rich " nor the " poor " would have understood that argument.

Stranger still was the prohibition to gather anything whatsoever after the time fixed. Consequently, those who, for lack of workers, could not finish the harvest within the stated period were forced to employ their less occupied neighbours, if they did not wish to lose their barley or potatoes; for the day after the date fixed the cattle were let loose in the fields to nibble the stubble, and no claim on the part of the farmer whose grain was destroyed in this way would have been admitted.

The produce of their herds, their potatoes, and their scanty barley crops were not sufficient to feed the Lachen-pas. They required wheat, rice, tea, salt, and many other things. In order to procure them they went down to Sikkim or up to Tibet, where they exchanged their wool, potatoes, butter, apples, etc. for what they needed. This necessity entailed periodic expeditions, the dates of which were as rigorously fixed as those concerning agricultural labours.

On the chosen day, all the population set out; only the old people and children were authorized to remain in the village. It was not to be tolerated that some should stay at home, making profits or simply resting, while their absent fellow-citizens were bearing the fatigue of a journey. Equality! All must march in company.

Following the Tibetan custom, there existed, in Lachen, a corvée of porterage. This service, however, was not entirely gratuitous; an official schedule of wages determined the amount to be paid to each porter.

All travellers holding a requisition order delivered by the Sikkim authorities had the right to ask for porters. The corvée was obligatory on all the villagers, with the exception of the chiefs, councillors, and *trapas*. The rich could also be exempted from duty by paying an annual contribution. As to the needy, it would have been in no way displeasing to them to receive money, occasionally, for a day's work, but they were not permitted to retain such earnings. The whole of it had to be given into the hands of the chiefs. When the sum produced by these wages together with the amount of the exemption tax paid by the rich had reached the price of a yak, a banquet was decreed, during which the animal was eaten.

Some poor wretch who was badly in need of a pair of trousers might think the money he had received from the travellers could be better employed; but he would never have dared voice such an individualistic desire. He would get his bone to gnaw, and have to pass the winter bare-legged.

The women were also subject to the corvée of porterage as well as to all other corvées imposed by the chiefs, and, like the men, they had to pay their wages into the municipal fund. But, they did not even have the consolation of participating in the feast, which was exclusively reserved for the male population of the village. It was declared that the feminine members of the community should find sufficient satisfaction in the knowledge that their fathers, husbands, and brothers were feasting.

A WOMAN OF THE SINO-TIBETO-MONGOLIAN BORDER

Giving way, one day, to an access of feminism, I attempted to offer a banquet to the martyrs. The triumvirs scowled, for such an innovation interfered with established customs. Nevertheless, after some reflection, they told me that they would authorize a little feast, if I undertook to give one, exactly similar, to the men. I retorted that they gave no place to women in theirs; it was only to waste breath. Men could enjoy advantages that were not granted to women, but it was impossible to imagine the reverse. And, after all, there are many so-called civilized people who think as these barbarians.

It happened that, while the majority of the Lachenpas were away on one of their journeys into Tibet, it became the time for me to lay in a supply of firewood. I therefore let it be known what price I was offering for a load and also that whoever would like to work for me as a wood-cutter could present himself. Some men, whose positions exempted them from making the journey (the schoolmaster had deserted his post on this occasion), and a number of women arrived, delighted at the windfall that had come their way. I had tea and food distributed, and for four days everybody worked happily, singing and laughing.

Everything seemed most satisfactory; but the chiefs, on their return, judged otherwise. According to them, no one had the right to undertake any work whatsoever, if he had not been given it to do by the council. The supplying me with wood had brought a profit that the whole community should have shared. I ought to have applied to them, the triumvirs told me. They would then have ordered each head of a family to supply me with an equal quantity of wood, the price of which would have been paid, as always, into the banquet fund. The result was that all my woodcutters, both men and women, found themselves inflicted with a heavy fine.

I had already experienced what could be the result of this convoking of all the men to work together, when building a rustic cottage. The council had agreed to build it for me by contract. The chiefs began by asking an advance of half of the price, with which to buy food. Having received the money, the whole male population installed themselves in a glade below the spot where my building was to rise and feasted. They feasted for ten days, while, from my tent, I watched them, wondering when they were going to begin the work.

At last, giving way to my oft-repeated remonstrances, some of the men began to fell the trees and to cut planks with axes; they did not know how to use a saw. The rest of the company did not attempt to move. When the workers had laboured for two hours, they returned to eat and drink in the glade. Then, the time fixed for one of their journeys arrived, and they *all* went away, because no one must work longer than another. I remained facing a roofless structure, a fortnight before the rainy season.

I called in three carpenter *trapas*, who consented to finish the cottage. When the " community " came back, they were furious with those who had received the wages that *ought to have been* theirs. But the members of the monastery were only answerable to their abbot: the triumvirs could do nothing in the matter.

It was when there was a question of supplying provisions that the odd conception of equality formed by the Lachenpas reached the maximum of absurdity. I was compelled to buy my butter from herdsmen who lived on the other side of the frontier, in order to prevent each one of the eighty families that constituted the commune from each bringing me their quota, which I should have had to accept, whether fresh or rancid, without the right of refusal.

Misfortune again befell me upon another attempt at encouraging individual initiative. I asked to buy big potatoes from anyone who might have them. Peasants climbed to my hermitage carrying sacks, the contents of which had been carefully chosen. I wanted thirty sacks; these were duly paid for and stored away.

Once more the unavoidable triumvirs turned up and reminded me that by the terms of their Constitution, unwritten, but binding, no individual member of the community must be favoured. Each family should have provided me with a sack of potatoes. Moreover it was contrary to the principle of equality to ask for a selection. With great gravity, as if they were initiating me into the profound mysteries of agriculture, they explained that potatoes are dug up in mixed sizes: small, medium, and large. Why should some eat the small ones while I would be having the big ones at every meal? . . .

Why indeed? . . . Doubtless in virtue of the same eternal injustice on the strength of which they, the chiefs and the *piukpos*, ate the best pieces of the yak, drunk the buttered surface of the tea, and left the gristle and the bones and the wash at the bottom of the tea cauldrons to the others.

I did not take the trouble to discuss this point with them, all the same I was obliged to show considerable firmness in order that my hermitage might not be buried under a pile of potatoes brought from each house, in loads equivalent to those I had bought from the other villagers. These last had, as indemnity, to pay the money they had received from me into the voracious fund for collective treats.

I had not come to the end of my surprises. Shortly before the last winter that I passed in the country, the cottage where my servants lodged was, during their absence, visited by thieves. This adventure decided me to buy a watch dog. Therefore I sent one of my boys to the village. He brought back a great big black beast, very savage, eminently suited for the service that I required of it.

Some days later, one of the three chiefs who shared the supreme magistrature presented himself at my door.

On coming before me, he began, in a severe tone, without preamble, to say:

"You have purchased a dog from Tundu. Yet you know that no one must be favoured, that each family must enjoy equal rights. Why should he, Tundu, alone, benefit. You ought to have applied to us, we would have sent . . ."

"Eighty dogs, perhaps," I interrupted, aghast, thinking of the number of families in Lachen.

"No," the other continued coldly. "There are not eighty dogs available in the village. We would have sent you *a few* dogs."

That evening the winter snow began to fall, and a few days later all communication was cut off between Lachen and the Plateau of the Beatitude (Dewa thang), above which, in among the rocks, hung my anchoritic dwelling. Even had they had the intention, it was then impossible for my primitive socialists to come back to me. I remained with my one dog.

IV

THE MONASTERY OF LABRANG TASHIKYIL

THE next stage of our journey led me to Sasoma, which in the local dialect means "new earth". In fact, it was just an embryo village consisting of a few houses that had been recently constructed round a large building—at once inn and commercial stores. A trader, a Chinese Mohammedan, had established himself there and was now exploiting the guileless natives. These last may be fine brigands, but they make poor traders, and in business the Chinese always outwit them.

The Sasoma store-keeper bought wood, wool, and fur of them. He sold them everything they needed and, in addition, a number of superfluous articles, which he artfully displayed among the other goods to tempt innocent clients. Also, as is usual in the East, the head of the store practised usury, and from this source he probably derived the best part of his income.

His inn, however, was perfect. All the same, he could hardly have counted on the passing of many travellers through that out-of-the-way spot, therefore, I feel sure that the sumptuousness—very relative, of course —of the shop-hotel was deliberately planned for the purpose of impressing the simple-minded, and, in this way obtaining ascendancy over them. But the designs of the trader-landlord were of little interest to me. I was simply overjoyed at having found comfortable quarters. Yongden and I were each given a clean room, both of which opened into an anteroom with a balcony: quite a princely suite!

Sitting on this balcony, I see, standing before the house, two of those strange figures of which I have already spoken: two princesses who are wearing fur trimmed pointed hats and trailing sheepskin robes that are held in at the waist by silver belts. The women look as if they had stepped out of a XIIIth century painting.

Each of them carries a load of wood on her back. The Mohammedan approaches and laconically says: "Three hundred sapeques." Three hundred, which, according to the custom of the country, means one hundred and fifty.

One of the women protests; she finds the price insufficient. The buyer, correctly dressed as a Chinese gentleman, in black robe and waistcoat, looks at her with a complacent smile, pinches her chin, glides a playful finger down an opening of her fur robe, and rounds his libertine gesture off by sliding 150 sapeques into the non-plussed princess's hand. She, not daring to remonstrate, passively puts down her load and goes away with her companion.

The next day is again to take us through a region that has the reputation of being unsafe. As eight muleteers in charge of a caravan of merchandise happen to be staying at the inn, I decide to travel with them.

These people have the habit of starting well before dawn, therefore, lest they leave without us, we cord our luggage soon after midnight. Finally we sally forth beneath the meagre light of a moon on her twenty-first day.

The track, bad up till then, has become execrable. Narrow, strewn with rocks, sloping steeply up and down, it sometimes overhangs the river from high up, supported in space by only a few pieces of rotting wood that have been wedged in among the rocks. We have to cross many

THE MONASTERY OF LABRANG TASHIKYIL
North-Eastern Tibet

bridges, no easy task, for the engineering art of this country is of a special kind. Two trees, sometimes more, bound together are thrown across the river, and on top of these a platform made of planks and poles is fixed. When several animals cross this platform at the same time, it takes on an undulatory movement, and to watch the mules negotiate these wooden waves is very entertaining.

However, there is no road so difficult that the end cannot be reached. We get to Labrang in the afternoon.

Labrang is in the centre of the province of Amdo; a region where the population is even more rough and primitive than the one that we have just been through. Foreigners are hardly tolerated in this country. Fortunately, I had previously made the acquaintance of a monk who enjoyed considerable influence in the great Labrang monastery. This made matters quite easy for me and helped me to keep up my character of lady-lama, before the natives; for although he who acted as my sponsor knew that I was in reality a lady-lama, he nevertheless was well aware that I was by birth a foreigner.

This monk's name was Tsöndu and his story was truly eastern, one in which tragedy and greed mingled freely. He had been chief-steward to the Grand Lama *tulku*, Jamyang Shadpa, abbot of Labrang Tashikyil. In this capacity the monk had acquired considerable influence over his old master; had, in fact, managed all the abbot's affairs, free from control. Such a case is often to be met with in Tibet, and Tsöndu, as many another steward, had amassed great riches. His prosperity excited the jealousy of the Labrang monks, but as that kind of thing is quite usual, they probably would have put up with it had not Tsöndu given them cause for further criticism.

It appears that, unfortunately, he became the lover of the abbot's sister, and, so it is said, pushed his contempt of monastic rules to the length of advertising his failure.

to keep the prescribed chastity, by installing his mistress in a house belonging to the monastery.

Jamyang Shadpa, old and very attached to his steward, shut his eyes to this flagrant infringement of the precepts that govern the "Yellow Hat" sect; and, as he said nothing, his monks dared not publicly express their sentiments.

However, Jamyang Shadpa died. The abbatial throne had to remain empty until the child who was reincarnating the deceased should manifest himself. The dignitaries and lower clergy of Labrang took this opportunity for taking their revenge. Tsöndu was first of all dismissed from office; then his possessions were seized; and, finally, incensed at the obstinate resistance that he continued to display towards the monastic authorities, by refusing to accept their judgment, crying out against the injustice done to him, and claiming what he called his rights, his enemies decided to put him to death.

The day before he was to be executed, he learned what they were plotting against him. Although he was kept under strict observation, he managed to elude the watchfulness of the *trapas* who were posted round his house and escaped during the night. Outside the monastery he found a horse ready for him and galloped away.

Nevertheless his disappearance was at once discovered and the alarm given. Expert riders went in pursuit of him, and then, in the darkness, a dramatic man hunt began along the terrible mountain paths.

Tsöndu succeeded in reaching Chinese territory. He had friends there, commercial agents with whom, in his prosperous days, he had done important business. They helped him and procured for him relays of horses. He arrived at Sining.

It was there that I made his acquaintance and that he described his tragic flight to me. Naturally he was careful to remain silent concerning his own wrongdoing, and equally careful to bring out in full relief that of his enemies. If the steward had the bad grace to pose as an innocent victim, his adversaries were, for their part, probably not sinless.

However it may have been, Tsöndu did not consider himself irremediably beaten. He was clever enough to interest the Chinese General—the then ruler of the Tibetan borderlands of Amdo—in his cause. As a good politician the general no doubt saw in this monk's quarrel an opportunity for consolidating his authority in Amdo, where at the moment it was hardly more than nominal. He ordered the monks of Labrang to re-establish Tsöndu in his former office and to give him back his confiscated possessions. The General, who was a Mohammedan, anticipated a refusal, and, just as he had foreseen, the monks haughtily declined to obey him.

He then sent his Moslem soldiers to enforce his command. Some peasants, who were devoted to the lamas, led these soldiers into an ambush and massacred them. War was declared. The Labrang monks called the natives to arms. A little troop was formed, who, believing implicitly in the charms distributed by the lamas and the magic rites they celebrated, resolutely faced the Mohammedans.

Badly armed with old-fashioned barrel-loaded muskets, with forked supports, but animated with exceptional courage, the poor wretches put up a desperate fight. Never for a moment could the result of such an unequal struggle have been in doubt. The general had issued definite orders. The independent spirit of these tribes, who had so systematically refused to recognize Chinese authority, was to be broken, and the brigand infested routes were to be opened up to commerce. The Mohammedans gave no quarter. The night before the enemy's entry into the village of Labrang, the terrified Tibetans fled into the mountains. It was winter, snow was falling, and the fugitives, who had neither food nor shelter, dared not attempt to go back to the places that were occupied by the troops, for even the children who had been sent to ask for quarter had been killed.

It is said that about two thousand natives died of cold on the summits.

The monks of Labrang had very prudently not taken part in the fighting. This fact saved their lives, all the same they were made to pay a big war indemnity. By way of reprisals, the soldiers freely looted the temples and set fire to the palace of one of the Grand Lamas, he who had shown himself particularly violent in inciting the villagers to resistance.

Upon the order of the Chinese General, Tsöndu was reinstated, not however in his former office, which he declined to assume again, but in all the privileges that were attached to it, and, in that which he cared for most, the possession of his costly house and of all his property.

While the people of Labrang were surrendering, the struggle was being continued, close by, at the monastery of Amchow.

The laymen who had defended it having for the most part been wiped out, the Mohammedan troops besieged the lamasery, where the *trapas* had taken refuge. From there the monks fired on their assailants, who retaliated by setting fire to the monastery. The flames spread from one building to another until the whole *gompa*[1] became a glowing furnace. Whoever attempted flight fell under the bullets of the soldiers that were stationed round the burning monastery. One of them, an eye-witness of the fire, told me that the *trapas*, courageous to the last, entoned liturgical chants and then jumped from the upper stories of the houses into the flames.

They all perished with the exception of their abbot, a *tulku* lama, who, according to what was related to me, was saved by a miracle.

When the *trapas* saw that they could not possibly

---

[1] Tibetan name for monastery.

MARKET IN AMDO

escape, they wrapped the Lama in some *thankas*[1] representing the terrible deities who have sworn to protect the Religion and the faithful. Firmly enveloped in these pictures and surrounded by a wall built of volumes of the Sacred Writings, the lama was not touched by the flames and, when night came, he succeeded in escaping from the smouldering ruins of the *gompa*.

I do not know what to think concerning this miracle; but it is a proved fact that the lama did escape and did take refuge in the grassy desert, among the Ngolog tribes.

When I arrived in Labrang, the child who "reincarnated" the deceased Jamyang Shadpa had been discovered near Litang, in the Kham country, and was installed as Grand Lama of the monastery. In his beautiful house, among his recovered riches, Tsöndu triumphed with prudent modesty.

As soon as he was informed of my arrival in Labrang, Tsöndu sent some *trapas* to invite me to come and live at the monastery, in a house that was reserved for distinguished guests. However I had already found suitable accommodation at an inn, so I declined the invitation. A little later the ex-steward came himself, accompanied by servants who carried the customary gifts of welcome. He pressed me to move into the monastery and accept the suite of rooms that he was offering me, but my big room, with its windows overlooking the market place, greatly pleased me. From it I could watch at leisure the crowd of peasants and herdsmen who strolled among the open-air stalls and haggled noisily over the articles displayed for sale in the surrounding shops. I, therefore, warmly thanked Tsöndu and stayed where I was.

The successor of the deceased Grand Lama—or, as the Tibetans would say, Jamyang Shadpa once more rein

---

[1] Unframed religious pictures painted on soft material, which can be rolled in the same way as the Japanese *kakemonos*.

carnated—was still very young. Therefore his parents had accompanied him to the monastery and lived with him. According to custom, when the child was old enough to pass out of his mother's care, she and her husband would go to live at a little distance from the monastery, in the palace set apart for the family of the Grand Lama.

Tsöndu had informed the young lama's father of my arrival, and the latter hastened to send me provisions. Since I had refused the apartments that had been offered me, it was only right that I should be provided with food. Such is the usual practice in Tibet, but the munificence of the "yab chenpo" ("great father," because he is the father of a *tulku*) exceeded by much the quantity demanded by the custom of the country.

I was sent many carcases of mutton—some fresh, others dried—, about twenty big pieces of butter, some cheese, sugar, tea, barley, flour, and also some grain for the mules. There was enough to feed us all for more than a fortnight.

During the evening more presents were brought by people who said they had met me in Kum-Bum or in the Koko Nor. Most of my visitors I did not recognize, but, in order not to hurt anyone's feelings, I pretended to have pleasant recollections of each one of them.

Others came simply to present their offerings, without really knowing who I was. Rumour had it that a wise *Khadoma* had come and that Tsöndu, the father of the young Jamyang Shadpa, monastic dignitaries, the Grand Lama of Lob's commercial agent, and other notables had welcomed her; this was enough—the impulsion had been given. The villagers came in flocks, ranged themselves in files, and were introduced by the imperturbable Yongden. A heterogeneous mass of things, edible and otherwise, rose in piles about the room until it had the appearance of one of the shops round the market place.

Seated in the "lotus"[1] position on the platform that served me for bed, until nightfall I received those who, filing past, solicited my blessing. I distributed *sungdus* that protected the wearer against illness and accidents, and I also gave medicine to some sick people.

To make the people accept medicine called for a certain ingenuity. To give it to them as medicine that had been prepared in oversea countries would have been to have them refuse it point blank, or, if one of them had risked swallowing even a minimum dose, the regret for his (or her) action, the certainty that it would produce disastrous effects, the anxiety and commiseration of those around him, would not have failed to aggravate his malady. It is quite conceivable that, suggestion aiding, some might have died in consequence. In which case the unfortunate doctor would then become in the eyes of every one, a malevolent sorcerer, a diabolic poisoner, and I would not wish any stranger to gain such a reputation in Central Asia: it might cost him his life.

A doctor-lama, no more than his lay colleague of the West, has anything to fear of this kind. His patients can leave this world without causing his peace to be disturbed in any way. For this reason, therefore, the medicines I distributed were transformed into orthodox remedies. The quinine pills or aspirine tablets became *tsering rilbu*, "pills of long life". Sometimes I consecrated them myself, at others I gave them as having been consecrated by some very saintly hermit, in a far off region; or, again, I dissolved the medicinal powders in supposed holy water. To what subterfuges have I not had recourse when dealing with these guileless natives of the frontier. For the most part my ruses have been entirely successful and my remedies have occasionally produced results of which they seemed little capable. Those who believe in the

[1] That is to say cross-legged, in the position shown in the statues of the Buddha, which is the usual way of sitting for men in India and Tibet. A lady-lama receiving the faithful can permit herself this posture, which is not allowed to other women.

55

power of magnetism and of thought can think, if they like, that the very keen and sincere desire I had to relieve my patients intensified the natural virtues inherent in the Western drug, which they absorbed under an Eastern form. Their faith undoubtedly did the rest.

All Tibetans do not share this superstitious fear of foreign remedies. On the contrary, in other parts of the country these are greatly appreciated and are held to have almost miraculous efficacy. There exist at the present time in Tibet native doctors who have received their diplomas from the English Faculty of Medicine in Calcutta.

The next day I visited the child Grand Lama. With great ceremony I was first introduced to his parents, who were living in a sumptuous apartment. The father, a handsome giant, such as one often finds in the Kham country, was, it was said, chief of a small territory situated in the neighbourhood of Litang. He had a haughty, noble bearing and an expression that indicated both intrepidity and intelligence. His wife, the mother of the young *tulku*, was really beautiful. She, too, had a bold air; her big brown eyes sparkled in her golden face. Apart from her height, which was that of a Nordic goddess, she made me think of a lovely Neapolitan girl.

Besides the Grand Lama—their youngest child—this fine couple had a son and a daughter.

A plenteous meal was served, to which both Yongden and I did ample justice. However, there was little fear of our appearing greedy; even if we had wanted to, it would have been impossible for us to have swallowed even half the amount of food that was consumed by the fortunate father of the young lord of Labrang.

When everyone was satisfied, we were conducted to Jamyang Shadpa. He also had his private apartments—those of his predecessor—, and was surrounded by a little retinue of officials. Among them was the tutor whose duty consisted in teaching him monastic " good manners "

56

Later. he would have as masters the most learned professors in Labrang, and, still later, he would go to Lhasa to perfect his education at the University of Sera or Depung. This is the unvarying programme of study for a great *tulku*.

Meanwhile, the present tutor could be complimented on the beginning of this training. Correctly clothed in the monastic dress, which had been made to fit him, and wearing the traditional hat of Jamyang Shadpa, many sizes too large for his little head, the child already knew how to sit gravely on his throne, with an open book on his knees, and to look at the pages as though he were meditating on the meaning of what was written there. He also knew how to knot *sungdus*,[1] and to blow gently on them for the purpose of communicating to them a virtue that emanated from him. He could bless ritualistically as well, placing his tiny hands on the head of the notables among the faithful and lightly touching those of lesser degree with a little whisk of ribbons, which his chamberlain put into his hand.

It was not until the next day, when he was receiving a band of pilgrims, that I saw him exercise all his precocious talents. During my previous visit he had seemed a little frightened. What had his guardian told him about me?—Those around him knew me for a foreigner, but one well versed in everything that concerned Tibet and the Lamaist religion; and doubtless they wished their lord, in his new incarnation, to impress me favourably.

While I was talking to the monks present, the little fellow, seated on a high pile of cushions, remained motionless, with down-cast eyes, in the studied attitude that his master had taught him. But, all at once, his curiosity got the better of him and, looking me straight in the face, he smiled mischievously. Then, in spite of the monastic clothes in which he was imprisoned, he became for the moment a simple child, who, doubtless, would have liked

---

[1] *Sungdu* see previous note.

57

to jump down from his little throne, throw away the heavy crushing hat and restricting toga, and begin to play, as do all those of his age. It was but a flash of merriment. Subject already to strict discipline, did he think of his tutor, of the possible punishment the latter might inflict on him, or, as the faithful would have preferred to suppose, was the spirit of Jamyang Shadpa, who inhabited his infantile body, dominating its natural impulses?—The child became instantly grave again, recited some sentences he had learned, and offered me a book enveloped in yellow brocade, which one of the monks had handed him. It was the gift that had been prepared for me. At this the audience ended.

As I have just mentioned that the young Grand Lama might fear punishment, I will take this opportunity of mentioning that the high ecclesiastical dignitaries of Tibet, the Dalai Lama included, are not in early youth exempt from corporal punishment, which is freely administered to them by their Tibetan masters. The professor of grammar or history or the one who initiates the young lama in philosophical doctrines does not fail to inflict a good beating on him when he cannot recite his lesson correctly. Among these hardy people the spiritual directors themselves are not averse to pushing their disciples on the path of perfection by means of blows and kicks. After receiving such punishment the disciple must prostrate himself before his master and thank him for his vehement care of him. If I am not mistaken, some similar practice prevails in some Roman Catholic Orders.

What is striking, in the case of the great *tulkus*, is that, as soon as the punishment has been received by his pupil, the master who has inflicted it prostrates himself three times before him. He has chastised the imperfect instrument, which the young lama still is, then pays homage to the exalted personality (deceased god or sage) that animates and uses it for the purpose of con-

THE NEW GRAND LAMA
THE DAY OF HIS ENTHRONEMENT

THE LATE GRAND LAMA
OF THE LABRANG TASHIKYIL MONASTERY

tinuing his career and of accomplishing his work in this world. At least, this is the way in which Tibetans explain these contradictory acts.[1]

The following day I visited the monastery. After this visit, Tsöndu, who had been our guide, took Yongden and me to dine in his beautiful house. It was very luxuriously furnished in the style of the country. The two enormous teapots placed ready for the meal and the braziers full of hot cinders on which they stood were of solid silver decorated with gold ornaments. The cups were of jade, their saucers of chased gold, and their pagoda-shaped gold covers set with pearls and turquoises. Piles of cushions with covers made of leopard skins and beautiful rugs were placed as seats, and fine specimens of Chinese and Tibetan art, pictures and statuettes, decorated the room. In jarring contrast to these last, but perhaps more appreciated by the master of the house and his visitors, some chromolithographs of Paris showed here and there : views of the Place de la Concorde, of the Opera House, of the Seine near the Châtelet. I had already noticed copies of them in the home of the Tashi Lama's mother. Tsöndu thought these pictures represented Moscow. I undeceived him, and he was delighted to see my native city.

Casually, I was told that a Chinese chef presided over the kitchen. In Tibet, a Chinese chef is esteemed by gourmets as highly as his French confrère is in the West. For a host to have one in his service is a guarantee of his opulence and nice epicurism. Tsöndu made a point of emulating the rich Tibetans of society.

The dinner began with slices of dry bread. The people of Amdo are very fond of bread, which they eat as we eat biscuits and cakes. I do not share their taste for it. I can only eat bread when it is supplemented by

[1] With reference to *tulkus* and Tibetan theories concerning incarnated Lamas, those whom foreigners incorrectly call "Living Buddhas", see my book: *With Mystics and Magicians in Tibet*, page 113.

other food, and nothing appeared with which to eat the dry slices that lay piled on a big silver dish. Yongden, who likes bread as much as if he had been born in France, smiled ironically at me while Tsöndu was pressing me to partake of this unappetizing dainty.

When, at last, my host became convinced that his entreaties were in vain, he rang. He had one of those pretty table bells that were so generally used in our countries before electricity came into general use.

In answer to his call, the servants brought in some Chinese biscuits as well as two tins that contained others of foreign make. I nibbled a few. Rice cooked with butter and sugar and freely besprinkled with currants came next. This is the national sweet dish of Tibet; it is excellent when well prepared. I welcomed it. I then began to feel more hopeful about the meal; other courses would follow. The rich Tsöndu was offering me a feast in the Chinese fashion, where the dessert is served first and the soup last. And, indeed, dish succeeded dish: fish, meat, a variety of vegetable stews, tasty *momos*—minced meat enclosed in balls of steamed paste—and, to end with, soup with *pechis* in it, little triangular pieces of paste made with eggs and filled with highly seasoned minced meat.

We had begun eating at one o'clock in the afternoon, and we had barely finished by six in the evening. After having again talked for a while with Tsöndu and some friends of his who had arrived towards the end of the dinner, I rode back to my inn, escorted in procession, by servants carrying lanterns.

In order not to disappoint a very worthy man, the commercial agent of the *tulku* Grand Lama of Lob, I was obliged to accept another dinner the next day, at his house.

Other days were spent in more serious work: in consulting books and questioning learned lamas. I also went to a *ngagspa* monastery, which was situated in the country at a little distance from Labrang. The *ngagspas*, "men of secret words", are magicians, descendants of the Bön Shamanists,[1] who, before the introduction of Buddhism into Tibet, held the place now occupied by the lamas. Dispossessed of their power by the lamas, the Bön Shamans have taken their revenge, thanks to the tendency towards superstition that is innate in their adversaries. The thing has come about naturally, without any conscious trickery on the part of the conquered.

The Buddhism that was preached in Tibet by Hindu missionaries in the eighth and following centuries was far from being the original Buddhism. It contained, side by side with some excellent philosophic developments of the primitive doctrine, a number of theories and rites that were borrowed from the religious system called Tantrism that then dominated India and Nepal and that still flourishes there to this day.

There can be no question, here, of even briefly examining the very obscure origins of Tantrism. Suffice it to say that it comprises grossly superstitious or even vile practices,–magic rites, methods of psychic training, and philosophic theories of very varying value. Now the elements of which Tantrism is composed are to be met with elsewhere than in India. Theories and practices, which were analogous to those that the Indian missionaries introduced into Tibet, existed already among the Shamanist Böns.[2] Therefore, there was nothing to prevent a partial amalgamation of the alien religion with the one that the natives had practised up till then. In fact, many Bön beliefs and rites continued to exist under other names in Tibetan Buddhism, while the Böns—more

[1] Concerning Böns see Chapter VI.
[2] Perhaps, in addition to the Böns, there were in Tibet followers of other doctrines about which we have no information. It is written in a biography of Atisha, the celebrated Buddhist philosopher who lived for a long time in Tibet and died there (XIth century), that he exclaimed: "What a great number of doctrines exist in Tibet that are not to be found in India."

especially the " white " Böns—embodied in their religion a good number of Buddhic doctrines and rites.

It is thus that, disguised under the name of *ngagspas*, genuine Shamans have become incorporated into the Lamaist clergy. Still, they occupy a distinct position at the side of the regular clergy and their role principally consists in dealing with the demons.

There are independent groups of *ngagspas*, who possess temples of their own, where they meet together at certain times, living the rest of the time at home (the *ngagspas* marry). Other *ngagspas*, who do not belong to any group, but who have been initiated by a master of their sect, independently practise the rites that he has taught them. This they do either for their own benefit, or for remuneration at the request of people who want to be delivered from ills that have been caused by demons or who cherish less innocent wishes, such as the desire to harm an enemy or to destroy him. That which is commonly termed black magic lies within the province of the *ngagspas*, and they are all thought, if not actually to practise it, at any rate to be capable of doing so.

Some of the great lamaseries of the "Yellow Hat" sect have thought it useful to attach to themselves a group of *ngagspas*, who, outside the monastery walls, can in their stead hold constant intercourse with the evil spirits. The celebration of those rites that consist, not in subjugating these spirits, but in giving them the kind of worship that pacifies them, having been forbidden to the monks of this sect, they have devised an indirect means of assuring themselves against the attacks of the wicked of the other world, by making the *ngagspas* pay these malevolent beings the homage that satisfies them and offer them the nourishment for which they crave. In this way illness and accidents are diverted from the monastery and its prosperity as well as that of its members is assured.

In exchange for their services, the *ngagspas* who are

attached to the temple dependent on the monastery receive a grant from it.

The temple belonging to the *ngagspas* of Labrang was large and very well kept. The frescoes decorating its walls represented the subjects, at once gruesome and picturesque, which are to be seen in all buildings that have been consecrated to the terrible deities. Most of these deities are ex-demons who have been converted and forcibly subjugated by a magician saint and who have afterwards been constrained by him to use their power for the defence of the Lamaist religion and its faithful. Nevertheless, it is said that some high mystical personalities occasionally assume a terrifying and demoniacal appearance for the purpose of terrorizing and punishing wicked beings.

Around these mysterious figures of the Tibetan pantheon, the artist, in his frescoes, had grouped a whole world of grimacing beings, both male and female, who were busy flaying unfortunate human beings, tearing at their entrails, devouring their hearts, or giving themselves up to other equally delectable sports. Tibetans, however, are no longer impressed by pictures of this kind; they abound in their country, but, apart from scholars who understand their symbolic meaning, no one there pays any attention to them.

With the exception of a few *ngagspas*, who are held to possess very extensive supernormal powers and who, in consequence, rejoice in a great reputation, the rest of them are generally pleasant people, free from the haughty bearing that the magicians belonging to the regular clergy affect. The simple manner of many of the *ngagspas* is probably due to their status in the ecclesiastical world, which is definitely inferior to that of the monks who are members of a lamasery. However, I have met some whose particular courtesy was the outcome of their rather sceptical ideas, which prevented them from taking anything very seriously. In them, it took the form of a sort of universal benevolence, slightly pitying, slightly ironical, and essentially detached, which they extended to all and everything, not forgetting themselves.

I was very cordially received by the *ngagspas* of Labrang. I passed some hours talking with them, while drinking tea, and then I returned to my inn.

At dawn next morning, I continued my journey.

V

THROUGH KANSU AND SZECHWAN

YONGDEN has travelled with me for eight years. I have had ample time in which to become accustomed to his sometimes strange ways, yet, he has just amazed me, and what is more curious still, he himself is just as astonished at what he has done as I am.

Notwithstanding our early start from Labrang, we have not been able to get as far as we intended to. Some people who wanted to wish me a good journey, offer me presents, and receive my blessing arrived at the inn after I had left. They then followed me, caught me up and delayed me. Later, the cords on the mules' packs loosened, and the beasts had to be unloaded and bales re-corded. . . . In short, night is falling when we reach a small hamlet and realize that it is impossible for us to go further that day.

One of the servants goes to knock at the door of a farm and asks for hospitality. It is curtly refused him. He returns to tell us of his rebuff and is on the point of seeking shelter elsewhere, when Yongden stops him.

The young lama has a sudden inspiration. Boldly hailing a woman who is looking at us from a window, he imperiously demands to be directed to the house of a certain Passang, of whom I have never heard. It turns out that he is the owner of the finest house in the hamlet. Yongden goes there, and always in the same imperious tone declares that we have been sent by Kushog Leszang of the Labrang monastery, who orders the master of the

65   E

house to receive us and give us the best accommodation possible.

Who is Kushog Leszang, and how is it that Yongden knows him? I have not the least idea. But what I do know is that there never has been any question of his recommendation or of our requiring hospitality in this hamlet. Only the lateness of the hour has induced us to halt here.

Nevertheless, the door is immediately opened to us, and we are welcomed with great respect. I am shown into a pleasant little room, where I shall pass the night. While my people unload the mules and bring in the bags that contain my blankets and camp bed, my hosts busy themselves at preparing a meal for us.

Very soon I do justice to a copious and excellent supper. Then all the inmates of the house, masters in front and servants behind, march in file before me soliciting my blessing. They want to call in the neighbours, but I say I am tired, and promise to receive them in the morning.

However, before going to bed, I detain Yongden in my room. I am anxious to know what caused him to think of this lama who is unknown to me. I question him.

"Who is Kushog Leszang? When did you meet him? Why have you never spoken of him to me?"

"I don't know him."

"You don't know him! . . . And Passang?"

"I don't know him either. . . ."

"Come, let us understand each other: I can quite believe that the idea of saying we had been recommended and that we must be received was a ruse on your part. But the names of these people, how did you know them, and how did you know that Passang was a *jindag*[1] of Kushog Leszang?"

---

[1] Written *spyinbdag*, literally "Owner of gifts"—a householder and, more especially, one who, by means of gifts, provides for a monk's material needs.

" I am quite as astonished as you are. I can only think that during our stay in Labrang I heard this lama and his jindag spoken of, but I don't remember having done so. And, what is stranger still, rack my brains as I may, even now I cannot remember when and how I learnt of their existence. These two names and what I had to say in order to obtain lodgings flashed suddenly into my mind when Tobgyal told us that we had been refused hospitality. I did not stop to think, I acted on impulse. . . ."

I thought it all very extraordinary. However, the sudden flash that had kindled Yongden's memory had come at a most opportune moment. So, putting off all other reflexions until later, I sent the young man away and was soon fast asleep.

I woke early, but I was already awaited by some twenty people who had come in quest of blessings, charms, and divinatory rites.

One by one they told me of their wishes. They begged me to consecrate and distribute water of longevity and to magnetize some barley, which they would share among themselves at home or send to relations and friends who lived in other villages. Both this grain and the water of long life are held to possess a special virtue that preserves soundness of body, this virtue having been communicated to them by the officiating lama.

I thought all the ceremonies were over when Passang respectfully begged me to exorcise his house. He had not noticed anything particularly suspect in regard to it, but he thought that as the demons are so many and so cunning, it were better to prevent any consequences of their malice than be obliged to fight them later. This argument could be supported. It is one that we apply to illness and upon which the laws of hygiene are based. I therefore proceeded with a preventive exorcism of the farm. It is possible to accustom oneself to anything. I have come to officiate with the solemnity of an archbishop, but these performances distress me.

When I first began living among the country people of Tibet, I had tried to show them the uselessness of these rites and to convince them that belief in their efficacy had been explicitly condemned as a fatal error by the Buddha, of whom they declare themselves the disciples. It had been labour lost. In no way was I able to shake their perfunctory attachment to secular superstitions; doubts even arose in their minds as to the genuineness and orthodoxy of the Buddhism that I pretended to profess. The villagers began even to suspect me of being a Christian missionary who was trying to corrupt their religion.

Later on, in other regions of the country, when my standing as a member of the Buddhist Religious Order could no longer be called in question and when it was also recognized that I possessed the power of effectually celebrating certain Lamaic rites, I still openly showed my horror of ceremonialism. I then continued, and with more authority, to point out its baleful consequences and to show how, in rites, a series of gestures and words take the place of mental action, which alone is of consequence. I had with me the opinion and the example of the great mystics and contemplative hermits of Tibet, who also reject all rites, but the ordinary people opposed me with an obstinate humility.

They said that *dubthobs*[1] and *gomchens*[2] could, if they thought proper, dispense with ceremonies. They were greater than the gods, and could force obedience from them as well as from the demons. But it did not benefit poor ordinary men to dare imitate these spiritual giants; therefore, they, simple laymen, would keep to the customs of their fathers.

At Kum-Bum I had formed the habit of constantly wearing the Lamaic monastic robe and I continued to do so while travelling. Under this presentment, it was more

[1] *Dubthob*, written *grubthob*: a magician saint.
[2] *Gomchen*, written *sgomchen*: a contemplative hermit.

68

difficult than ever to evade the "ecclesiastical duties" incumbent upon me.

Yongden, who is very sceptical with regard to the importance of outward forms, laughed at my scruples.

"Pshaw!" he said, "blow on the back of this cripple and into the ears of this deaf woman. They will be none the worse for it, and you will greatly please them. Then, you, who have practised thought concentration, cannot you emit a beneficent force, which your breath or the water and the pills that have been consecrated by you will communicate to these poor people? You must have compassion on them and treat them after their own fashion, just as the learned lamas and saintly anchorites do."

Alas! even without being unduly modest I could not regard myself as a very "learned lama", and my saintliness did not appear to me to be devoid of alloy. But Yongden, always eminently practical, continued.

"You and I, are we or are we not genuine lamas? Yes, we are. Well, we have decided to present ourselves as lamas during this journey, we must therefore consistently play our parts, otherwise people will become suspicious of us and imagine that we have disguised ourselves for some bad purpose, and, as a result, harm could come to us. Moreover, if, through our fault, people were to commit the sin of doing harm to real lamas—as we are—, we would have to take the responsibility for their wrongdoing and bear the consequences."

There was nothing unsound about these arguments, and the most telling of them was that it was essential for us not to become suspect, seeing that we could avoid it without hurting anybody. It was in this way that I became resigned to the performance of my ecclesiastical functions. These were not always confined to simple ritualistic gestures, sometimes my character of lama gave rise to some touching incidents.

At Passang's, a woman, who had stood apart during all the ceremonies, came to me when the others had left.

"My father died last week," she sobbed out. "What has become of him? I want to know. Will he have a happy rebirth? Will you look and tell me?"

To try and reason with her would have been useless. This woman did not seek any empty consolation. She wanted to know something definite. Where had her father been reborn.

I did not know, and, also, my ideas on the subject of rebirth differed greatly from hers. But it was necessary to give an answer to this agonized enquirer. Charity demanded it.

"Come back in half an hour," I said. "Let me be left alone. In meditation, I will try to see your father's fate."

I did not feel at all inclined to treat the matter lightly. A daughter's sorrow at the loss of a beloved father is not unknown to me. I had myself too poignantly experienced the bitterness of it to ridicule in another the strange fancies it can induce. An answer was required of me, but I was very loth to invent any kind of story and to tell it to the woman who had faith in my clear-sightedness.

It would be better to leave it to chance, or to that which, being ignorant of its source, we term "chance".

I sat down in the posture of meditation, with half-closed eyes, driving away all thought, making my mind a blank, until I gained that state where all consciousness of my surroundings was lost. Then, spontaneously, a subjective picture rose before me of a Chinese commercial house. I saw the employees busy with clients and the goods displayed all around. Everything gave the impression that the place belonged to a rich merchant. I saw the master, tall and smiling, dressed in black silk, and I *knew*—without being told, as it happens in dreams—that he had quite recently become the father of a boy. Then the picture faded, and I gradually regained my normal consciousness.

Why had I seen a Chinese shop? It seemed to me

70

that it would have been more natural if I had seen some pictures of the Tibetan life in which I had been immersed since I left Sining. I did not attempt to reason about it, it would have been useless.

Whatever might be the reason of my vision, it supplied me with an answer that would spare me the remorse of having lightly treated an earnest enquiry.

The method that I had used is in practice among the Tibetan mystics, and any lama, acquainted with it, would have employed it to obtain an answer for the unhappy girl. Therefore I did not feel guilty of any fraud.

"Your father did not linger in the *bardo*,"[1] I said to her. "He has already been reborn in our world. It is not in Tibet that he has been born, but in China. He is the son of a rich merchant, whose house I have seen. I cannot tell you in which town it is, but it must be in the north of China, for the men who appeared to me were tall like those of Kansu.

"Do not cry any more, your father will live in comfort and in a country where the religion of the Buddha exists. He will be able to hear it preached and to practise it."

The woman still wept, but much less bitterly. She now only grieved over her own loss. As to the deceased, she felt reassured about his fate. Her filial love rejoiced at knowing that her beloved father had been reborn in happy surroundings.

The country continues to be picturesque and beautiful. It is sparsely populated, and for this reason we are obliged to travel far each day. Although we are at the end of March, the temperature is still low in these highlands, it is scarcely possible for us to camp. We, ourselves, would

---

[1] The state in which the " spirit "—or to use a more correct translation of the word, the consciousness: *rnanshes*—of the deceased remains after death and until rebirth in this or another world. *Bardo* literally means " between two ", that is, between death and birth.

not suffer much from cold in the tents, but nights passed motionless in the open might be harmful to the animals; after the fatigue of a long day's march they need the shelter of a stable. Also, we must find straw or some other kind of fodder and dry peas (the usual food for horses in Amdo), so as not to use up our emergency reserve.

Apart from the care required of us by our beasts, other reasons urged us to refrain from camping there. The region was not held to be very safe, and our fine big Sining mules might prove a temptation to robbers, who would not find it hard to dispose of them to their advantage.

Unfortunately, the villages were few, and the inns far apart from one another: distances that forced us to make a tiring "trek" each day. The weather remained fine and dry, although snow fell one night during our stay in a village called Kargnag (perhaps originally Karnag: black rampart).

It was in Kargnag that I became the heroine of an amusing comedy, which Yongden had started without foreseeing its absurd developments.

Seeing an urchin staring at me, the Lama had jokingly said to him:—" You are looking at Jetsun Kushog, do you know that she is a hundred years old! "

Extremely astonished, the boy had run with the extraordinary news to his father. The father had immediately repeated it to his neighbours, and thus, spreading from mouth to mouth, it had rapidly circulated the whole village. A centenarian, looking very agile, had just arrived on horseback! Everyone wished to see this phenomenon. My room was soon invaded by people who went into raptures over my healthy looks.

The women scrutinized me very closely: no white hairs! They asked me to open my mouth: all her teeth! I held myself erect, I had no wrinkles, my sight was good,

72

and my hands did not tremble! Wonder of wonders! Never had anyone so aged come to the village, they declared, and they never could have imagined it possible for a centenarian to have such a youthful appearance.

Then since, in Tibet, all sentiments—joy, pain, respect, admiration—express themselves materially by presents, the natives' admiring astonishment turned into offerings, which arrived from all quarters in edible form: butter, wheat and barley flour, cheese, meat. I could not stem this flood of provisions, which ran from the door to the *kang* upon which I was seated. In strict honesty, perhaps, I should have proclaimed that I would have to live many more years before attaining my hundredth birthday, but virtue does not always lie where the rigid moral codes would have us believe. It depends upon circumstances, and I think that, in these matters, charity must be the criterion. To be kind to others, to cause no pain, is the best rule of conduct. Now, the good people of Kargnag rejoiced exceedingly at the spectacle I was giving them. In their monotonous lives, the advent of a vigorous centenarian was a conspicuous event, one that would be remembered of an evening for many years to come. Perhaps with the aid of the imagination of the most inventive among them, a legend would spring up, which would become the glory of Kargnag and the envy of the neighbouring villages.

It would have been very cruel of me to rob them of their present joy and all that this innocent joke reserved for them in the future. What matter the few pounds of butter, meat, and flour that they paid for this pleasure. The farmers were sufficiently well-to-do to give me presents without depriving themselves of anything. Besides they counted on being repaid in their next lives, with full interest too, for these meritorious tokens of respect. Meanwhile, they hoped that the blessings, which they forced me to distribute, the woollen threads, which they made me pull out of my robe to serve them for charms,

73

would communicate to them something of my ever-green longevity.

The incident that marked my stay in another village was less agreeable. There is a fairly large *gompa*[1] there, and as, in these out of the way monasteries, some of the monks usually have provisions to sell, two of my servants went to enquire what we could buy. They returned to say that they had been rudely treated. They had been recognized as *Sentuanpas*[2] and the monks of the place, for reasons best known to themselves, did not like the people of that tribe.

Matters would have rested there, had not some blustering clericals, who are known by the name of *dobdobs*,[3] come to the inn where we lodged and insolently tried to pick a quarrel with my men. Without showing myself —which would have been contrary to custom and have shown a lack of dignity—, I ordered their immediate ejection. A dispute ensued, blows were exchanged, and the *dobdobs* went off, vowing they would presently return with friends and guns. After their departure, the innkeeper securely barricaded his door, and my servants loaded their rifles in readiness for an attack.

I was very worried. We could expect no outside help, for, according to the innkeeper, though the villagers had no sympathy with these quarrelsome *trapas*, who dishonoured the monk's habit and only dreamed of evil deeds, they would do nothing in our defence. What kind of a man was the head of the monastery? Would he, and could he, check the fighting spirits of his *gompa*? It was practically certain that he knew nothing about what was happening, but I did not see any way of bringing it to his notice. I would not let my men go out, lest they

[1] *Gompa*: lamasery.
[2] A tribe that inhabits the province of Kansu. The *Sentuanpas* are of Mongolian origin but often have Chinese blood in them.
[3] On the subject of *dobdobs* see *With Mystics and Magicians in Tibet*, page 109.

should get molested, and another messenger might not be able to reach him.

Whilst I was reflecting, Sotar, my head-servant, fearing the return of the armed *trapas*, disclosed my true identity to the innkeeper, assuring him that if any harm came to me, to those who accompanied me, or to anything that belonged to me, the Chinese General at Sining would send troops to burn the monastery and also very probably the village.

The threat must have frightened the landlord; the memory of the terrible reprisals carried into effect by this general's soldiers in the neighbourhood of Labrang was still fresh in the minds of the Amdo people. He evidently managed to let someone at the monastery know what he had just heard. As to Sotar, he did not at the time breathe a word about the initiative he had taken, and we sat up all night waiting for the expected attack. Seeing that everything remained quiet, before dawn I ordered our departure, and by sunrise we were already far from that inhospitable spot.

Only the next day did Sotar confess to me what he had done. I was very annoyed; for to be regarded by the natives as one of themselves is the only means by which to obtain real knowledge of their thoughts and ways.

Proceeding in the direction of Szechwan, we began to hear vague rumours of the fighting that was taking place in the south. As it is usually the case in China, bands of soldiers had detached themselves from the regular troops, either after a defeat or because the promised pay had not been forthcoming, and were wandering about the country living on brigandage. These men were totally devoid of that vague nobility of mind that makes the Tibetan brigand a kind of chivalrous barbarian. To meet them was dangerous. In such an encounter, the greatest good fortune that a traveller could hope for would be, after abandoning all his belongings, to come uninjured out of their clutches.

Strictly speaking, if the traveller seemed a person of note, above all if he were thought to be a foreigner, they would accost him, with a polite request. " My horse is tired," one of them would say to a rider, " please *lend* me yours."

In this way, they would likewise " borrow " the carts and horses, and merchandise of every kind; these things being always precisely what they most " needed " at the moment. They exchanged their rags for the new clothes of their victims. But all this was only play, an innocent pastime along the road. Tragedy supervened when the hordes took possession of a village or small town and plundered it.

At Minchow, where I stopped, the villagers had a great deal to say about these bands, although as yet the brigands had not come near the town.

Minchow is only a little town, but one that is full of commerce and bustle. I lodged outside the fortifications, in an inn that had several large walled-in courtyards. From among these, I had chosen the furthermost in which to put up the tents belonging to Yongden and me. Notwithstanding the cold, which was still intense, I preferred to be in a clean tent than in the evil-smelling and dirty room of a Chinese inn.

We had been in Minchow four days, waiting for one of my servants, who had sprained his ankle, to be able to travel, when at sunset our landlord came to warn us that a band of robbers had been sighted and that we would need to be on our guard during the night. As to our tents, he begged us to have them moved. The walls of the yard in which they stood gave directly on to waste land, and he did not think that the height of the walls was sufficient to give us adequate security. He begged us to sleep in rooms, or, at any rate, to have our tents taken to a large inner court that was surrounded on every side by buildings.

We chose the latter alternative. All our baggage was

CHINESE TEMPLES IN THE PROVINCE OF KANSU

carried to a room near the stable, where our servants were quartered, and the lama and I continued to sleep in our tents, keeping with us only our bedclothes.

All night watchers relieved one another on the town walls and also in the houses situated, as our inn was, outside them. The night passed peacefully. The sound of shots in the far distance made us think that some marauders had attempted an attack, but the firing was too slight for it to come from a regular band.

Complete calm reigned the next day.

Contradictory rumours circulated. Some said that the brigands had gone eastward, others that the Mohammedans were preparing an insurrection and might come to Minchow. My people were of the opinion that we should leave the region at once. Sönam's ankle was better; he declared he was ready to start. I had some clothes sold, also bedding, and various other things that we could do without. The getting rid of these superfluous articles would lighten the mules' loads and permit us to hurry on, or, if necessary, to carry more provisions should the villages where we hoped to obtain fresh supplies be in the hands of the bandits, and we were obliged to keep away.

The night passed again without incident. We left Minchow the 16th April at dawn and travelled fast.

The road we followed was at first wide and flat, but it did not remain so for long. We soon came to mountain paths, narrow and steep, which traversed rock-strewn slopes and often, from high up, skirted a tributary of the Heishiu ho. We crossed the river many times and, at one place, very nearly took a bath.

In that country, there is nothing to indicate the exact position of the fords, which is, moreover, frequently changed by the floods. We had put our trust in a mountain path that ended at the river. Sotar was riding in front. Unable to see the bottom through the turbid rushing water, he relied, as usual, on his beast's instinct.

The water was deep; we were obliged to take our feet out of the stirrups and hold our legs up. Suddenly, Sotar's horse lost its footing and began to swim awkwardly, impeded by the weight it carried. Sotar was a good rider; he managed to turn his animal round, which immediately touched ground again and recovered its footing. On seeing the accident, the other boys at once stopped the mules. I ordered everyone to return to the bank. It was not possible, with laden beasts, to try to find the ford. If need be, Tobgyal, who was a strong swimmer, could take off part of his clothing and with an unsaddled horse explore the passage before we again attempted it.

However, we could perhaps spare him the trouble of doing so. Close by, there was a little hamlet perched on the cliff. Its inhabitants certainly knew the ford and, for payment, should be willing to guide us across it. Yongden climbed up to the cottages.

A mischievous sprite was surely hidden there, who wanted to amuse himself at our expense. Yongden had barely reached the level of the village when his mule—usually so docile—began to kick and then unexpectedly to rear, without apparently any visible reason for its change of temper. The poor lama was thrown on to a little platform, which fortunately was bordered by a wall on the river side. But for this wall, which held him back, the young man would have been hurled into space and then crushed on the rocks below or drowned by the current.

Badly bruised, he picked himself up and resumed his quest. Nobody consented to cross the ford in front of us, but everyone was willing to point out the way. They declared that we had entered the water at the right spot, only after that we should not have tried to go in a straight line, but to have borne a little down stream and then a little up stream, then have done this, then again that. . . . The river was wide, and indeed there was much room in which to make many evolutions . . . and also to drown. . . .

In these regions men and animals are often drowned while crossing the fords. These accidents trouble the natives as little as to-day the fatal motor car and aeroplane accidents trouble the Westerners. Each mode of travel has its particular risks!

We tried again, and, more kindly than we had judged them to be, some of the villagers followed our movements from above and shouted the course we must take.

We were aiming for the small town of Siku. I knew nothing about it, not even from hearsay. On the map a red lozenge showed it to be a Chinese *ting*,[1] which was situated practically on my route, at the extreme south of Kansu, where the province joins the great grassy solitudes of Northern Tibet. It could not be an important place, but I imagined it as a small trading centre, like the frontier town of Dangar near the Koko Nor, and I counted on finding all the provisions I needed there.

The valley we followed opened into a much larger one, along which flows the Heishiu ho. Ascending the course of the river we continued in the direction of Siku.

Night was falling and it was beginning to rain when we came in view of the town. We had probably been seen by the sentinels who were posted in the watch tower on account of the unsettled condition of the country, and I do not know what kind of optical illusion can have caused our modest party of five to appear formidable to them. Even before we came near it, the town gate was hurriedly shut, and half a dozen soldiers, gun in hand, showed themselves on the walls, ready to defend the place.

Never before had I created such a sensation. Although I did not fail to register a correct degree of pride, I was also very worried. The rain increased, and the China-

---

[1] A town where there is a resident administrative officer.

men, who, complacently fingering their weapons, regarded us from the top of the crenelated walls, did not inspire me with confidence. It is unwise to put dangerous toys in the hands of children, and the Chinese soldiers, often very young in these outstations, sometimes give way to playful impulses that prove dangerous to others.

At length, while we were still wondering at the strangeness of our reception and asking the reason for it of the "braves" ornamenting the walls, the gate was slowly opened, with studied solemnity, and a herald appeared. He was on horseback. This fact did not permit him to advance towards us with the dignity he had doubtless premeditated. Our laden mules had instinctively sought shelter from the rain by standing close to the gate, and my men waited behind them; in this way the passage was almost blocked.

The envoy could only partially emerge, his horse's croup remaining in the shadow, under the arch. The darkness, which was rapidly increasing, added to the phantasmal aspect of the scene; man and beast had the appearance of animated figures in a bas-relief.

"Who are you, you who carry arms? (We had three guns, he could not see our revolvers.) From what country do you come, and what are your intentions?"

I foresaw that Sotar was on the point of proudly reciting my titles and qualifications, and I felt very anxious. Now that we were so near Tibet, where news travels miraculously quickly, it was more than ever necessary to safeguard my incognito. Happily my son, who had already realized this, hastened to anticipate any indiscretion on the part of my boys.

"I have official passports," he answered. "I cannot unpack them in the rain, but I will show them as soon as I am under cover. I am a lama and am on a pilgrimage; my servants are authorized to carry arms for our protection against robbers. I have come here to buy provisions."

This statement seemed to satisfy the messenger. The rain now fell in torrents, he probably wanted to get home as quickly as possible.

"I will report your words to the magistrate," he said.

He did not add that he granted us leave to enter the town, but he also did not issue any order to prevent our doing so. While he was turning his horse round, my boys quickly pushed the mules in behind him. When the gate was shut, we were all inside.

An inn stood just by the wall. I rushed into it. Several muleteers had already found lodging there. Still the landlord managed to give me a little room, where I could pass the night alone. The stables were full; my poor beasts had to remain tied up outside. The men tried to put up a sort of tarpaulin lean-to, but it was too small and only partly covered the animals. Very soon, however, my lot resembled theirs, the rain cascaded into my room.

The bad weather did not prevent the magistrate from coming to verify the lama's statements regarding his identity and his papers. Two subalterns and four armed soldiers formed the official's escort. He was very courteous, which is usual in China, where the civil servants are, with but few exceptions, people of good education. Moreover, Yongden is an authentic lama and a Tibetan: the papers, which had been officially given him, certified these two facts and authorized him to possess arms for his defence. There was not the least deception in his case. As to me, I was esteemed a negligible quantity and remained unquestioned.

All that we gained from our visit to Siku was the amusement of assisting at an absurd comedy and the discomfort of being drenched to the skin. We found nothing to buy but a little salt pork. The widespread rumours concerning the brigands who wandered over the country kept the merchant caravans from travelling. The inhabitants of Siku had only sufficient provisions for themselves, and they lived in constant fear of a raid which would rob them of even that little.

The rain ceased during the night. When I awoke, the weather was fine. From my window I could see a lone dark mountain, rising directly in front of the town, and, on the right, the entrance to a short valley, which opened out into a sunny plain. Peace reigned, and the valley that led to the sunlit *thang*[1] conjured up, to us who knew them, the radiant solitudes of Northern Tibet, with their lakes of sapphire water set between banks of silver spangled pink and mauve stones.

"Look, Sotar," I said to the Lhasapa,[2] who was standing by me, "if we were wise we would stay here. We would build hermitages on that mountain and end our days in meditation. What is the use of travelling over the earth. . . . All the worlds, and all that which lies beyond them, are in our mind."

I can scarcely imagine a traveller speaking in this way to his European servant, but Easterners are different. The Tibetan understood me and thought as I did. But like me, he also lacked wisdom. He sighed and pensively went to rejoin his comrades who were strapping the luggage on the mules. Soon after we left Siku. The happy hour when all ties are severed had not struck for us.

The next place on our route that the map indicates as being of some importance is called Nanping. Perhaps it will be possible to get provisions there; meanwhile, unless unexpectedly favoured by fortune, we must considerably reduce our rations. It is with this unpleasant prospect before us that we retravel the road of the day before. In going to Siku we had slightly gone out of our way.

The region we are crossing is cultivated by farmers

[1] *Thang*, Tibetan for large, flat plain.
[2] A native of Lhasa.

of Tibetan descent. It is a mountainous country, where the scattered villages are separated, one from the other, by vast tracts of woodland. The natives of these parts are often cross-grained and inhospitable. We usually sleep in our tents, but as close as possible to the villages, for the sake of the relative safety that such proximity affords.

At nearly every stopping-place sick people come to beg me to heal them. They describe the symptoms and causes of their maladies in a most fantastic way. The number and the strangeness of the various painful sensations that poor human beings are capable of experiencing surpass all imagination.

One afternoon, a *trapa* comes to tell me that several of his family have recently died and asks me whether these deaths may not have been due to the fact that the house in which they lived faces the wrong direction. The direction in which a building faces is held to be of the utmost importance in China and Tibet.

Probably what this man says is true and his enquiry genuine. But, as I notice another *trapa* standing outside the tent, who seems to be listening to what I am saying to his comrade inside, I wonder if these people are not setting a trap for me, in order to find out if I am a true lama? In the uncertainty of not knowing whether this is so or not, it will be best to make my answer sound strictly orthodox from a Lamaistic point of view. This will not prevent me from slipping into it some advice on hygiene.

I get him to explain the exact situation of the house. I ask for a little earth to be taken from the four sides of it and brought to me in four separate packets. The *trapa* immediately rides away to get what I require. In the evening he returns with it. I take the earth and postpone my answers until the next morning.

I already know that one of the rooms in the house has no window, that the sun never enters it. I am also in possession of several other details. I ponder deeply, and the next morning I give the oracle.

"Given that the front door receives the sun's rays, its position is favourable, but the dark room must be provided with a window that will give access to the beneficent light.

"All the house shall be thoroughly cleaned. All that it contains shall be taken out, and the dwelling purified with the fumes of *sang*[1]. When all the household utensils have been cleaned and the clothes, carpets and blankets been beaten outside, everything shall be put back into the house and *sang* burnt there again.

"A picture or image of the Buddha shall be placed in each room, and all the rooms shall be kept quite clean, so as not to show lack of respect to the Buddha, who will be there in effigy. For the same reason, no one shall spit on any floor in the house (such abstention will be difficult to obtain, but, perhaps, piety will perform the miracle).

"Finally, you will go to the Abbot of the neighbouring monastery and ask him to bless a Sipao (a particular drawing printed on paper or cotton fabric that is supposed to be a powerful charm), and you will place it on the front door."

All these things can do no harm, they may even do good, and they are, at the same time, in conformity with Lamaic customs. The Grand Lama of the monastery—whom I shall never see—will be pleased at the indirect compliment I pay him in recognizing his authority and power, and, consequently, if anyone should happen to cast a doubt as to my genuineness as lama, he would take him for a fool.

[1] *Sang* is the name given to the dried needles of some varieties of coniferae, to cypress leaves, to young fronds of some ferns and shoots of several other plants, which are burned on charcoal to produce perfumed smoke. This smoke is considered to have the virtue of purifying people and things.

Apart from the few presents that consultations of this kind bring me, our provision bags remain unfilled. The successive bad harvests of the past years, the raids carried out by the brigands, and the levied taxes have ruined the country; there is nothing left to buy. We are even without flour and must content ourselves with the little sun-dried mutton that I have brought from Kum-Bum, in anticipation of just such an emergency. Now and then we are able to find some dandelion leaves, which we pick and eat without condiments. This makes a change from our dried meat diet, but we do not come across the leaves every day. If our beasts were not so laden and the country so hilly, we could rapidly reach Nanping; as it is we are forced to proceed slowly.

Occasionally, too, we are obliged to go out of our way, the Shawa pass, which we want to cross, has been blocked by the inhabitants of a village who are fearing an attack from bandits coming from Szechwan. The pass is at the top of densely wooded slopes. The natives have cut down some of the big trees and have laid them along the path that crosses the mountain. A pedestrian might be able to thread his way through, but not riders, nor laden beasts.

We have to go very far out of our way. This delay causes us another disappointment; we had hoped to find food the other side of the mountain.

One consolation, however, is allowed us. That same evening we come upon a large and prosperous farm, such as is rarely seen, even in Tibet proper. I count about a hundred cows as they return from the fields, and I can see others in the distance. The house is an immense stone building, the rather large windows of which are protected by heavy wooden shutters. We are received with politeness, and a huge room, more than sixty feet in length, is placed at our disposal. In Tibet, masters and servants, women and men, very often share the same room, especially when travelling. As Tibetans do not undress at night, they do not, as we do, feel the need of private rooms.

Servants place the cushions and blankets that constitute their master's bed on the floor. The master, if he be richly clad, may perhaps take off his outer garment and go to his couch in just his vest and trousers. Once under the blankets, if these are warm enough, he will often discard his vest and sleep naked down to the waist. This is what is done by the majority of Tibetans of both sexes, when they are at home.

As to the women, after removing their jewellery and outer robe, they sleep in the long petticoat and chemise that they wear under the latter.

As regards the servants, peasants, and the common people, who neither have thick cushions nor warm blankets, they go to sleep fully dressed, with just their belts loosened.

In the big room that was offered us, my boys make a kind of shelter with one of my tents and put my bed in it . . . in this way I was at home. The grand lamas, when travelling, seclude themselves in this way, by means of curtains, in order to perform their religious exercises in private. It did not appear extraordinary for me to imitate them.

There, too, I had to pay for the hospitality that had been shown us, by blessing the whole house. The farmer's chaplain assisted me as acolyte, carrying the grain and water that I had consecrated.

Many people are under the impression that to the traveller who leaves the beaten track each hour brings some joyous or dramatic adventure. The truth is less romantic. Most of the days pass uneventfully. Monotonously? Indeed no. For the one who knows how to look and feel, every moment of this free wandering life is an enchantment. Also, in such journeys, the periods of blessed repose never last for long. Something always "happens" to interrupt them.

An adventure awaited us while we were quite innocently going through a wood full of blossoming trees and rejoicing in the excellent condition of the paths.

We were approaching Gomi, when a farmer of the district came along and for a few minutes spoke with us. He very kindly asked us to spend the night at his place, giving us careful directions for finding the house. Then, having no luggage, he rode quickly away, repeating again from the distance that he would have a meal prepared for us.

This agreeable meeting, the prospect of a comfortable lodging and a good supper makes us all feel exceedingly cheerful. We hurry on and, about two hours later, as night is falling, we reach the village.

The first thing my boys do is to ask where the farmer lives, but before anyone can answer, they are confronted by an individual who, shouting at the top of his voice, proclaims that, by order of the local chief, no one is to give us shelter or sell us anything. Attracted by the noise he makes, the people come out of their houses and gather round my men.

I had remained a little distance behind with my son. When we arrive upon the scene, it has already become animated. Quickly making my way through the crowd to see what is happening, I find my three servants being harangued by a maniac, who, with eyes starting out of his head, gesticulates threateningly. The villagers are still quiet and silent, hesitating as to the course they should take. But situations of this kind are dangerous; they must be dealt with quickly, otherwise they are liable to get out of hand. The natives may turn on my men at any moment.

I cast a rapid glance at those about me, there are about fifty unarmed men. With our weapons, we can·

hold out for some time against them, if matters grow worse.

" Shall I hit him? " Sotar says briefly.

Of course he must, and quickly, unless we wish to receive blows ourselves.

I answer him in one word:

" Dung! " (hit).

Bang! the brawler receives a good punch in the chest. Sönam immediately follows with a blow capable of stunning an ox, while the third boy belabours the man's sides with his heavy cudgel. The enemy falls prone. The desired effect is produced, no one will interfere with us.

We catch sight of a clean and empty spot, which looks like a threshing floor. I give my orders:

" Let the guns and revolvers be seen, pitch the tents, and advise the people not to come wandering round us in the night. Tell them there will be a watcher on guard, who will shoot at sight, without warning."

We are left severely alone and we begin to settle in. Bravely disregarding the magistrate's commands, an old woman brings us a bundle of firewood. The lama recompenses her generously.

An officious intermediary cautiously approaches Yongden and tells him that the local official has soldiers posted at the top of the pass that we mean to climb the next day and that no one is allowed to cross it without a letter bearing his seal. He also says that this official will examine our luggage in the morning, and then goes on to relate many other things likely to impress us. The good man has evidently been sent by the " official " about whom he talks so emphatically. It is likewise apparent that the great man himself does not dare to face us. This proves that he has no soldiers at his command, and, probably, too, that he is not certain whether his subordinates will support him against lamas, and energetic lamas, at that. Tibetans greatly admire strength, and we have just proved that we are not afraid of any-thing.

The conversation I overhear, hidden in my tent, enlightens me as to the meaning of the scene that has passed. The magistrate takes us for genuine Tibetans —rich merchants or lamas—and is trying to extort a generous bribe from us in return for a free passage. He is endeavouring to do it by a process of intimida-tion. It is an old trick and one that nearly always succeeds with the natives. Shall I pay or shall I let him know who I am? I would almost rather pay for the sake of keeping my incognito. But to give way to that brute is to bring discredit upon me, in the eyes of my servants, and, to lose their respect is to jeopardize my authority.

I go outside and briefly tell the messenger to report to his master that I will not allow my luggage to be examined, that his soldiers mean nothing to me, and that later I will send him my card that he may know who I am.

Soon after, my boys take Yongden's card and mine to him. This produces the expected effect. In a little while an embassy arrives, with the magistrate's representative at its head. He presents me with a complimentary silk scarf and begs me to accept his chief's excuses, who, he says, was unable to guess who we were. Behind him come men bringing enough straw and peas to feed my beasts for ten days and an ample provision of flour and butter for us. This procession, preceded by lantern bearers, must greatly impress the villagers. The apology is all that can be desired. My servants swell with pride.

"Since the magistrate has soldiers at his disposal," I say to the ambassador, "I desire him to send me four, to-morrow morning, to act as guides and escort as far as the top of the pass." I abstain from demanding the letter bearing the "great man's" seal to show to the officer in command of the fifty soldiers up there.

To do so would be unnecessary malice on my part.
"You can all go quietly to sleep," I tell my boys.
"No robbers will trouble our rest to-night."

I was the only one who could afford to laugh at the
comedy that had just been enacted; it had provided me,
free of cost, with the provisions we so greatly needed.
As to the magistrate, he had "lost face", and the villagers had been obliged to give him gratis the straw,
peas, flour, and butter that he had offered us. In the
East, it is in this way the chiefs generally procure the
gifts that they offer to distinguished visitors.

The one to suffer most was the brawler, whom my
servants had, I feared, badly hurt. He was expiating
his excess of zeal, and it was quite certain that the official
on whose account he had received maltreatment would
not give him a word of sympathy. He could deem
himself fortunate, if his master did not hold him respon-
sible for all that had happened and punish him.

The next morning, instead of the four soldiers I had
demanded, four peasants present themselves as guides.
One of them is undoubtedly a leper. I release him
from his corvée, without letting him know the reason
for my generosity, and in order that he may have no
regrets when his comrades return with a little present,
I give him some money.

Whereupon we start. It is a long steep climb, hard
on man and beast. Fortunately, my big black mule
bravely carries me and spares me all the fatigue of an
often very muddy road. The approach to the pass is
treeless on the side that we are ascending, and the path
winds in long zigzags through swampy pasture-land.

No picturesque view makes up for the weariness of
the climb. The mountains are shrouded in mist, and,
as soon as we descend the other side, we enter a dense
forest. The path then becomes a mere track, which
the rains have traced, laying bare rocks and roots, and
our passage is continually obstructed by the thorny

shrubs that edge this semblance of a way. We have to dismount and perform a variety of tiring gymnastic feats in order to surmount these difficulties. The incline is very steep and twilight overtakes us. I go slowly because of an acute pain, probably neuralgic and due to a chill, which stiffens one of my legs. Foreseeing that I shall be a long time on the way, I send Sotar, Sönam, and two of the guides on in front with the beasts, so that, on arriving at the stopping place, they may pitch the tents and make tea. The lama, Tobgyal, and one guide remain with me. I have taken the precaution of providing myself with a Chinese lantern and this feeble beacon helps to guide us when darkness envelops us.

Things go from bad to worse with me. I feel feverish, my leg grows more and more painful, and the descent seems interminable. Becoming exhausted, I have often to stop and rest. Yongden tries to encourage me: "Come, make an effort, otherwise we shall never get there!" or "You must hurry on; the candle will soon be consumed and then we shall no longer see the way." He offers to carry me on his back, but along such a path, he would be certain to stumble before long, then we would run the risk of breaking both our necks.

Our guide chooses one of these moments of rest to inform us that this forest is infested with leopards. The men of his village have themselves killed six that year, and those from the other villages many more. Occasionally, too, one or two tigers have been seen in the vicinity.

Neither the lama nor Tobgyal are pleased at hearing this, and the former earnestly implores me to "make an effort". I would gladly do so, only my leg is getting increasingly painful and my temperature is rising. I do not mind about the leopards, but I would like to reach my tent, get between warm blankets, and drink some boiling tea. As I still linger a little, Yongden improvises a variety of rhythms on a policeman's whistle. Each of us wears one of these whistles hanging at his neck, for the purpose of calling to his comrades or of letting them know where he is. Up to the present they have been of little service, for we have been following more or less well defined paths, but they may become useful in other parts of the country, when some of us will be obliged to go on in front to reconnoitre. Meanwhile, the young man doubtless believes the noise will scare the wild beasts away. I think it is much more likely to attract robbers. It is said that some of them are usually to be found wandering in such places, on the look out for travellers. I silence the musician.

We continue our way down for some time; perhaps for over half an hour. Then, suddenly, we hear shouts in the distance. Men are calling. . . . Who are they? and whom are they hailing? I am inclined to think they are villagers who have been sent to meet us. However, it is always necessary to be on one's guard in this country. Our guide, himself, advises caution and that we do not answer at once. He urges us to leave the path and hide ourselves in the underwood, until we are quite certain that the people who are looking for us are friendly.

"We must not fall into a trap," he says. "If those who are shouting have designs upon us, they know we are coming down from the pass, but they do not know exactly where we are. If they do not meet us here, they will go on climbing. If they are armed brigands, we will let them pass by, and, when they have gone a certain distance, we will go as quickly as possible down to the village, before they can turn back."

Whereupon the worthy man blows out our candle and leads us far into the thicket. How will it be possible to distinguish from there, in the darkness, whether those who pass be friends or enemies?

"It can be felt," emphatically declares our guide, to whom I have expressed my doubt.

This rustic seems a clever rascal. The sense I am lacking in and of which he boasts, can he not have developed it during unlawful expeditions?—Such an idea is very amusing.

I discreetly suggest it to him.

"Bah!" he answers, "everyone cannot sit in his chair waiting for merchants to come along, as does the *pönpo* (the chief) of Gomi, who wanted to examine your luggage."

The rogue is not wanting in humour.

But now lights begin to appear, coming up towards us, and the calls sound louder. Unless these people are deliberately trying to deceive us, they are not thieves. We appear ridiculous crouched in the shrub. My reputation will suffer if I am found hiding, like a frightened hare.

"Let us get out of here," I say. "If they are thieves, we shall soon know. I am not afraid of them."

I relight the lantern and lead the men back to the path.

Just as I had surmised, those who were searching for us were animated by the best of intentions.

At their head walked an old *trapa* who had, long ago, stayed in a monastery in Lhasa. He asked my blessing, and we set off in procession.

The path had become much better. The strangeness of the scene roused me, held my attention, and made me forget my tiredness.

Men holding flaming pine boughs, lighted the way. Others joined them coming from different directions, and long before their forms could be distinguished, gleams from their primitive torches danced in the distance. The forest became a fairyland of dazzling lights and deep shadows.

Rustic thurifers, marching ahead, burned fragrant herbs in pots filled with smouldering charcoal. The rising smoke, spreading under the big trees, added a nebulous escort of phantoms to the barbaric procession.

In this way we reached a forest hamlet, and scattered huts appeared in the wood. My guides stopped from time to time, then the perfume of the burning herbs

93

became more pungent, the cloud of smoke more dense, and, close to some other braziers, I glimpsed vague human shapes prostrating themselves before me, which I blessed indiscriminately.

At last, in a clearing, I found myself facing my camp. Our three tents had been pitched. I rushed into mine, found my bed made, and learned that the villagers had provided us with huge teapots, filled with excellent buttered tea. I drank several cups of it, ate a hearty supper, and went to bed quite refreshed. I had completely forgotten all about my fever and painful leg.

All the same, it would be as well to give our animals a day's rest. In doing so I seemed to condemn myself to twenty-four hours' inaction, but, by taking a little trouble, there is nearly always something worth-while to be discovered. The very position of this hamlet, right in the middle of a virgin forest, made me think that surely some legends must be attached to the place, or else I could learn some interesting details concerning the worship of the local deities. Although nominally Buddhists, the majority of the Tibetans, with the exception of the learned lamas, are really Shamanists.

When the old *trapa* came to see me in the morning, I did not fail to question him on these subjects.

"This village is especially blessed," he said. "It has now the honour of your unexpected visit, for you told me that originally you had purposed crossing the Shawa pass. If you had not heard it was blocked, you would not have passed through here; it is the gods who have led you to us. And then, about three months ago, a *dubthob* (holy magician), certainly brought by them also, stopped not far from here and still remains there. His protection extends over all beings: men and animals. Since his arrival, no one has been ill, and, without doubt, because of his good will, the harvest will be plentiful this year."

Oh! I thought, here is something better than a legend. And I promptly voiced my intention of going to see the *dubthob*. This created difficulties. The hermit had ordered the villagers not to disturb him and not to approach the hut that they had built for him, except now and then to bring him food. However, yielding to my entreaties and tempted by the promise of a present, the *trapa* consented to conduct me there.

The *dubthob's* hut was in the middle of the wood. No path led to it, and, to reach it, we were obliged to force our way through the bushes that grew under the great trees.

A vague attempt at a clearing had been made near the hut, which was encircled by some *dochöds*.[1] Little flags floated from its thatched roof and others hung from cords stretched from tree to tree round the hermitage. Ornamented in this way, it resembled one of those altars that are dedicated to rural deities of the mountain and forest.

In keeping with such a scene, I thought to find the *dubthob* seated in the orthodox posture and plunged in deep meditation. Nothing of the sort, the holy man was performing the very ordinary act of eating. He had just made tea and was now drinking it while partaking of roasted maize.

Although he did not appear pleased to see me, he was nevertheless polite. I offered him the usual scarf, the customary token of civility in Tibet. Knotted in the corner of the silk, I had put a little silver. He did not seem to be aware of the fact, but placed the scarf beside him on a small carpet and invited me to sit on a block of wood, which stood in a corner.

The hermit told me that he proposed resuming his journey the next month. He was one of those wandering *naldjorpas*[2] of whom there are hundreds in Tibet.

[1] Written *rdo mtchod*, literally, stone offerings: piles of stones heaped up in honour of local deities—gods of the mountains, forests, etc. . . . There they were raised to the anchorite, as a mark of respect.

[2] Written *rnal hbyor*, and means "the one who has attained calm, serenity". It is the name given to mystics, to yogins. It has been much misused, and a number of religious impostors belonging to the irregular and roving clergy appropriate the title.

I asked him if, during his stay in that forest, he had
been in communication with the local deities, and I gently
teased him about the *dochöds* that the villagers had
erected round his dwelling, as if he himself were a sylvan
deity.

"A god!" he declared with scorn. "He who has
mastered *jinas* and *lhagthong*[1] is far superior to the gods.
Yes, the *lhas*, the *lus* and the *tsens* who dwell in this forest
come sometimes to pay me homage, and I bless them, as
I also bless men and all things. I do nothing but that;
it is for this reason I travel. I go among beings and things
and I bless them, sowing happiness. *Sarva mangalam!*,
Sarva mangalam![2]

"Calmness of mind, the deep insight that discerns
what the vulgar cannot perceive, this is what must be
acquired. There is nothing beyond it, and it is the source
of the infinite and supremely powerful charity of the
Bodhisattvas."[3]

This wandering ascetic possessed a ready tongue. Had
he read the words he spoke and was merely repeating
them, or had he fathomed their meaning? Whichever
it was, in his hut, empty except for an old rug, a ragged
blanket, and two kitchen utensils, the *dubthob* enveloped
himself in an atmosphere of quiet dignity and serene
benevolence, which, perhaps, was not without an element
of pride.

We had hardly left the hut, on our way back to my
camp, when the *trapa* said:

"Those *dochöds* about which you spoke to him, they
were not built by the villagers, but by the gods of the
mountain, the *lus* and the *tsens*. They all pay homage
to him, as he told us. These *dochöds* increase in number;

---

[1] Written *ji gnas* and *lhag mthong*: the perfect calm and superior
vision, that is to say, an understanding which surpasses the ordinary understanding. The real meaning of *lhag mthong* is "see more", "see beyond".
[2] Sanskrit phrase that has been taken into the religious language of
Tibet. It means: "Joy to all!" or "May all be joyful!"
[3] Beings who have attained the degree of spiritual perfection immediately below that of the Buddhas.

each time our people take him food, they discover fresh ones.

"Ah! it is most unfortunate that this *dubthob* should think of leaving us. What a pity that he cannot die here, we could then preserve his bones; they would make powerful talismans!"

On the highest ridge visible from our camp stands a row of isolated rocks, each shaped like a *chörten*,[1] and from among them, the tallest one shines forth luminously white. At sunset, these curious monuments turn golden, and then, pass through all the shades from orange to burnished copper, and dark purple, before fading in the shadow. But long after darkness has engulfed the surrounding landscape, the great white *chörten* still remains visible, its cold radiance lighting the inscrutable night.

My people declare it to be a *chörten rang jung*, and respectfully prostrate themselves before the pure wonder that rises in the clouds.

Tibetans revere the lovely forms of nature. They are particularly affected by the beauty of rocks; these they regard as self-created works of art (*rang jung*)[2] animated with a spirit of their own, which those that owe their existence to human labour do not possess.

I too linger in admiration, contemplating the majestic spectacle, and, for the morrow, I promise myself the great joy of reaching, if not the ridge with the *chörtens*, at least a spot from where I can see them close to. But on my voicing this thought, Sotar, with a knowing toss of his head, remarks:

"It is not possible to reach *chörtens* that appear in this way. They are inaccessible. We shall probably no longer see them to-morrow when we wake. They have brought us a good omen. That's all."

---

[1] *Chörten*: a religious monument of the kind that the Buddhists of India call *stupa*. Tibetan spelling: *mchod eten*.
[2] In Tibetan spelling: *rang byung*.

G

The good man is mistaken, but only partly so. I see the ridge with the *chörtens* at dawn next morning; the largest, the King among them, has taken on a pearly lustre and emits a roseate light.

I jump in the saddle with the combined feelings of a climber who is setting out to conquer a mountain and a pilgrim journeying to a shrine.

In the wood, at the side of the path, we come across two coffins: one is intact, the other crumbling to pieces.

My servants, good Tibetan *trapas* that they are, examine the bones, hoping to find the femurs with which to make *kanglings*, those macabre flutes that are used in the performance of certain rites by the *naldjorpas* of their country. Perhaps they have been forestalled by some other searchers of femurs, for these particular bones cannot be found.

One of the men then ingenuously proposes to open the other coffin, to see if it does not contain what he wants. His suggestion makes me think how diverse are the world's various customs and ideas. The violation of a tomb is considered to be a crime in the West, but the Tibetans, who abandon their dead as a supreme act of charity to the wild beasts, do not see anything reprehensible in it.

Tibetan laymen would perhaps hesitate to open this coffin, for fear of disturbing or annoying some bad spirits, who might then attach themselves to them and do them harm. But my boys are monks. They are convinced that the *naldjorpa* to whom they will give or sell their find will be capable of subjugating any demon who might attempt to hurt them. Moreover, they are accustomed to gruesome musical instruments and ornaments. Such things are to be found in the possession of many lamas and most Tibetan ascetics. I, myself, have a *kangling* in my luggage and wear a rosary of little discs made from human skulls round my neck. The Christian hermits, too, had often a skull in their caves. Death is an inexhaustible subject of meditation in all religions; but that which the Tibetan mystics see through this dismal display of images is not death itself, but its unreality.

As to me, instead of the dread of demons, I have the fear of microbes. Last year cholera raged in this region. I persuade my people not to touch the coffin. I explain to them that the Chinese have not the same ideas as they have upon the treatment of the dead and that the natives would think it very bad of us if we dared to open a coffin.

We pass on our way.

For some time yet the fairy *chörtens* remain in sight. We gradually get closer to them, then suddenly the path turns in another direction. Between us and the crest on which they stand other summits interpose themselves, and as we continue to climb, we leave below us the vision that, since the previous evening, has bewitched us. Never will we touch those "miraculous" aerial monuments.

A small adventure awaits us on the other side of the pass. After having dismounted at the beginning of the descent, we follow an indescribably muddy track. I let the servants go on in front with the animals and I walk behind with the lama. Farther on, the path becomes good, and, as the weather is fine, we stroll slowly through the forest.

All of a sudden we hear shots. Someone has fired close by. Probably some hunters, and as the undergrowth is very thick, they may, on seeing indistinct forms through the bushes, take us for game and put an ounce of lead into us. I urge Yongden on, we must show ourselves.

But lo! at the turning of the path, climbing up towards us, we meet two of the most extraordinary individuals I have ever come across. They are dressed in rags, and their matted hair, falling to their shoulders, half hides their faces. One of them carries a gun, the like of which I have never seen outside a museum of antiquities, and the other a pike. In order to let us pass the two men draw back into the bushes, and then a third one comes into sight. This one holds in his hand an extraordinary weapon; a kind of dagger-knife with a triple-edged blade, as long as a forearm.

We can only stare in amazement.

"They are hunters," I whisper to Yongden, unable to imagine what else these savages can be.

"No," he answers, "they are soldiers."

Soldiers! I have seen some pretty odd specimens of soldiery in China and Tibet, but not any that have approached in grotesqueness these we have just met. While I am still wondering, we hear more shots.

It would certainly be wise to show ourselves; moreover we have now been seen by the three men.

Hurrying on, we come out into a clearing where we find about twenty natives, all of whom more or less resemble those we have just passed.

Lolling on the grass, these ragamuffins are firing into the air, at nothing. Have they seen us coming from afar, without our noticing it? Do they wish to appear important by making a noise, or are they amusing themselves by trying to frighten us?—Among them are some little boys carrying pikes, the handles of which have been shortened to suit the height of their owners.

A photograph of this group would make a good picture, but unfortunately my camera is in my saddlebag. Another thought quickly chases away any idea of securing a snapshot.

What has happened to our beasts? If there are another twenty men similar to these a little lower down the mountain, the animals run a great risk of being stolen. Yet no sounds of fighting have come to me through the stillness of the forest, and I know that my three men would not let themselves be robbed without putting up a strenuous defence. They are better armed than these ragged soldiers.

The pseudo "braves" do not say anything to us as we pass on our way. Then, one of them risks the usual question:

"Where are you going to?"

Without stopping, I answer:

"To Nanping."

We quietly continue the descent. We have not gone a hundred yards before the whole band gets up and follows us. The three men whom we had met going up to the pass have returned and joined the others.

We go on for some distance with this escort, then I catch sight of my mules in a meadow. They are all there, and my boys are sitting by them. The lads open their eyes wide with astonishment on seeing the lama and me in such strange company.—

We must not now appear in a hurry to get away, as if we were afraid. That would be unwise. If these people have no bad intentions, to act in this way would only be to put such ideas in their heads. If they already harbour them, calmness, coolness, and an assured air are the best means of making ourselves respected.

I therefore sit down, ask for my thermos flask, and drink a cup of tea. It is the moment for a chat, I begin questioning the one whom I think is their chief.

"Who are you?—What are you doing in these parts?"

"We are soldiers from Nanping," he replies. "We were sent to meet the troops that are expected from Kansu, but some passing muleteers have told us they will not arrive to-day. So we are returning."

The ice is broken; the savages talk. They admire my American boots, the marvellous bottle that keeps the tea hot, and my big Sining mules. Then I stand up, get into saddle, and we set off accompanied by the bearers of absurd guns, revolutionary pikes, and farcical daggers.

After all they are good fellows, they do not intend to rob us. We are probably congenial to them, for, in a veiled way, they give us good advice.

"Do not enter Nanping," the chief says to us. "The town is full of soldiers, you will be robbed there."

We will profit by this advice, but by interpreting it in our own way. As to those who have given it us, they lied when they said they were soldiers from Nanping; they do not go as far as the town, but stop at a mountain village, while we continue our way.

Yongden, who is prone to suspect people of nurturing bad designs and who is, perhaps, not altogether wrong in doing so, thinks that our shaggy friends, not wishing to attack us in the day time, have urged us not to seek lodgings in the town in order that, if we decide to camp outside it, they may be able to steal our beasts during the night.

I do not believe this, but as three of my mules need shoeing and we must buy food, we will go to Nanping.

The town lies in a large valley through which flows the Paishiui ho. We find the place crowded. The Governor of Szechwan, who has been beaten by a rival general and is in flight, has taken refuge in Nanping. From a distance I see the house where he is staying. Triumphal arches, made of branches and decorated with red paper garlands and multi-coloured lanterns, stand conspicuously in the garden in front of it. The "triumphal" arches seem to me to be a little out of place, under the circumstances, but it is not for me to criticize.

Some thousands of soldiers in decent uniforms, who do not in the least resemble the beggarly crew we fell in with, are roaming about the town, and at first it seems impossible to find lodgings. We hesitate to camp in the open, in a garden where some kind market-gardeners offer us a place. The confusion that reigns in Nanping may encourage thieves to attempt an attack, and Yongden still remains mistrustful of our late companions' intentions.

It is almost night when a Mohammedan currier invites us to shelter in a shed next to his house. He can also put the beasts in a closed stable, built in the courtyard. The last proposal decides me. Here we will enjoy the greatest possible security.

My host immediately has the shed swept and cleaned, as best he can. Mohammedans have usually a greater regard for cleanliness than the other natives. However, the good man can do nothing against the terrible smell of the skins that lie piled in his shop. It makes me feel ill, and I hasten to forget it in sleep.

Once more it is impossible for us to replenish our empty provision bags. No eggs, no butter, no milk, no vegetables can be bought, only a little salt pork and flour at a ridiculous price. There is also no straw for the animals, and both peas and barley cost ten times their value. The troops requisition all they find.

We learn that the soldiers expected from Kansu are a band of brigands, who want to plunder the town. The inhabitants are filled with dismay. They are afraid lest the defeated governor's troops should not be strong enough to defend the town, or their chief should deem it wiser to retire without fighting.

I am now of the opinion that the strange wanderers in the forest were the vanguard of this army of bandits.

We had counted on resting for a few days; travelling in the mountains along barely defined paths, the bad weather, the indifferent food, all these things have tended to tire us. The mules, having long since cast most of their shoes, injure themselves when walking, laden, over the uneven and stony ground. Nevertheless to remain in Nanping and run the risk of finding ourselves in the midst of war and pillage is imprudent.

We decide to leave the town before daybreak.

VI

A BÖNPO MONASTERY

FOR a time after leaving Nanping we ascend the Paishiui ho, then we once more cross the mountains. Notwithstanding the fatigue, privations, and difficulties, our journey is a delight. Unfortunately the weather becomes rainy, and on the second day we are overtaken by a violent thunderstorm. The next day, at the same hour, the storm breaks again.

I do not know of anything that is more wretchedly uncomfortable than a camp hastily pitched on soggy ground, in the rain, and a night spent in damp clothes and blankets. However my servants, who have been underfed for several weeks, appear so tired that I shall camp again to-day, if they want to stop. I consult them.

"Oh!" answers Sotar, "we have no opinion on the subject. If Jetsun Kushog tells us to stop, we will stop; if she tells us to go on, we will go on."

The others nod their approval. It must not be thought from this mental attitude that these men are fools, far from it, but their views concerning the relation between master and servant differ from those in the West. Their answer does not denote any abject servility. It merely expresses an unbounded confidence in me and a recognition of the superiority of my intelligence. They expect me to provide for their well-being and take it for granted that whatever I decide to do will be wise and for their good.

At last, after going from hamlet to hamlet, we find

shelter in the house of a young Chinese couple and pass the night under cover. My boys are radiant, once more my perspicacity has asserted itself—they call it prescience. While drying themselves in front of a huge fire, they joyously prepare our meagre supper.

The next day, we continue our way through dense forests that have the reputation of being unsafe. With eyes searching the undergrowth to catch the least movement among the twigs and ears straining to detect the slightest suspicious sound, we ride for the greater part of the time in silence. At night, the men relieve one another in keeping guard. I also take my turn at watching; the only privilege I allocate to myself is the choice of the first or last watch, so that my sleep may not be interrupted. It is possible to become accustomed to all things. The sharp little thrill that the Lama and I experienced the first few times when loading our weapons before a start and thinking of the brigands who might show themselves, is, if not actually dead, at least greatly weakened. As to the others, they have long since become accustomed to frequenting dangerous regions, and, during their childhood, brigand stories took the place of fairy tales.

Travelling by easy stages we finally arrive before the Bönpo monastery at Tagyu.

The Bönpos are the adherents of the ancient religion of Tibet, the one the Tibetans professed before the introduction of Buddhism into their country. At least, that is what they say and what is repeated by Orientalists when writing about Tibet.

All the same the real facts are much more complicated than this simple definition would lead us to believe. There exist in Tibet many varieties of Bönpos and it is doubtful whether, at present, any of them exactly represent the religious forms that prevailed before the seventh century of our era.

What were the doctrines of the primitive Bönpos?

We really do not know. To say that these Bönpos were
Shamanists throws little light upon the question. There
exists no clearly defined "Shamanist religion". The
Shaman is a sorcerer, sometimes a magician or even an
occultist expert in secret lore; his habitual clients are
called Shamanists. But these facts do not imply either a
common doctrine or common practices; quite the reverse,
each region and each *Shaman* have their own.

Up till now we have found no genuine documentary
evidence to enlighten us on the "Shamanism" of the
ancient Bönpos. According to Tibetan chronicles, no
writing existed in that country before the reign of King
Srong btsan Gampo (seventh century), who sent some
learned men to India (or perhaps to the frontier countries
of Nepal and Kashmere, of Indian civilization), to look
for the elements of an alphabet, in order that the Buddhist Writings might be translated.

Some Bönpos declare, on the other hand, that a
kind of writing did exist in Tibet before this time and
that their sacred books date from long before the reign
of Srong btsan Gampo. Such a thing is possible. Moreover this would not mean that the Tibetans possessed
a writing of their own. These books could have been
written elsewhere than in Tibet. Those who know the
habits of the people of these regions are well aware that
books that are reputed to be sacred form the object of
a worship that does not, necessarily, entail a knowledge
of their contents on the part of the worshippers or even
the simple possibility of their being able to read them.
There are a great number of illiterate people in Tibet
who possess libraries of sacred books. These works are
placed in rows above an altar, and before them the
faithful prostrate themselves, burn incense, and light
lamps in token of veneration. This is—as they themselves are aware—the cult of a wisdom that they do not
think themselves as yet capable of reaching, but that
they hope to attain to in another life.

However, up to the present, the Bönpos have nevei been able to produce either books of proved antiquity or archeological evidence in support of their statements. The modern Bönpos divide themselves into two great groups, which in their turn sub-divide themselves into many branches. The two main divisions are those of the White Böns and the Black Böns respectively.

The White Böns have slavishly imitated the Lamaists. Their dignitaries call themselves lamas, their monks wear exactly the same costume as the *trapas*, and their monasteries resemble in every way the Lamaist *gompas*. In their temples you find statues identical with those of the Buddhas and the deities venerated by the Lamaists, the only difference is that the Bönpos have given them other names. With them Guru Shenrabs[1] holds the same place that Gautama Buddha occupies with the Buddhists. Just as Gautama Buddha is said to have had several predecessors, Buddhas like himself, so the Bönpos name several predecessors of Guru Shenrabs. These last, Buddhas or Bönpo Masters, have no historical existence. As to Guru Shenrabs, although we are not so well informed with reference to him as we are with regard to Siddhartha Gautama, (the historic Buddha) it is probable that he actually lived. He is reported to have been born in the country that was formerly called Shang-Shung, situated in the south-west of Tibet. His real personality has disappeared in legend and the mania for imitating, which rages among the Bönpos, has led them to create a biography of him that reproduces all the chief features of the one of the Buddha.

As to their doctrines, the White Bönpos pride themselves on professing the same as those of the Lamaists. They practise the *dubthabs*,[2] the evoking of the deities

---

[1] Written *Gshenrabs*.
[2] Written *sgrub thab*, literally " method to succeed ". See explanations concerning *dubthabs* in *Initiations and Initiates in Tibet*, page 91.

for the purpose of obtaining peaceful or terrible results. Their discipline differs but little from that of the non-reformed Lamaists of the *ñingma* sect of " Red hats ". As it is with these last, marriage and the drinking of alcoholic beverages is permitted to the clergy.

Bönpos sacrifice animals during the performance of some of their rites, but this applies chiefly to the Black Bönpos.

The Black Bönpos are more original than their White co-religionists. Perhaps they have better preserved the primitive character of their religion. They are not so numerous as the " Whites " and do not generally form themselves into groups. The natives of the Himālayas make a distinction between the Bönpos and those whom they simply call Böns. According to them, the Bönpos are all those—whether laymen or members of the clergy —who repeat *bön la kyab su chi wo* instead of *chös la kyab su chi wo*[1] and do the ritualistic circumambulation of the religious monuments by keeping them on their left instead of on their right, as do the Lamaists. Now the Bön, on the other hand, is a veritable sorcerer and medium, one to whom all have recourse when the magic power of the lama does not appear to be strong enough to obtain the desired effect: usually the overcoming of the demon who is the cause of the evil, but also, in more secret cases, the harming or killing of an enemy. The Bön hardly ever performs other than bloody rites, the sacrifice of an animal is always demanded when he officiates. Women as well as men can be Bön, and, very often, the kind of natural gift that, so the natives think, makes a person a Bön, is transmitted hereditarily.

Among these mountaineers there is no antagonism between the Lamaist clergy who belong exclusively to some " Red Hat " sects and the Böns. The Lamas do not oppose the Böns and the Böns perform their

[1] Written *bön* or *chos la skyabs su mchiho.* " I take refuge in the doctrine " (respectively that of Böns or that of the Buddha).

devotions in the Lamaist temples. I even know a *trapa* of high position in his monastery, who is the husband of a Bön woman and who assists at the rites conducted by his wife in the villages.

In the north of Tibet, the black Böns are very similar to the *ngagspas*—magicians, who are classed as Lamaists. Just as among the *ngagspas*, there are men of distinctive character among the Böns, some of whom are really remarkable either for the originality and abstruseness of their philosophical conceptions or for the development of their psychic faculties.

So, we found ourselves in front of a Bönpo monastery. It was not yet mid-day, hardly the hour at which to stop and camp, but I was travelling for the purpose of observing and learning and not at all for breaking a speed record. I have always travelled slowly; a habit that has enabled me to see many things and listen to many people. I was not going stupidly to continue my way that day. On the contrary, I determined to gain admission to the monastery.

Permission to enter within its walls was given us; but there was no room available. The next day the monks were to celebrate a solemn service for a man who had lately died. A great number of villagers were coming from a distance, and, as it would be impossible for them to return the same day, they had to be given lodgings. In fact, many of them had already arrived and were installed in the houses that surrounded the temple. However, we needed no roof, all we required was leave to pitch our tents. This was granted us, and I was even allowed to choose a place for my tent in the principal courtyard, in front of the peristyle of the temple. . . . It was an excellent spot from which to witness the ceremony that was in preparation.

I sent the customary scarf and present to the head of the monastery, and, after unpacking, waited to be asked to go to him or for him to come to me, according to the degree of esteem of which he deemed me worthy.

He simply sent an officer of his household, who brought me the tea of welcome and, as present, some big pieces of butter. This small show of courtesy was sufficient to enable me to preserve my dignity. I drank the tea, and, when the monks had gone, began to look at the faithful, fresh groups of whom were arriving at every moment.

If I was interested in them, they were equally interested in me. Many of them came to see and to consult me, either concerning maladies from which they or their relations suffered or about the care of their crops and cattle.

At nightfall, the Abbot paid me a visit. He began by apologizing for not having come to welcome me on my arrival, and gave as the reason for the delay, the preparations that had to be made for the next day's ceremony. He courteously questioned me as to my well-being. Was I comfortable in my tent? . . . Had I sufficient provisions? . . . He was going to send me supper.

Finally, he approached the subject that he had at heart. Relying on my discretion, he confided to me that the affairs of the monastery were not in as flourishing a condition as he could have wished. He was inclined to think that this unfortunate situation might be owing to the position of the temple door, which had perhaps been made to face the wrong direction.[1] He begged me to tell him if this were so, adding that, should it be necessary, he would not hesitate to pull down the facade of the edifice and build it up again facing another cardinal point.

He had a second cause for anxiety. He had to

[1] The Tibetans, as also the Chinese, attach great importance to the direction in which the principal entrance of a building, especially that of a temple, faces.

choose the site for a new cemetery.[1] What spot was most suited to this purpose. It was of the utmost importance to avoid irritating any of the local deities and to be safe from the bad spirits that haunt the tombs.

These things were all very complicated. He felt the weight of his responsibility and would be very glad to have the advice of a *Khadoma*.

I put off giving my answer until the next day, and, the promised supper having been brought, I began to eat, thinking to have no more visitors that night.

I was mistaken. I had not finished my meal when a *trapa* pulled back the curtain of my tent.

"I would like to speak to you," he said.

"Come in and sit down," I answered.

He sat down on a rug and, without preamble, began:

"My Lama[2] and I live in a hut that belongs to the monastery, but we are not Bönpos. We are *nangpas*.[3] ... My Lama is ill. I have heard that you were distributing medicines; perhaps you have one that will cure my Master. ... He does not know that I have come to you. ..."

"Why do you live among the Bönpos, if you are not Bönpos?" I asked.

"My Master knows," replied the *trapa*.

I saw that he would not give me any explanation on the subject.

"What is the nature of your Master's illness?" I then asked. "I cannot give you any medicine without knowing what is the matter with him. Can he not come here to-morrow morning? ... If he is too weak to walk, I will go to him."

[1] The Bönpos bury their dead. The Lamaists do not; they burn them, throw them into the river, leave them exposed on the mountain, or, in Central Tibet, cut the bodies into pieces for the vultures to devour.

[2] My "Lama", that is, my spiritual guide: my "guru", according to the Sanskrit term, which is also used in the religious language of Tibet.

[3] *Nangpas*: "insiders", meaning, those who belong to the spiritual body of Buddhist adepts. The faithful of other religions are called *chyirolpas*: "outsiders".

"Perhaps he will die," murmured the *trapa*.

Was the case then so grave? If that were so, I did not possess sufficient medical knowledge to be of use, but charity demanded I should go and see the sufferer. It was possible his disciple magnified the evil; ague due to a simple attack of fever might appear to him as a premonitory symptom of the death agony.

"I will go and see him at once," I said.

I called Yongden and we left together, guided by the *trapa*. The hut was in a little wood, close to the monastery.

"Wait," whispered the monk, as we neared it. "I must first go in and announce your visit. The Lama did not order me to fetch you; he may be angry at my having done so."

He went in. Instead of remaining discreetly at a distance, Yongden and I crept to the door, urged forward by curiosity. How would the zealous disciple be received by his spiritual master? Gurus are often hot-tempered in Tibet.

At first we only heard indistinct murmurs. Doubtless the *trapa* was telling his master about the initiative he had taken and our arrival.

Crack!

There was no mistaking the sound; it was that of a blow. At all events some energy remained to the dying man.

My son laughed, quietly.

"That was the kind of thing I received from my professor of grammar," he remarked.

I had long been familiar with this detail of his school-days. I signed him to be silent.

The sufferer was now speaking in a broken voice.

"I will not see her. . . . Medicine! . . . Fool! . . . You have no faith in me. Oh! poor me! The bad actions I committed in my past lives have brought me this despicable disciple."

The voice grew muffled.

"Why did I reveal the secret to him! . . . His sins have become an obstacle in my path. . . . Medicines. . . . It is the manuscript I want, it is there. . . . I shall then know how to live forever. . . . Inside one of the statues, but which . . . ?"

"Be quiet, be quiet, *Kushog*,"[1] implored the *trapa*, who suspected we might hear.

As the result either of anger or weakness, the patient began to breathe noisily, as if he were choking.

"Wretch! I have told you a hundred times!" he continued, becoming excited again. "The Bönpos do not know that the book is hidden there. . . . And you fetch this woman. . . . Perhaps you have told her. . . . Perhaps you have told the Bönpos. . . ."

"I have said nothing. Be quiet, *Kushog*," again implored the distracted disciple.

"Go away! Go! . . . go! . . ."

The voice gradually weakened, the words became confused. The *trapa* cried repeatedly: "*Kushog!* my Lama!" But I could not distinguish any response. Had his master fainted, or had the old man's anger brought on a stroke? Yongden wanted to go in, but I kept him back. By showing ourselves, we would only run the risk of increasing the harm of which, quite unwittingly, we had been the cause.

I heard the *trapa* moaning, as he walked to and fro in the hut. He was evidently trying to come to his master's aid.

I waited, thinking perhaps he would call me and that I might be able to help the sick man in some way. Presently the *trapa* came out. As he opened the door I caught a glimpse of an old lama leaning against the wall, propped up on either side by cushions. His eyes were wide open, but he did not move.

We had stepped back a little, but not far enough

[1] Sir.

114

to prevent the *trapa* from realizing that we had both
listened to and heard what his master had said. For
a moment he remained as if nonplussed, then said:

"*Kushog* does not wish for your medicines. He is
not ill. He will not die. He will never die . . .
never . . ."

He spoke strangely, like a man who is out of his
mind or who dreams.

Nevertheless, I once more offered my services, only
to have them energetically refused.

"*Kushog* does not want anything. . . . He is not
ill. . . . He is not going to die. . . ."

And as I turned away, the thought came to me that
perhaps the old lama had just died.

The search for the secret of immortality has been
as resolutely pursued in China as that for the philosopher's stone has been in the West. Moreover, it is
said by some, that what, in our countries, was exoterically described as the transmutation of base metals into
gold, meant, to the initiates, the science of becoming
immortal.

The ancient Chinese Taoists openly boasted of
possessing the secret of immortality, and more than one
credulous prince has died from the effects of the magic
elixir that, he believed, would assure him eternal life.

In our times, less is heard concerning this secret of
secrets, but there are still some who search for a means
by which their personality may be forever retained in
their present bodies.

On the other hand various theories regarding the
possibility of indefinitely prolonging individual existence,
either in a spiritual or in a material form, but outside of
the body to which it is at present attached, are, even in
our days, part of the esoteric teaching of some Asiatic
spiritual masters and occultists.

Immortality in our actual body has never interested
the Tibetans to the same degree as it has the Taoists.

For to the one who firmly believes in the theory of reincarnation or of repeated rebirths, the problem of immortality is solved. Nevertheless, according to several traditions, among the many secret books hidden by Padma Sambhava in out of the way places, there are to be found treatises that describe ways by which death can be evaded, and, among the seekers of these hidden books, a small number specially look for those on that subject.

The Bönpos, more particularly the Black Bönpos, who resemble the Taoists in many ways, still hold traditions concerning the secret of immortality. The old lama, of whom I had caught a glimpse, might have heard, or have imagined, that a Bönpo manuscript dealing with this subject was somewhere among the sacred books that had been stuffed into the temple statues of this monastery. Such a thing could have been done without the nature of the manuscript becoming known to those who had handled it. These men might have been illiterate, or, as is often the case, completely indifferent to religious literature.

All the statues that are venerated by the Tibetans, either in private houses or in temples, contain sheets of paper on which passages from the Sacred Writings are printed, or, in the case of small statuettes, just short mantras or magic words.

Very often a complete collection of canonical books is placed in the giant statues. It is the writings that are hidden in a statue that give it life, make it worthy of being worshipped, and communicate to it a certain power, which is strengthened by the rite of consecration celebrated by a lama.

The next morning I was awakened by the clash of cymbals, with which the sound of gyalings soon mingled. Although it was still dark, dawn would soon break. The Bönpos were beginning the office for the dead villager.

By degrees the peasants who had arrived the day

before awoke also and began to walk inside the monastery enclosure. It was not that they had any intention of assisting at the office; such is not the habit of Tibetan laymen, whether they be Lamaists or Bönpos. They are not prohibited from being present at the ordinary religious rites, but neither are they required to be. The celebration of these rites is the affair of the clergy, and whoever is not a member of that community need not participate in them. No merit is attached to a layman's presence in the temple where rites are performed. The object of them consists in procuring the particular end in view: whether that end concerns a specified individual (for the purpose of assuring his prosperity, bringing back his health, or, in the case of a dead person, of guiding him to a happy rebirth) or aims at a more general effect (that of producing fertility, plentiful harvests, or of averting sickness among men and animals).

These rough mountaineers, passing guests at the rustic monastery, therefore paid little attention to the monks' noisy chanting. They simply wished to prepare the morning meal that they had to offer[1] the monks and, also, to breakfast themselves. So they looked for fuel and glowing embers by which to light it. Very soon smoke curled out of the windows, or rose from the corners of the court, where those who had been obliged to sleep outside improvised open-air kitchens. Then the tea-churns began to play their part in the concert of hautboys, trumpets, cymbals, and drums that groaned and thundered in the temple. An entertaining discord, to which the guests of the stable added their neighs and raucous brays.

By degrees fresh groups of faithful appeared, made up of those who lived near the monastery or who had slept on the way. Before ten o'clock, about three hundred men and women had assembled, all dressed in their best

---

[1] When offices are performed for the special benefit of an individual, he or his family must feed the celebrants for the duration of the rites.

clothes. They were not a pretty crowd. Out of every twenty of them, at least a dozen would have goitre, in a more or less advanced stage.

The gathering organized themselves into processions, which circled round the temple, keeping it on the left; the reverse of the Lamaists' custom, which is to keep it on the right. Many of the faithful held a *mani*-wheel, but instead of the *Aum mani padme hum* of the Lamaists, they chanted *Aum matriye sa len du*, as they turned them.

The crowd's participation in the rites should have consisted in fasting for a day. But this was not strictly carried into practice by everyone. At any rate, as I have already shown, both the local clergy and their servants were exempt from any such obligation.

A fast, in Tibet, implies not only abstention from eating, but from drinking and speaking as well. Most people find it difficult to keep silent, and the Tibetans, both men and women, are not exceptions.

Around the temple many old women were to be seen struggling with a desire to wag their tongues. Pursing their lips, they then pushed them out in the form of a snout, and somehow from behind this barrier they managed to mumble inwardly what they were not allowed to articulate distinctly. They seemed able to understand one another very well; and their silent conversation, accompanied by smiles, grimaces, and winks, was very animated.

In this mute fashion the young girls flirted with the boys of their own age and, with taps from their prayer-wheels, incited them to playful scuffles. I saw one seized by a lad as they walked in procession round the court of the temple. He held his smiling and delighted prey with both hands, while, with his feet, he defended himself against the attacks of his victim's friends, who, laughing too, tried to rescue her.

As the day advanced, the people's shouts of *Aum*

matriye sa len du increased in volume. When night came, those who were not fasting or who had broken their fast—there seemed to be a great number of them—began to drink spirits, until, in a few hours, fatigue and drink had lulled the whole herd to sleep.

In the meantime, during the afternoon, while I was watching the crowd, the abbot had come to remind me of our conversation of the day before and of the advice I had promised him. I gave it.

It was not necessary to displace the temple door; its position was not prejudicial to the prosperity of the monastery. As to the new cemetery, the usual direction of the winds must first be carefully observed, and, then, a site chosen that was not swept by them before they passed over the monastery. It was also expedient to bury the dead deep down in the earth.

These simple directions could cause no harm.

Other monks also came to see me during the intervals between the ritual ceremonies. During this time, Yongden made discreet enquiries about the sick man whose disciple had come to fetch me the evening before.

He learnt that, some months previous, these two travelling monks, one old and one young, had asked hospitality of the monastery and had had it granted them. As a matter of fact, this is never refused to members of the clergy, if there is a place available. The two *trapas*, who said they belonged to the Sakyapa sect, had installed themselves in the hut and remained there. No one thought of driving them away. The abbot sent them a few provisions, and the young monk, from time to time, toured the neighbourhood, begging for food. They both lived very isolated lives, and the Bönpos of the monastery paid little attention to them.

Yongden, wishing to pursue his enquiries still further, returned to the hut. He found the door closed and, on knocking, received no reply.

At Sungpan we discover good lodgings on the first floor of a newly built wooden house belonging to a Mohammedan artisan. It is situated close to the town gate. The rooms are large, light and airy, but scantily furnished in the Chinese fashion, with only a few tables and chairs. Some planks on trestles serve for beds. The natives of Szechwan do not sleep on *kangs*, those ovens that I have already described.

The pleasure we felt in establishing ourselves in such agreeable quarters was to be immediately followed by a disappointment. The first words Yongden utters concerning the buying of food brings a reply that completely shatters all hope of a satisfactory supper. There is nothing but dried pork and some flour to be bought in Sungpan. Our stomachs are tired of this unchanging diet. I had dreamed of butter, milk and vegetables, and my boys of fresh beef or mutton. We shall have to go without them again.

Were my men less strict observers of their religion's rule, they would have a few chickens or even a sheep killed, but they are Buddhists and members of the lower clergy. If they lack the necessary moral force to give up all animal food, they nevertheless refuse, merely for the sake of satisfying their stomach's bestial desires, to order the killing of a being that, like themselves, wishes to live. Their selfish gluttony does not go that far. When the harm is done and the meat is for sale at the butcher's, they waver and yield to the temptation. A human weakness, which they recognize with humility, and one that I cannot severely censure, for I sometimes give way to it myself.

After a long search, however, our host ends by finding some eggs. Hope stirs again within us. Who knows what will happen if we continue to search? . . . The gods of Sungpan, indeed, do favour us; the next morning we are brought some turnips.

At Sungpan I was definitely out of Kansu, not only

according to the official boundary line of that province, but in a way that was much more effective from my point of view. For between Sungpan and the Chinese villages in the centre of Kansu where white foreigners travel and where I was personally known by some Chinese of high position, I had put a large tract of country that is sparsely inhabited by people of Tibetan origin or even completely uninhabited. Western travellers are rarely seen in those parts. Perhaps not one passes through in ten years. And, as to me, after having left Labrang, I had soon become an unknown Tibetan nun of high rank. This was what I wished. Also, I took good care not to forgo the benefits that my incognito assured me, by paying a visit to the Chinese magistrate at Sungpan. The protection that these officials can afford to travellers is purely theoretical, and often only leads to unpleasantness. Apart from the pleasure a foreigner who speaks Chinese fluently can experience in conversing with these generally amiable and intelligent literati, there is no practical advantage in making their acquaintance. Now, neither Yongden nor I knew enough Chinese to be able to talk about interesting things with the magistrate of Sungpan, and it was on the other hand very essential for me to keep my freedom of action and to be able to go where I pleased, at my own risk, and without anyone troubling about me.

This time, I succeeded in completely keeping my incognito.

For the moment, no one thought of enquiring into the object of my journey or of upsetting my plans. But I could not be certain that this would always be the case, when, on going South, I should pass through populated Chinese regions where the natives are more wideawake than those who inhabit the borders of the Tibetan solitudes. Would it not be better, instead of continuing my way south, towards Mochow, to verge towards the west and pass through the country that is occupied by independent Tibetan tribes?

While I hesitated, not knowing what to decide, I learnt that the chief of one of the frontier tribes was in Sungpan. The man was known to be a powerful brigand. The Chinese officials, who were being harassed by his bands, were at that moment discussing the knotty question with him of the boundary line of a territory that he claimed to be his. Full of quiet courage, the old bandit had come to Sungpan with his son and a few servants to treat on an equality with the Chinese authorities. No doubt he felt confident that his adversaries, for fear of terrible reprisals, would not dare to take advantage of his lack of protection to capture him. However, he could not have been absolutely certain of this; sudden anger on the part of the magistrates whom he was defying might cause him to be, within an hour, beheaded or shot. He accepted the risk with that ease, that lofty calm in face of supreme danger, which are usual with gentlemen of his kind.

Yongden went to see him. He told him that a reverend lady from Tibet, an "*incarnated Khadoma*", wished, from fear and dislike of the infidel Chinese, to continue her journey through country that was occupied by Tibetan co-religionists of hers.

The interview was cordial. Without difficulty the chief understood the reasons that were given him, and promised to provide us with a safe-conduct, which would not only be binding on the people of his own tribe but on those of the two neighbouring tribes, with whom he was upon friendly terms.

This safe-conduct would assure us free passage, and he guaranteed that we would not be robbed. Such a thing was easy for him to promise, since the robbers were his own subjects. Further, he would help us by giving us provisions and guides, also pack-mules, so that ours could rest by travelling unloaded. I am certain that this programme would have been strictly carried out. I should have relied, without reservation, upon the old chief's word.

Tibetan brigands are gentlemen and in addition usually very "pious", therefore in my capacity as *Khadoma* I should have been very well treated.

But the advantageous protection that was to be accorded us stopped at a certain point. Of this we were honestly informed beforehand. The chief at present at Sungpan was at war with a Grand Lama, the abbot of a monastery whose land we should have to travel over.

This consideration naturally lessened our enthusiasm. What kind of a reception should we get in the enemy's camp?

The chief came to see me one morning. He was a curious type of half-savage, at once cunning and dull-witted. He repeated to me what he had said to Yongden, without trying in the very least to influence me either into accepting or rejecting his offer. This lordly brigand showed a haughty indifference towards everything. Perhaps he was a philosopher and held the things of this world to be "images seen in dream", as it is written in the Prajñā Pāramitā, which is greatly read in his country.

After he had left us, Yongden and I went into matters, and, having carefully weighed the pros and cons, we decided it would be too dangerous to venture among tribes that were at war with one another. Therefore we would continue our journey in Chinese country, as far as Lifan, and start the next day.

We had stayed four days in Sungpan. Must I say we remained one day too long? A shorter stay would have spared us the gruesome sight of a public execution; but, as it had to take place, it was just as well perhaps for us strangers to be able to note this lugubrious scene of Chinese justice.

The condemned man was a traitor. He had betrayed some strategic plan of the Northerners to the chiefs of the Southerners, in this way bringing about the loss of a battle

123

and during it the death of a general. At least, this was what was said in Sungpan.

The man had then been foolish enough to return to his own village, and had been arrested there. He was now to suffer capital punishment.

Towards the end of the afternoon, he passed in a procession through the village. At its head strode a minor official carrying the thin, narrow strip of wood that in China represents what the bundle of rods with an axe in the middle, the lictor's fasces, symbolized in Rome: Law, Authority. Near him walked the executioner, holding a naked sword straight in front of him, as he would have a tall candle. The magistrates followed, and lastly, surrounded by soldiers, came the prisoner with his hands fastened behind him. He did not appear to be at all affected; his step was as firm as that of an ordinary pedestrian.

The party, marching quickly, went beyond the ramparts, on which the people thronged to watch the spectacle. This was, however, very brief, not at all solemn, and, judging by the faces of the onlookers, not at all impressive.

While one of the magistrates appeared to put further questions to the captive, the executioner suddenly plunged his sword into the man's back, or perhaps into his side. The movement was so rapid that I could not discern exactly where the blow struck. I was standing—as may be imagined—some distance away from the place of execution.

The man staggered and fell. The little procession of officials, minus the one whom they left behind, returned in the same order as it had come, preceded by the same emblems; and the crowd quickly dispersed.

Late in the evening I saw the body still lying in the same place. One man alone remained by it. Perfectly calm, with an impassive face, he explained to me that he was a relation of the deceased and muttered some excuses for the incorrectness of his dress; he had not yet been able to put on the white robe of mourning. This breach of etiquette seemed to sadden him much more than his relation's tragic end. He said he was waiting for a coffin to be brought in which to place the body, he would then take it to his native land for burial.

It all appeared very simple, not in the least dramatic. The dead man lay there at my feet. Around him the blood-soaked earth had taken on a golden brown sheen in the faint glimmer of departing day, and he seemed to rest on a velvet carpet that had for border some tufts of grass and a few wild flowers.

I waited for a time. Darkness was creeping slowly upon us and the coffin did not arrive. I bowed to the mournful watcher, and left him.

When I had gone a little distance, I looked back. The Chinaman's black robe had melted into the surrounding shadow; all that could be seen of him was a motionless white face, fantastically suspended in space.

VII

CONCERNING DEMONS

TO all travellers who may be tempted to wander
through the extreme west of China in Spring or in
Summer, I give the friendly advice: refrain from doing
so. This half of the year is the rainy season there, and
such things as landslides that carry away roads, floods that
fill valleys, bridges that break up, sudden rushes of water
that fall through dilapidated roofs on to the sleeping
traveller, mud and damp that increase the dirt of the
native inns, all put the wanderer's enthusiasm severely to
the test.

As concerns me, I had the sacred fire of adventure,
and no doubt, that sufficed to keep me physically as well
as morally warm, for my health remained good and I
escaped even the ordinary cold.

The distance from Sungpan to Mochow is not far.
For a great part of the way, the mule path we followed
bordered and, caught as it was among the rocks, even
overhung the river. Probably in ancient times it had
been made in the Chinese fashion, which was also that
of the Romans, that is, paved with flags. When the
incline became too steep for a single slope, steps were
inset along stretches of several miles. Want of repair had
left these antique works of art in a state of ruin. The
big blocks forming the steps had broken away and rolled
in different directions, consequently in many places our
mules were obliged to emulate the chamois in order to
climb and, what was worse, to go down among the chaotic

mass of loose flags and rocks. As to us, we had to follow on foot. A proceeding that was not easy for me, owing to my lack of height. Often my legs were too short to reach the steps, and, descending, I had to jump from one to the other of them.

To those days of fatigue were added nights that tried me much more. It was impossible for us to camp. All that part of the country is cultivated; the path winds among wall-encircled fields, or else skirts the perpendicular face of the mountain. The inns are few, far between, and horribly dirty. The muleteers who travel that way sleep in the stables with their beasts and merchandise. In such quarters it was impossible for us to undress before going to sleep; we did not even dare to take our blankets out of the bags, so loth were we to put them in contact with the surrounding filth. I had to content myself with dozing a little, enveloped in my wide Tibetan robe. Fortunately, a few minutes' walk in the pure early morning air soon refreshed me and reawoke in me the great joy I felt at having left the beaten track.

Besides, the country through which we were passing was not without interest. Its history should be worth studying. Who were the enemies who had attempted to enter those narrow valleys, enclosed by precipitous mountains, and justified the fortifications that had been constructed there? Where had the invaders come from, where had they been going to? In many places were to be seen buildings with unusually thick walls and, here and there, watch towers rose overlooking the road. The smallest hamlets were encircled by enormous walls. To-day all these defence works are falling into ruin. When veiled by the rain, or emerging from the nocturnal mists, and touched by the weird light of the moon hidden behind the mountains, they added to the phantom-like character of the landscape.

Nevertheless, it was with keen pleasure that we found ourselves once again on an honest path, free from the pretentious flag stones, and where the slopes were less steep. To add to our comfort, the rain ceased, and some generous hearts gave me a present.

We were skirting a field in which peasants were digging up potatoes. Potatoes! The very sight of them made my mouth water.

" Will you sell us some? " asked the Lama politely.

" No."

" We will pay you a good price for them. How much do you want? "

" We don't sell them."

The people were Chinese. With them, my Lamaic robes might not necessarily command the same respect as they had obtained for me among the Tibetans. However, pushed by greed, I tried my luck.

" Will you not help a lady-lama to live without eating meat? " I said.

I had hit the mark. Those to whom I was speaking no doubt belonged to one of the numerous Buddhist sects in China, whose adepts are strict vegetarians. Some of the women stopped working and smiled at me.

" Here are some potatoes," they said. And they filled the sacks hanging from my saddle.

Yongden pulled out his purse.

" No, we don't want to be paid, we give them to you. A safe journey! "

" Thank you. May your crops and beasts prosper. May you all have long lives, free from illness."

We continue our way.

The news given us by the muleteers whom we meet is contradictory. For a moment a relative calm seems to reign in the region, but the fighting is expected to begin again before long.

I want to be far away before hostilities begin afresh. Therefore I find myself obliged to deny to my poor beasts the rest of which they stand so much in need. Two of the mules are lame, having hurt their feet on the bad roads, and nearly all of them have sore backs. Notwith-standing the padding and the blankets that are placed under the native wooden saddles, the animals are rapidly galled by them.

It is feared that the disbanded and plundering soldiers have reached the vicinity of Mochow, where we have to pass. What is actually happening in Mochow itself we cannot discover. Shall we find the town in the hands of bandits? Shall we run the risk of having our mules seized under the pretext of being requisitioned? Who knows.

After having pondered for some time upon the wisest course for me to take, I decided to abandon my semi-incognito for the moment, and, on the contrary, to emphasize my foreign nationality. At this time, Euro-peans in China still enjoyed a remnant of prestige, and I counted on this as a means of overawing the thieves, should we meet any.

Would I appear sufficiently European in my Lamaic robes? This question rather worried me. I had a pass-port, but before an official would be found who could examine it, many disagreeable things might happen. I should have had some Western clothes, or, at least, a Chinese dress, such as is worn by the missionaries living in the interior of China. I did not possess either. Masters and servants, we were all Tibetans from our hats to our boots.

However, we were not entirely destitute of " foreign " clothes. Before starting on the journey, I had had some mackintoshes sent from America: coats for Yongden and me, capes with hoods for the servants, and also, for me, a cap with a neck piece. In spite of the bad weather we had encountered, we had hardly used them, for fear of making ourselves conspicuous. They would save the situation.

Yongden and I would put on our coats, I would wear my cap and my son a soft felt hat. By pulling its brim down over his eyes, perhaps, he, too, would succeed in looking a "foreigner". We would both put gloves on. As for the boys, their capes would loudly proclaim the foreign origin of the masters who had provided them.

I have never seen a more comic looking party than ours was, when we were all dressed up. With their pointed hoods over their heads, the servants had the appearance of Spanish penitents, all they needed to complete the picture was a candle in their hands. Even our beasts looked at us with an astonishment that was not unmixed with concern.

Thus, all of us dressed for rain, we entered Mochow; although it chanced that, just that day, the sun beat fiercely down and uncomfortably burnt my skull under the mackintosh cap.

I rode in front of my people, hoping to draw attention to myself. At first, nothing happened; the natives ignored me completely. However, on reaching the centre of the little town, some Chinamen deigned to notice me. I assumed a dignified air and, pushing my head forward, pointed as conspicuously as possible my very Aryan nose.

The Chinamen looked at me more attentively.

" She's a *Hsi fan* woman," one of them said quietly, telling the others the impression he had derived from his examination, and his companions nodded their heads in assent.

How humiliating! . . . *Hsi fan* is one of the names the Chinese give to Tibetans, and one that is scarcely complimentary, for it approximately means "savage", thus, notwithstanding my American coat, my gloves made in France, my white woman's pointed nose, and the foreign garments of my escort, I resembled a *Hsi fan!*

Having recovered from our surprise, we laughed at the unexpected result of my beautiful stratagem. No one else took any notice of us and, without awaking

The lama Yongden also dressed as a foreigner. With him our three servants from left to right, Sonam, Tobgyal and the youth Sezang Tales.

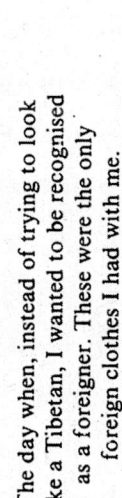

The day when, instead of trying to look like a Tibetan, I wanted to be recognised as a foreigner. These were the only foreign clothes I had with me.

CONCERNING DEMONS

the least curiosity, we arrived before a house, the pro-
prietor of which stopped us, offering to let us some
rooms for the night.

On seeing we were going to put up there, some men,
such as are always to be found loitering in the streets
of Chinese towns, hastened to help my boys unload
the beasts, take them to the stables, and fill the mangers
with straw.

When they had finished the job, Yongden called the
Chinamen to him to give them each a small gratuity.
He was seated, having placed beside him a sack full of
big copper pennies. All of a sudden, while he was speaking to them, one of the men standing in front of him
darted to the sack and plunged his hand in it. Before
he had time to withdraw it, the Lama seized the thief's
wrist and, gripping it firmly, forced him to let go of
the money he held. The man's hand came out empty.
The other Chinamen began to abuse him, and my servants, having rushed in on hearing the noise and understanding the cause of it, overwhelmed him with blows.
I interrupted the punishment, and the thief was sum-
marily ejected by his indignant compatriots.

What reason could have induced him to commit this
foolish act, which never could have resulted in success?
Was the man mad, or was misery and hunger so affect-
ing his mind that the mere sight of the bag full of big
pennies had made him lose all sense of prudence?

He remained standing in the middle of the road,
opposite the open door, apparently still fascinated by the
contents of the sack, which now lay on the table.

The Chinamen and my servants, with Yongden's approval, had decided that the least penalty we could inflict
on him would be to deprive him of the gratuity that
was to have been his. They had told him of this decision, adding that he should deem himself fortunate to
have escaped being sent before the magistrate, who
would certainly have had him beaten. Nevertheless,

131

the poor wretch continued standing where he was. The other Chinamen went away, after having received their money; but he obstinately refused to move, his eyes fixed on our door, in the attitude of a hungry animal.

He reminded me of an incident that had happened one evening, when I was camping in the snow amid the great solitudes of the *chang thangs*.

A black speck moved on the white plain: a wolf in the search of prey. It had seen my mules, which were tethered close to the tents. Wolves, when alone, do not usually attack such big beasts, and, born in that land of herdsmen, the animal knew perfectly well that under the tents were men, killers of wolves. But, for the moment, hunger obliterated all other instincts. It sprang forward . . .

Hidden behind the curtains of my tent, I had been watching it for several minutes. My movement answered the wolf's: I ran out, shouting. The creature stopped, not having had time to reach the mules, but it did not go away. In the meantime, my servants had rushed up, and, on seeing a wolf, one of them went to get his gun. He asked permission to shoot the beast, saying that its skin would make me a good carpet. Very naturally, I forbade his shooting it.

As to the wolf, it remained rivetted to the spot. It had seen the men, it might even have seen the gun, the look of which was perhaps not unknown to it; still none of these things could break the spell that the mules . . . the food, cast on it.

In our bags we had some big pieces of meat. I took one, and told the servants to leave me. Then, I went slowly towards the still motionless animal. When I reached to within about fifty yards of it, I showed it the meat, threw it as far as I could in its direction and retreated backwards. Bounding forward the wolf flung itself upon my gift, seized it in its jaws, and rushed away.

The unhappy Chinaman in the road reminded me of that wolf.

Taking advantage of a moment when my servants were occupied elsewhere, I threw him a dollar. The big silver piece did not shine long in the dust. The man seized it with the same frenzied avidity that the hungry beast had shown and, like the wolf, rushed away.

Was that justice? No, indeed. The thief, by his " reprehensible " act, had gained a bigger reward than the others had earned by their " honest " work. Perhaps his need was also greater than theirs. I could not tell, and to presume to set myself up as judge in our chaotic world would seem absurd to me. Certainly the best moral rule for us poor mortals to follow is to give one another the benefit of a generous pity.

We did not rest at Mochow: having arrived there early, we were at once able to buy provisions, and we left again next morning. Our water-proofs were re-packed in the bags, and we had again put on our costumes of *Hsi fans*. Laughing, although a little anxiously, we asked ourselves, if, now, we did not resemble " foreigners ".

The road and the weather were both better, but the effects of many weeks of torrential rains continued to make themselves felt. The very day we left Mochow, we came across, not as previously a landslip which, for the moment at least, had ceased to slide, but a high cliff, which was actually in the process of crumbling away. There was already a long row of porters seated some distance up the road, placidly watching the rolling of the stones and sand.

For over an hour, we were forced to do likewise, then, the quantity of earth and the frequency of the falls lessening, my boys declared themselves ready to attempt a passage. They first had to level the heaped-up earth, in order to mark out a path for the mules. It was slow work; the men lacked tools, and, in place of spades, they were obliged to use some of the flat stones that lay about.

While they worked, I watched the spot from where the falls came and when a movement showed at the top of the cliff, I shouted to my boys to rush for shelter. In spite of these precautions I did not feel reassured; an unexpected fall might cause a grave and even fatal accident.

As soon as the passage was made, the beasts were led one by one along the improvised path to beyond the dangerous place. After that, the servants carried the luggage across it on their backs. All this took a long time, and I felt very anxious at seeing my brave boys make the crossing so many times.

Finally, when everyone else had gone, I went, and I joined the others without receiving on me anything worse than a shower of sand.

Weichow, to where our way led, is a town of some importance, surrounded by magnificent market-gardens. It had just been plundered by a band of soldiers who had become brigands. Perhaps some of the thieves still lingered there?—It would be wise for us to keep at a distance. We therefore did not enter the town.

At this place we intended leaving the road that went down to Chengtu by Kwenshien and to turn westward, in order to reach Lifan and the Tibetan country. The road to Lifan lies beyond two rivers: the Hsi ho, which is nothing else but the Sungpan river under a different name, and the Hsiao, which comes down from the neighbourhood of the Dza pass and flows into the former.

The passage of these rivers is effected at their confluence by two suspension-bridges, which are only separated from each other by the extreme end of the tongue of land that divides the two streams.

Four enormous cables, apparently made of straw,[1] support what stands for the platform of the bridge, that is to say, a series of planks placed in a row and not joined or fixed together in any way. On either side, four or five other cables support those on which the planks rest, and, at the same time, form a sort of parapet. The whole thing resembles a gigantic hammock.

A native told me that on windy days the passage is closed. The bridges then become veritable swings, and the planks, which otherwise would be swept into the river, have to be hastily removed.

The crossing of the first bridge was accomplished without incident. Not so, however, the second; one of the mules started sliding as soon as it stepped on to it, and thrust one of its legs down into space. Its driver instantly tried to hold it up, but, in the effort of trying to regain its balance, the beast dislodged more planks, then fell and remained suspended with only the cables under it.

I am always pleased to testify to the friendliness of the Chinese peasant; for everywhere, where I have been among them, I have found them kind and ready to oblige. Everywhere, except at Weichow.

Far from trying to help my boys, who were striving to keep the mule from falling into the river, many of

[1] Cables made of straw are frequently used in the west of China, either in the construction of suspension-bridges or of rope-bridges. The latter usually consist of a single cable that is fastened to the two banks, by means of which travellers, animals, or merchandise pass over the rivers, hanging on from a hook that runs along the cable. Some of the rope-bridges, however, consist of two cables, in which case the traveller begins the crossing at a much higher level than the one at which he lands on the opposite bank. The slope obtained in this way greatly diminishes the sagging of the cable, and by the speed attained in the descent the passengers are able to mount the slightly sagging part and reach the landing place. These bridges can be negotiated without help. The cable that is used for the departure from one bank is not the same cable as the one used for this purpose on the other. The bridges with a single cable serving for the two banks sag considerably more; and except over narrow rivers, where it is possible for people with strong wrists to pull themselves up from the bottom of the dip by their hands, the travellers have to be hauled by the aid of a rope that is manœuvred by professional ferrymen.

those present started crossing the bridge, making it swing, and in this way rendering the rescue more difficult and the danger greater. Others hastened to remove more planks, so as to cut off the passage and prevent us from reaching the opposite bank. In the end, I discovered the reason for their strange behaviour: some of the people of the place made a profession of leading animals across the bridges and required to be very well paid for their services.

Wishing not to lose face entirely, I said I would pay them for the rescuing of the mule and for the leading of the others to the farther side, beyond the bridge; but, as regards the planks that had been taken away in order to stop us from going across, I would give nothing for the replacing of them. If these were not immediately brought back and placed as they should be, I would send my card to the local magistrate, who would know how to punish those who had caused the difficulties. Whereupon I gave my card to one of my boys, who set off for Weichow.

He had not got far, when he was stopped by a number of men, who promised instantly to replace the planks and to take my beasts and luggage to safety for the sum of eight dollars. I had to content myself with this pretence at amends.

The rogues were decidedly clever. In a trice they passed a cord round the body of the fallen mule, lifted it, and set it down, all trembling, on its feet; then, without giving it time to recover, took it by the head and tail, pushed it along the planks, and went and tethered it near a house, where it could meditate at leisure on the vicissitudes of life in general and of travel in particular.

The other beasts, having been unloaded, were in their turn forcibly dragged across; my boys transported the luggage; and I followed last, when everybody and everything was in safety. The pirates of the bridge now showed themselves exceedingly gracious. In order to help me to walk, they offered to support me under my arms. The enthusiasm roused in them by the thought of receiving eight dollars filled them with zeal. If I had allowed them, they would have pushed and pulled me as they had done the mules; some even wanted to carry me. I calmed their belated and interested good will and crossed the bridge at my own pace.

At the other end, after paying the scamps, we quickly remounted and rode away.

First the landslip, then the eventful passage across the river, had made us lose a lot of time. Night overtook us when we were still far from Lifan. We stopped at a hamlet called Kucheng, which lay quite close to the path. Its inhabitants seemed to be very poor; not one of them had a stable where we could put our beasts. Finally, a peasant, anxious to gain a little money, offered to put them in a room in his house. As to us, we found lodgings in the house of a good-natured old man, who was possessed of three wives almost as ancient as he was. For want of anything better we had to accept this arrangement.

The news we hear is thoroughly bad. The Gyarongpas have invaded Lifan; the Chinese official and his personnel have flown; and the bands of Gyarongpas are wandering in the vicinity of the town, robbing travellers.

We are in an embarrassing position. The narrow valley in which we find ourselves has for only practicable mule path the one we are now on. There are but two things possible for us to do: to go to Lifan, where the situation appears to be disturbed; or else to go back, with the prospect of having to recross the bridges that we have just passed over with so much trouble, and of falling into a region that is overrun by soldiers who have deserted from the regular army and given themselves over to brigandage.

The mules, too, are causing me anxiety. By not having been attended to in time, their sores have increased in size. I am unwilling to inflict further suffering on the poor animals, by making them continue to carry our luggage. We must either stop and let their sores heal or hire other beasts. But at the first words I utter on this subject, the peasants tell me that I shall not be able to get any.

Muleteers are only to be found at Weichow, which is situated on the other side of the two bridges, or at Lifan, where most of them have sent their animals away, for fear of having them stolen by the brigands.

Night has come. To-morrow we will consider what is best to do. For the moment we need rest.

The boys set up my camp bed in a little room that is already obstructed by two plank beds, from which my host has taken the blankets. These bare planks will serve me for tables.

A disagreeable surprise awaits me. When I open my saddle-bags, I cannot find my revolver. Yet its usual place is in the right hand one, out of sight, but within instant reach. I make enquiries. Neither Yongden nor any one of the servants has taken it from the bag, and nobody has seen it. They search carefully for it. It is not discovered in any of the other bags.

It may have been stolen while the mule that was in danger of falling into the river held our attention. It may also have slipped from the bag when the servants were carrying the luggage, either across the bridge or, in haste, under the crumbling cliff. It is useless to waste time on conjecture. We shall never know how the thing happened. One fact only is of importance: I am now deprived of a weapon, which, on occasion, could be useful, and I do not see any possibility of being able to replace it by another.

We remain eight days in Kucheng. The mules' wounds do not heal, despite the care that is given them.

We have no news concerning Lifan. Not a muleteer goes by of whom we can ask questions. As for the inhabitants of the hamlet, they are no better informed than we are. Being all of them Chinese, they are afraid of the brutal Gyarongpas, who are stronger than they; for fear of encountering them, they do not venture beyond the limits of their fields.

Life during this period of waiting is not very agreeable, but one of the happy sides of my nature is that I can accustom myself to and even find pleasure in any place, no matter where. I read some Tibetan books, which I have with me, stroll by the river, and listen to my hostesses, who quarrel from morning to night.

What are the points of contention that make them fill the house with cries of startled hens?—I can only understand a little of what they say. However, Tobgyal, who knows Chinese very well, assures me the disputes only relate to trifles: a badly lighted fire, some spilt tea, a misplaced chair. . . . The common spouse of these cross-grained women is a taciturn old fellow, rather shaky and unsteady on his feet. He remains seated for the most part of the day, staring into space. Is he thinking of anything. If so, of what? . . .

He pays no attention to the noise that his wives make. He must be accustomed to it. According to the Chinese law, only one of them has the right to the title of spouse, the others are only concubines; all the same, there is nothing discreditable in the avowal of this position. In better class families the demarcation between the legitimate wife and the concubines is sufficiently well defined. It is far from being so among the poor, where the whole family lives in a small house and where its members all work together.

It was not for the first time that I observed at close quarters a polygamous household of old Chinese peasants, and I again noticed the striking difference that exists between the effects of polygamy and those of polyandry among people of this class. The majority of polygamous old men I had seen had more or less resembled my host at Kucheng. They were poor depressed old fellows, who, having given up all initiative, had allowed themselves to be entirely dominated by their wives. These women had not all been crabbed and quarrelsome; I had known some very friendly and smiling old dames; but the one kind as well as the other asserted their rulership, and no matter how well they looked after him, their husband was no more than their chattel.

Neither does the polyandrous spouse among the Tibetan peasants efface herself before her old husbands, and all bent and toothless as she may be, she still knows how to keep them under her yoke. All the same, at this age, her supremacy becomes precarious on the day that her sons' polyandrous wife enters the family and takes over the management of the house. Then, there only remains to the old mother, as consolation, the reciting of thousands of *manis*,[1] while telling her beads or turning her *mani*-wheel,[2] and the endless gossips with other devotees of her age, on feast days in the precincts of the temple.

A zoological discovery, which I made at Kucheng, threw a gleam of mirth upon the monotony of the days passed there. In the first place the ambitious term " discovery " is only applicable to me. The animal in question has been well known for centuries, by millions of people, in all parts of the globe; but I had never seen it, and that, it seemed, was a marvel.

All the foreigners who tell of their travels in the East agree in their descriptions of the dirt of the natives, the number on them of these particular insects, and also in their complaints that they themselves have been subjected to their attacks. With me, on the contrary, more than

[1] The formula: *Aum mani padme hum!*
[2] The little portable cylinder that contains paper ribbons, on which the formula *Aum mani padme hum!* is printed. It is incorrectly called " prayer-wheel " by foreigners.

ten years of travel among Tibetans, Chinese, Indians, Koreans, and other Asiatics, had not only left me free of the visits of these undesirable guests, but, as I have already said, even of the sight of them.

When, lo and behold; one morning in Kucheng, while doing my bed and folding my sheets, I see a queer little being, white and transparent looking, with a black line running the length of its body. This, I say to myself, is a curious animal and doubtless very rare, for I have never yet come across anything like it; probably it belongs to the special fauna of Szechwan.

I had put the insect into the hollow of my hand and was examining it, when Yongden came in.

"Have you slept well," he said. . . . "What ever are you looking at?"

"A little beast," I replied. "Come and see. Do you know what it is?"

The lama approached, glanced at my outstretched palm, and began to dance for joy, laughing like a fool the while.

"There!" he said at last, "you have always boasted that you had never seen one. Well! you have seen one now. It's a louse."

More years have passed by, I have gone on living among Tibetans and Chinese, but the louse of Kucheng has remained the only specimen of its kind I have ever seen.

It was not possible for us to continue in the uncertainty in which we found ourselves. Yongden, accompanied by one of the servants left for Lifan. Both of them did the journey on foot, so as to avoid running any risk of having our only sound mules stolen on the road.

On their return, they told me that the Gyarongpas who had invaded Lifan had retired; their quarrel was with the Chinese authorities and concerned the levying of certain taxes by them. The local magistrate had fled, but there was no need for us to fear molestation. The lama had also been able to arrange with a muleteer there for the transport of our luggage as far as Tsakalo, a market town on the farther side of Lifan. Except for their sores, our beasts were in a healthy condition; it would do them no harm to travel after a week's rest, so long as they did so without carrying loads or saddles.

Next day the muleteer arrived with his animals, and the same evening we slept at his home, in a wooden house that reeked of opium. As Lifan had nothing of special interest to offer us, we left early in the morning for Tsakalo.

Our road ascended the course of the Hsiao ho. Above the opposite bank to the one we were following, high up on the mountain slopes, perched forbidding looking villages: huddled groups of many-storied wooden dwellings, with balconies. Watch-towers, of which there are so many around Lifan, continued to mark the valley.

The stage was a short one, less than twenty-five miles. We reached Tsakalo quite early.

Tsakalo is a village inhabited by Gyarongpas, that is, by people of Tibetan descent, who have lived for centuries in the Chinese (gya) valleys (rong).

On our arrival a crowd quickly gathers round us, but no one knows of a house where we can find rooms. Yongden leaves us in order to scour the neighbourhood in search of lodgings. While he is gone, a woman comes to tell me that she has some rooms she can let us have, but no stable large enough in which to put all our animals. Some of them will have to remain outside, in the yard. This suggestion does not please me, and I decide to wait for Yongden's return before accepting her offer. However, as he comes back without having found lodgings, there is nothing left for us to do but to go where we have been invited.

The woman who has spoken to me is a Chinese, the landlady of an inn. The courtyard into which we enter is small and muddy, and the stable at the end of it is still more muddy and very dirty. Our poor beasts will be very badly lodged. As to us, we are to have rooms on the first floor. This is reached by a wooden staircase, as steep as a ladder, which leads into a gallery giving on to the court. Up here, however, is an agreeable surprise. The first floor, built entirely of wood, is a recent addition to the house. It has not yet had time to become stained and smoke-blackened by the many passing guests. The wood still retains its light colour, and imparts to its surroundings an air of cheerful cleanliness. A large room near the staircase will serve my men for dormitory. Beyond is a kitchen, and, right at the end of the gallery, where it turns at right angles to run along another side of the court, is a little two-roomed apartment. I shall occupy the inner room, which has two windows: one looking on to the gallery, the other on to the open country. Yongden will occupy the outer room and, in this way, act as bodyguard; for anyone wishing to enter my room will first have to pass through his. He will thus be able to bar the way to intruders and ensure me this much quiet.

The days pass. The mules' sore backs slowly heal. My boys make up for the privations that they have undergone by eating almost without ceasing. Tsakalo is not rich in food-stuffs, but there is more than sufficient for proper nourishment.

The lama reads in his room; I do the same in mine, from which I never stir. The villagers are curious and would like to examine me at close quarters; a proceeding I dislike intensely. I have also another reason for wishing to live in retirement. At Tsakalo there is a fairly large lamasery, to which an enormous *chörten* adds a certain air of lofty dignity.

Monks, even more than merchants, form the travelling element in Tibet. Without luggage, without money, thousands of these itinerant clericals wander up and down Tibet and the adjoining regions. Some seek a spiritual master who will be capable of guiding them on to the path of supreme wisdom, others go in quest of mystic initiations, of secret doctrines. Others again dream of discovering one or other of the books that are said to have been hidden by saintly lamas of past centuries. There are also those who are animated by the desire for extraordinary encounters, for strange dealings with non-human beings. Lastly, the simple pious pilgrims whose only object is to visit sacred places.

All these people who wander from place to place are great gossipmongers. Therefore I did not want the *trapas* of Tsakalo to see me too often or too close to, lest they should discover my true identity and spread the news that a foreign woman was roaming across the country.

However, in spite of my efforts at retirement, I did not completely escape the attention of the lower clergy. The *trapas* came to talk to my servants, their confrères in the Lamaist Order. These visitors walked along the gallery balcony, outside my window, and tried to see what was happening in my room. They succeeded in doing so occasionally, but this manœuvre brought them little satisfaction; for they only saw me reading a Tibetan book, a sight with which they were quite familiar.

One afternoon, while I was sitting as usual on my bed reading, with my back to the window giving on to the gallery, I experienced that peculiar sensation which sometimes comes to us when we feel we are being looked at. I turned round and saw an eye framed in a hole in the paper that, in China, takes the place of window pane. It was not the first time I had been spied upon in this way; I therefore resumed my reading, but a voice from outside said:

"I have come to see you."

With this, the eye disappeared; then I heard footsteps go along the gallery and enter Yongden's room, and the same voice say:

144

"I have come to see the *ane*."[1]

"Jetsun Kushog," corrected my son, scandalized at the visitor's lack of respect.

"Jetsun Kushog, if it pleases you," answered the voice, in a tone of indifference.

Then, before Yongden had time to prevent him, the intruder opened the door of my room and began staring at me.

He was a grey-haired man, correctly dressed in a monastic habit made of fine serge. He seemed very sure of himself, very much at his ease, and a little overbearing. The way in which he had forced himself into my room displeased me, but I did not wish to run the risk of quarrelling with a lama, so close to a monastery that probably comprised several hundred, if not a thousand, monks. This might lead to unpleasant consequences.

I therefore pretended to laugh.

"Sit down, *Kushog*," I said to my visitor. "You have put yourself to a lot of trouble for nothing; there is nothing curious to see here."

"There is you," retorted the lama. "What are you doing here?"

"I am waiting for my mules' sores to heal."

"Where do you come from?"

"From the North, near Mongolia."

"Where are you going?"

"South, to my own country."

"Which country?"

"Gya Med."[2]

"But you are not Chinese."

"No, no more than are the Gyarongpas. The Gyamedpas are also different from the Chinese."

"Ah!"

---

[1] *Ane*, the term most often used when referring to an ordinary nun. Those whose rank, either ecclesiastical or social, compare with that of the lamas are respectfully called *Jetsun Kushog*, or by abbreviation *Jetsünma*.

[2] "Gya Med"="Lower China." For Tibetans of these regions, it represents a vaguely defined area that includes Indo-China.

Gya Med appeared to perplex the lama; he could not imagine what part of China was in question.

"Yunnan? . . ." he asked.

"Farther south. . . ."

"Is it far away?"

"Very far."

There was silence.

"And are people *nangpas* (Buddhists) in that country?"

"They are."

"Have you been a nun long?"

"Ten years."

He looked at me attentively for a moment.

"What did you do before then?"

"I was married."

"Your husband is dead?"

"No, he allowed me to become a nun. . . . He has two other wives."

The door shut quickly behind Yongden; he was rushing away, unable to restrain his mirth.

I was not nearly so amused as he; this examination annoyed me. I determined to put an end to it.

"What interest can all this have for you, *Kushog?*"

"It does not interest me at all. The *trapas* have told me that there was a foreign nun here, who recited the Sacred Writings all day long. This appeared to me to be rather extraordinary. What are you reciting?"

What an impossible person, I thought, and I answered him rather sharply.

"I do not recite, I *read*."

He looked at me again with what seemed to be a mocking air.

"O yes, I read," I continued almost angrily. "I read in order to try to understand how 'form is emptiness and emptiness is form,' and how 'outside of emptiness there is no form and outside of form there is no emptiness.'"[1]

[1] A quotation from the Prajñā Pāramitā.

146

He did not reply, but becoming serious, rose and went to examine the books that were lying on my table.

" The times are bad, Jetsun Kushog," he said, when he he had finished his inspection. " Men's minds are turned towards evil; they only think of harming one another. In selfishly seeking their own good, they are bringing about their own ruin. They are blind; they lack the calm in which the penetrating vision that produces wisdom is developed. The *chirolpas* (Hindus) and many others have thought and meditated, have had sages and saints, but. they have continued to believe in the reality of the separated, isolated *self*. Of this non-existent thing, they have made an object of adoration; for its sake they torment themselves and torment others. They have not reached that depth of vision which reveals the unreality of the self and of the world, as they see it.

" So long as they have not recognized the error of the belief in a *self*, they will be subject to the painful illusion of birth and death. He who can root out this error is forever freed from death."

He stopped speaking. I remained silent, not wishing to break the thread of his ideas, should he wish to continue the argument. However he passed on to another subject.

" Who is that young fellow who was here? He is a *tulku*,[1] isn't he? I do not think I am mistaken."

" You have doubtless been told this? "

" No, it can be felt, even if the *tulku* is not officially recognized. . . . He will have a curious life."

This life has already begun, I said to myself, thinking of all the journeys that Yongden had done and of those he would probably do in the future, having now become my son.

" He belongs to the Kahgyud-Karma sect," I said,

---

[1] A lama who reincarnates a noted predecessor. For theories concerning *tulkus* see *With Mystics and Magicians in Tibet*, page 113.

" he has studied under many masters. He is my adoptive son."

"My family comes from the neighbourhood of Gartog," resumed the lama, "I had for *guru* (spiritual guide) a lama who had attained enlightenment. He was not a *gomchen* (a contemplative hermit) he had never thought it necessary to retire into hermitage. He saw all things differently from the way we, through ignorance, perceive them. All that I have come to understand, I owe to him . . ."

"You are going to a far country . . ."

He looked at me and continued.

". . . Perhaps farther away than the one you named to me. The young man accompanies you? Since both of you love the 'Doctrine' and are trying to grasp its meaning, I will gladly communicate to you some of my master's teachings. They might be of benefit to the people over there. . . .

"I, too, do not think of staying here much longer. I am busy, and, for other reasons also, I cannot come back to this inn; but let the young man come to the monastery, I will dictate some notes to him, or let him read some pages of certain manuscripts. To-morrow I will send a *trapa* to fetch him and bring him to me."

The lama then drank some tea, talked a little to Yongden, and, later, left us.

The next day my son found the lama installed in a little house,[1] which was evidently not his own, for he did not appear to know where the most everyday things were kept. Yongden therefore concluded that the lama did not wish to receive him where he lived. Perhaps he did not wish those around him to become aware of what he was dictating to his temporary pupil. Judging, too, by the great respect shown to the lama by the two *trapas* who served him, Yongden also inferred that

[1] Tibetan monks do not live in community; each of them has a private dwelling in the precincts of the monastery.

his teacher must be somebody of importance. He inquired his name, but the personal name of a lama is seldom known, and etiquette does not permit it to be used in speaking of him. It is customary to call him by his title or official position in the monastery; by his residence, if he is a *tulku*; or by the name of his native country.

Yongden's benevolent master was Markham Kushog. Now Markham is one of the names for the region of Gartog in the Kham country, therefore this name did not shed much light on the identity of the lama. He was most likely one of those learned thinkers, of whom there are many in Eastern Tibet, who live in easy circumstances, without seeking fame, spending their time in the study of books, in friendly conversation with other scholars, and sometimes, in teaching a few chosen pupils.

During the few days we still spent in Tsakalo, my son took a number of interesting notes, and it was with real regret that he parted from the kindly lama.

The Tsakalo inn was the shabby setting of a poignant drama, the remembrance of which continued to haunt me for a very long time. The owners of the inn, Chinese people, had only one child, a son aged sixteen, who was in the last stages of consumption.

Every evening, at sunset, his mother lighted lamps before the image of I do not know what divinity of the Taoist pantheon, then, holding some joss sticks between her joined palms, she stood at the open door, and, with her head raised to the sky, sent a heartrending lament into the space. It must have been an appeal; the same word—perhaps the name of the deity invoked— sounded over and over again. The supplicant's voice never grew clamorous, but remained low, monotonous, filled with a painful weariness that was inexpressibly sad.

She was reciting an office that required responses.

149

A young boy of ten stood near the imploring mother and, at the proper moment, uttered the necessary words. No doubt, he would have often preferred to be elsewhere, and his part in this pathetic rite bored him. At any rate, he showed little reverence; for he turned his head from side to side, as he watched what was going on in the yard. Meanwhile the mother, her hands raised to the sky, plunged in thought, forgot everything but her dying son and the god who could heal him, if such was his good pleasure. She only became aware of her acolyte's inattention when he forgot a response. She then whispered it to him, and listlessly the urchin repeated it, his shrill voice cutting into the plaintive harmony of the chanter's appeal.

While she was absorbed in her prayer, people passed to and fro in the yard, each one engrossed in his own affairs. I looked at her from my window, my heart heavy with ineffable sadness at seeing her thus, alone, amid this general indifference, stretching out her hands to the void.

One day she asked me to go and see her son. I went down to the ground floor, where the owners of the inn lived, into a middle-sized room, which had for only opening a door that, under the shadow of the balcony, gave directly on to another part of the building. At the far end of this smoke blackened and airless room stood the invalid's bed. No medical knowledge was necessary in order to see that its occupant had only a short time more to live.

I advised a generous diet, if the lad could digest it. I also urged the parents to take him from that dark room and let him sit in the sun, when it was warm enough, or to move him to a lighter and more sunny room on the upper floor. I felt obliged to say something; no medicines would have been of any use.

I have never forgotten this sorrowing mother. I often think of her as perhaps still mourning the child whom the gods would not, or could not, save for her.

An opportunity presented itself for leaving Tsakalo without our having to wait for the mule's backs to heal completely, a process that was taking far longer than we could ever have imagined to be possible.

Yongden heard of a muleteer who had brought merchandise to Tsakalo and who was now returning home with unladen beasts. He immediately went to see him and arranged for our luggage to be carried over the mountain to the other side of the Dza pass.

We are late in starting from Tsakalo, so the first stage of our journey is a short one. The weather is cloudy. On quitting the village we see another watch tower that is admirably posed in the landscape, then we amble our way between fields and through hamlets of no special interest. The path, which has been partially destroyed by the recent rains, is almost cut off in several places. However we manage to pass without much difficulty; but our progress is slow, and it is nearly sunset when we stop at a place, which our muleteer calls Hsi-tien.

While we are looking for a suitable spot in which to camp, a *trapa* passes by. He is at the moment an *amchöd*[1] at a farmer's and volunteers to get rooms for us at the house. He also says that there is a big stable attached to it, where all the beasts can be lodged, and that the muleteer and his servant can sleep in an adjoining room. This proposal suits me perfectly; at least, as regards that which concerns the mules. As to me, after having been shut in my room for over a week, I shall be delighted to pass a night under canvas.

Tobgyal, Sönam and the muleteers unload the beasts, then, guided by the obliging *trapa*, they lead the mules

[1] A chaplain: often a *trapa* who resides either permanently or temporarily in the house of a layman or of a lama, to read the Sacred Writings or to celebrate rites.

to the village, where they will also buy straw and grain for them and give them their feed.

For his part, Sotar quickly takes a little dry wood from one of the bags, puts three big stones together in such a position as to support a saucepan, and lights a fire. While waiting for his comrades to bring him a more ample supply of fuel, with which to cook our supper, he prepares some tea.

Having nothing to do, I take a book from my saddle-bag, sit down on a sack, and begin to read.

As the place where we propose to spend the night is rather far from the village, the peasants have not seen us arrive, but when the *trapa* enters it leading my men and their beasts, our presence becomes quickly known. Several of the more curious of the inhabitants come out to inspect me.

Hearing me read in an undertone, as is the Tibetan habit, one of them comes close to me, in the hope of catching some of the words that I am uttering. Finding he cannot do so, he asks for the book. I hand it to him. After stammering out a few sentences in a curious pronunciation, he suddenly recognizes the work he has in his hand and, calling to those around him, cries:

"It is our religion!"

He gives me back my book, retreats a few steps, then, with intense fervour, prostrates himself three times in homage before the pages of the Sacred Writings that I hold in my hand. Many of the villagers hasten to imitate him. After having demonstrated his respect, this "scholar" rushes away and, in a little while, returns with some books. He shows me them and, with my help, reads a few pages. The peasants who are watching are filled with admiration. However, the sun has set, the light fails, and we are forced to cease our reading; but, while my attention has been occupied in this manner, a miracle has happened. Suddenly enlightened, the natives have discovered the object of my journey.

Their village has the signal honour of being the birthplace of a *tulku*. This eminent lama is now returning from Lhasa and, on his way to his residence in Mongolia, will pass some days in his native land. For the moment, he is staying in a small monastery the other side of the Dza Pass. As to us, we are pious people, who, having learned of the lama's presence in this region, are on our way to do homage to him and beg for his blessing.

I am delighted that these brave Gyarongpas should have themselves imagined this story. It saves me the trouble of inventing another.

The piety that has been ascribed to us has its immediate reward. Women bring us provisions for the road, among which are three eggs and a basket of nuts.

Night comes, and the villagers go away. Tobgyal and Sönam have returned. After drinking some tea, they are now going to pitch the tents, then, when all is in order, they will go back and water the beasts, which, on arriving, had been too hot to drink.

As we are unfolding the tents the wind suddenly rises, and almost at once becomes a gale. I begin to regret having refused the hospitality that was offered us. The night promises to be bad, and we could have passed it more comfortably under a roof. While I am thinking this, thunder rumbles in the distance. My servants want to know if they must continue to put up the tents; there is certain to be heavy rain later. Would it not be better for us to seek shelter in a house? . . .

Such a move presents difficulties. The farmstead where our beasts are stabled is at the farther end of the village. It would take too long for the men to carry the luggage there. . . . Can we not find lodgings nearer at hand?

Sönam proposes that we should go to a small house that he has seen close by, down a turning, behind a clump of trees that has hidden it from me.

The thunder sounds louder. I can quite understand that my boys have a great longing to get under cover. Then let them go and ask for hospitality at the little farm.

"Who would refuse to receive travellers during a thunderstorm!" declares Sönam, full of assurance.

The others share his optimism and are prepared to thrust themselves upon the owners of the small homestead. Besides, there is no time to be lost, if we do not wish to get wet. The servants quickly reclose the bags that have already been opened, carry away the half folded tents, and run to the house. As they have foreseen, they are well received. Yongden and I help with the removal. Great drops of rain begin to fall. Finally, after several journeys from camp to farmhouse, all our luggage is safe under cover.

The farmer and his wife are a middle-aged couple. Their home, which is built over the stables, consists of only two rooms: a kitchen and, separated from it by a terrace, a room that is filled with provisions, clothing, wool for spinning, dried faggots, sacks, boxes, and a heterogeneous mass of things, all covered with a thick layer of dust. The *nemo*[1] promises to make a place among them in which to put up my camp bed. The men will pass the night in the kitchen, with the owners of the house.

Such as it is, I congratulate myself on having found this shelter. The storm has broken, the wind rages, and the rain mixed with hail beats against the walls. We are better off here than under the tents, and we shall be able to have supper peacefully.

The *nemo* has offered to make the soup for us, with the meat and *tsampa* we shall give her. She, herself, will add some turnips and radishes, and she naturally counts on being asked, together with her husband, to share our

---

[1] *Nemo*: a familiar, but polite, term for the mistress of the house, when she is a woman of the people.

meal. While waiting for the soup to be ready, we drink some more buttered tea.

The squall is too violent to last long; indeed, in less than an hour after our arrival at the farm, the rain ceases.

Sönam and Tobgyal will take advantage of this fact to return to the village to water the beasts and fill their racks with straw. Since our hostess is kindly acting as cook, Sotar will go and help his companions.

The three men have drunk their tea seated on the floor with no table on which to put their bowls, so they put their empty bowls on the floor, close to the wall, in readiness for the next meal, and go out. The *nepo* (master of the house) follows them, to get the milk and the promised vegetables, and his wife goes to make an effort at tidying the room where I am going to sleep. Yongden and I remain alone by the hearth.

A few minutes later, a young man comes into the kitchen and, without saying a word, sits down in the corner. Our hostess comes back, glances casually at the newcomer, and, catching sight of a wooden bowl that is standing by him on the floor, fills it with tea and places a little bag of *tsampa* in front of it. Then, turning round to the hearth, makes up the fire, and starts preparing the supper.

The boy still remains silent, he has not even thanked the woman who served him. Awkwardly, he plunges his hand into the bag of *tsampa* and, on withdrawing it, lets the greater part of his handful of flour run through his fingers on to the floor. He throws the rest of it into his tea, then absent-mindedly, without looking at what he is doing, his eyes staring into space, he stirs the pap with his fingers. Finally, he puts the bowl to his mouth and holds it against his lips, without eating.

While she is cutting the meat up into little pieces for the soup, the *nemo* furtively watches this silent individual's strange ways. Then, as she goes to the

155

corner of the room to get some dry branches for the fire, he gets up, lets his bowl fall from his hands, and walks out like an automaton.

Both Yongden and I have understood.

" He is an idiot," the lama says to me in a low voice. I nod my head in agreement.

At the sound that the bowl makes in falling, the *nemo* turns round and she sees the poor fool disappearing out of the door.

" What is the matter with your servant? " she asks us. " He looks like a madman."

" What do you mean? This boy is not our servant."

" Is he not one of your people who have remained in the village with the mules? "

" Nothing of the sort. We don't know him. Only the two Chinamen have stayed with the mules. You have seen our three servants, here."

" Why didn't you say he was not your servant? "

" We thought he was one of the household. You gave him tea."

" I gave him tea because I thought he was one of your men."

" Do not regret having done so. It was a charitable act. You will gain merit by it. Poor fellow! he is certainly out of his mind . . . an idiot. He wasted all his *tsampa* and tea, without eating or drinking. He seemed to try to do so and could not."

Heavens! What indiscreet words had I uttered without suspecting their singular import? The woman turned pale.

" Ah! you remarked it too," she stammered. " He wanted to eat and could not."

She stood thinking. At this moment the dogs began to bark furiously, as they did when we arrived. My boys were returning.

On entering the room they at once noticed the spilt

156

tea and *tsampa,* and the overturned bowl. Tobgyal ran quickly and picked it up.

"What is the meaning of this?" he asked angrily. "Who has used my bowl?"[1]

I then understood that the bowl near to which the idiot had seated himself belonged to Tobgyal, who had placed it there. The *nemo,* seeing it by the man whom she took for my servant, had concluded that it was his and that he was waiting politely, in silence, for someone to fill it with tea.

The woman paid no attention to Tobgyal's indignation. She had given a start on hearing the dogs bark, as if a sudden idea had struck her.

"And . . ." she said, "when this man came in, the dogs did not bark, and when he went away they still did not bark. . . . *Kyab su chiwo! . . . Lama Kieno! . . .*"[2]

Whatever was the matter with her?

She called her husband and told him all that had happened. The man looked grave.

"That is bad," he declared. "It is not a man but a demon who has come. Tea and flour are not the food that his kind crave for; they feast on the 'vital breath' of beings. . . . Who has brought him here. . . ?"

"You are talking nonsense, *nepo,*" I said. "No demon has come, only a poor idiot boy. If he does not belong to your village, it is that he is wandering up and down without knowing where to go. You must find him and give him shelter. To-morrow you can try and discover where he comes from so as to send him back to his people.

"Take a lantern," I ordered, turning to Sönam, "and see if a boy is not wandering about close by. If you

---

[1] Every Tibetan possesses one or more bowls, personal to himself. Custom requires that no one except their owner drinks out of them.

[2] Current exclamations at the time of danger, misfortune, etc. The first one means: "I go for refuge," and the second "Know, O Lama!" or "The Lama knows it." It is an appeal to one's spiritual guide, or to the founder of the sect to which one belongs, entreating him to protect his follower.

meet him, lead him gently back here: he is a poor mad fellow."

On hearing this, the woman threw herself before the door.

"You shall not do it, you shall not go out!" she shrieked. "You shall not bring that demon back."

"He'll receive something, if he does show himself again," muttered her husband, taking a sword from the wall and unsheathing it. It was no longer a question of one lunatic; there were now two others in front of me, and these were certainly more dangerous than the first. To go against the peasants' superstitious ideas would have been imprudent. The unfortunate boy ran less risk in wandering over the countryside than in being brought back to this house, where they wished to kill him. I did not insist. Sotar cooked the supper, for the woman was far too upset to continue her job. We then ate quickly, and I retired to my room.

I am not yet in bed when my son raps gently at my door. I open it, and see that he is carrying his blankets under his arm.

"If you will permit me," he says, "I will sleep here."

"Are you too many in the kitchen; can't you find a place?"

"It is not that. This fuss about the idiot worries me."

"Oh! Why?"

"Because these fools have got it into their heads that he is a demon, and they seem to think that it is we who have brought him in our train. You know their ideas on the subject."

"What does that matter to us? . . . Sleep here if you like."

The young man spreads his blankets on the floor before the door, which I leave open. I am stifled in this room, among the many smells that come from the things that are piled there.

In the night an unusual sound wakes me. Somebody is walking slowly, bare-footed, on the terrace. Who is it? A thief. That is hardly probable. Nevertheless, I get up quickly, kneel down by Yongden, cover his mouth with his blankets, to deaden the sound of his voice should he speak on being suddenly awakened, and whisper in his ear:

"Somebody is coming; wake up!"

The lama has not yet disentangled himself from his blankets, when the nocturnal visitor appears. It is Sönam.

"I have come to warn you," he says. "The *nemo* is ill. She has moaned all the night, complaining of pains in her heart. She declares that the demon who came last evening has carried her 'vital breath' away to devour it and that she will die. Her husband accuses us of having brought the demon. He is so angry that he has cursed us the whole night. We have not been able to sleep. I have come out as if to satisfy a necessity of nature; I wanted you to know what was happening."

Yongden immediately determines upon a course of action.

"We must leave," he says, "leave at once, before the *nepo* has time to spread his absurd notions all through the village. The woman's sudden illness may create a bad impression. We must leave. . . . If she becomes worse, the peasants, already excited by the story of the demon, may handle us roughly. . . ."

"That is what I fear," acquiesces Sönam.

They are right. Ridiculous as it may seem, the situation is a serious one. The superstition, firmly established among the Tibetans, that wandering demons attach themselves to travellers, enter into the houses where these last are received, and, there, draw out and "eat" the life of both men and animals, may provoke an outburst of collective fury among the villagers. To try to reason with them, to nurse the sick *nemo*, whose illness is probably entirely caused by fright, would be useless. Flight is best.

"Listen," I say to Sönam, "in two hours it will be day. Go to the muleteers and tell them that I wish to go far to-day, in order to reach as soon as possible the Grand Lama, whom I wish to visit. Above all do not say anything about the demon. Let the three of you quickly bring the mules here. If the chaplain or any of the farm people wake up and ask questions, repeat to them what you have said to the muleteers: I am in a hurry to see the lama.

"Will it take you long to cord the luggage, here?"

"No. We packed everything last evening. Except for Jetsun Kushog's blankets and ours, all is ready to put on the mules."

"Good. Now be quick. The dogs have been chained up, so you have nothing to fear from them. The *nepo* saw you go out; he will think you are in the yard and will not be astonished if they bark."

"I think I can manage to jump into the field from the end of the terrace; as the dogs are chained up on the other side of the house, perhaps they will not hear me. The *nepo*, whose attention is centred in the invalid, will be less likely to notice my absence if the dogs do not bark."

Yongden approves, and I tell them to do as they please.

Sönam is tall, young and agile. The distance from the terrace to the ground is not great; he soon steps over the wooden railing, hangs there for a moment, then drops. Now he is running off into the darkness. The dogs have heard nothing. It almost seems as if he were enacting a romantic drama. I am half inclined to laugh, but the lama is serious. "Rotten business," he mutters.

It does not take me long to make my toilet. In Tibet, one does not undress much while travelling. I have only taken off my outer robe and my boots. My son and I silently refold my blankets and bed and put them back into their bag. Then, we wait.

It seems a long time before we hear the sound of the mules' hoofs splashing in the mud.

Yongden goes to tell Sotar and Tobgyal of our plans. He also retails to the farmer the story I have invented: " We are longing to see the Grand Lama, therefore we are making a very early start so as to be able to go far to-day." I think the fact that we are going to visit this saintly man rather impresses our host; he is not quite sure that it would be possible for such pious people to have demons following them.

I approach the sick woman, but her husband stops me and will not let me touch her. I do not insist. When in a few days' time she finds herself still alive and she is no longer terrified, the fever will leave her quite naturally.

The beasts are loaded by the light of our Chinese lanterns, and we set off.

The path that mounts to the pass is cut through virgin forest. The natives go along it either on foot or on their little Szechwan ponies, and for the convenience of these riders the trees have been ruthlessly lopped of their lower branches. As for me, seated on my tall Sining mule, I ride with my head in the foliage, often at the risk of having an eye put out by a twig. At one moment my way is completely barred. My mule not under-standing why I wish to stop, insists on trying to follow its companions in the file. The boys have to hold it and extricate me by cutting the surrounding branches with their swords.

Owing to our hurried departure we did not break-fast before leaving, and the mules are also fasting, there-fore towards midday I call a halt. While some of the men give grain to the beasts, others gather dead wood. A fire is lighted, and soon we are each enjoying several bowls of buttered tea. The rest of the meal follows: some pieces of meat that have been grilled on the glowing embers, and some bread that we ourselves had baked in Tsakalo.

As we are eating, a man on horseback comes along. "Where are you going to?" Tobgyal asks him, according to the Tibetan custom of questioning a traveller whom one meets. And, conforming likewise to the usage of the country, Yongden adds: "Come and drink tea with us."

"Thank you, I cannot stop," answers the rider. "I am in a hurry."

"Where are you going to?" insists Yongden.

"To the monastery on the other side of the pass. I am going to ask the lamas, there, to perform the rites for the dead in behalf of the woman at whose house you slept last night. She died at daybreak; a demon killed her!"

The man continues to ride as he speaks. His last words are shouted from a distance, when he is already hidden by the trees. It is the voice of an invisible being, who, through the dark silent forest, sends us the astounding news: "The woman died; a demon killed her!"

We remain stupefied. However, we must on no account let the muleteers become afraid, they might abandon us. I quickly recover.

"Poor woman!" I say. "She was very ill when we arrived."

This statement ought to reassure the Chinamen: if her illness existed prior to our arrival at her house, there can be no connection between it and our visit. But I see them turn pale. They look all around, they look at me. I can guess their thoughts: Has this murderous demon followed us?—Was it already with us when we entered the farm?—Do demons follow in my train?—Although less given to superstition, my servants appear uneasy.

The widowed farmer must, now, be completely convinced that a demon has devoured the " life " of his wife and that it is we who brought it to his house. Will he call his friends to his aid? Shall we be pursued, and will the villagers attempt to murder us?

Hurriedly we resume our march, my men pushing before them the terrified muleteers and their beasts. Yongden rides with me in the rear. On the other side of the pass, at the foot of the mountain, we shall find ourselves in territory under the jurisdiction of a Chinese magistrate. The magistrate has his seat at some distance from there, but it is almost certain that the tribesmen will not dare to attack us in his district. . . . The pass, however, is still far ahead. Suddenly, we hear clamouring voices from below us. Are the villagers coming?— Shall we, after having been, unfortunately, the indirect cause of the death of a poor woman, be compelled to use our arms to defend our lives against deluded hillmen? I would never do such a thing for my own sake, but my men are not willing to let themselves be killed without fighting. I see them unslinging their rifles. . . .

" Let us hāsten," I urge.

Haste is essential; nevertheless, the voices we hear may merely be those of wood-cutters, who are shouting to some distant co-workers. I want to communicate this reassuring idea to my companions, but the muleteers have already formed their own opinion as regards the disquieting clamour that rises from the mysterious depths of the forest.

" Demons follow us! " they suddenly cry. " The demon who has killed the woman and others whom he has called to join him. . . . Demons! . . . Demons! . . . They will tear us to pieces! "

There is now no longer any need for me to urge the men on. Panic is doing it for me. In front of me, at top speed, a troop of madmen climb the narrow rough path, whipping the terrified beasts of burden, which stumble over the projecting roots and rocks that obstruct

163

the way. Sometimes the men themselves fall, but only to regain their feet instantly and to rush on at once with the same maddening cry: "The demons! . . . demons!"

I hurry after them, unable to quieten them. It is a scene such as is lived through in nightmares.

At last we cross the pass. Men and beasts hurl themselves down the steep slopes. At the foot of the mountain, they reach deserted pasture-land, and the silence, the soothing influence of the peaceful verdant landscape have immediate effect upon their overwrought nerves. They look wonderingly at one another. What has happened? What have they done? They seem to be only half conscious of it and to be awakening from a dream.

"Unload the beasts and light a fire," I order. "We will camp here."

The men begin to work. A few minutes later, I hear one of them laughing. These childish folk have already forgotten the demons and their fear of them. I am the only one of our party who remembers the hospitable farmer's wife, whose cold rigid body now awaits the funeral pyre, and I think that had we not entered her house and, in this way, given her material upon which to feed her superstitious beliefs, she would still be alive. Yet . . . who can tell?

Was it their proximity to the Chinese magistrate that had inspired the peasants with a salutary fear, or was it that they hesitated to molest us on account of our meeting with the village "scholar", which had proved that we were people "learned in the Religion" and because of our pious desire to visit the Grand Lama. Whatever the causes might have been, we were left undisturbed.

Our hostess had died of fright. There could not be the least doubt about that. In itself, her death had nothing of the nature of a supernatural or occult "phenomenon", and I sought no explanation regarding it; nevertheless, I related the circumstances attending it to several lamas. Thus it happened that I had offered me the most extraordinary explanation imaginable of the real personality of the one whom I had taken for a simple idiot and whom I have continued to think of as such. A fantastic story is attached to this explanation, and since, apart from its strange character, it relates to some peculiar beliefs held by Tibetan occultists, I will relate it here.

Alak Ngags Chang, who was reputed to be deeply versed in secret sciences, did not admit that this strange boy, whose visit had proved so fatal to my hostess, was a genuine demon. He also hesitated to adopt my opinion that he was a simple madman. Without affirming anything explicitly, he insinuated that he might have been a *tulpa*, which had escaped from the control of the magician who had created it and was wandering about.

The Tibetans believe that adepts in certain secret lore have the power of forming phantom-beings (*tulpas*) that are able to behave in the world as ordinary mortals. However, the *tulpa* has no consciousness of its own. It is but an empty form animated and directed by the magician who has made it. Now, Tibetan occultists believe that, in certain cases, a *tulpa* can succeed in completing its personality, becoming, in some measure, a conscious individual. The desire to preserve its existence and make it independent of its creator can, then, wake in it and a terrible struggle—usually carried on by psychic means—ensues between the magician and his creature. The former endeavours to dissolve the latter and, in doing so, comes up against the resistance and attacks of the *tulpa* which is trying to destroy its master in order to gain its independence.

Could such a being, acting as a demon "eater of breath" have caused the woman's death? According to Alak Ngags Chang the thing was very doubtful but not impossible. Upon which, our conversation having centred round the subject of *tulpas*, he told me the history of Chös Tags.

It had come to his knowledge in this way: Immediately before his death Chös Tags, no doubt inspired by the example of the famous ascetic Milarepa, had dictated his biography to one of his disciples. While doing so, he had specially charged him to warn any of their fellow *ngagspas* (magicians) who might be tempted to engage in such an undertaking of the dangers of creating *tulpas*. This disciple, a friend of Alak Ngags Chang's spiritual master, had told his friend the story of the *tulpa* created by Chös Tags, and, in his turn, my informant had heard it from his master.

The *ngagspa* Chös Tags was neither a saint nor a sage. In his youth he had committed a crime. One evening, yielding to a sudden burst of passion, he had brutally violated a *dokpa*[1] maiden whom he had long desired. Then, his flaming frenzy extinguished and fearing punishment as the result of his victim's cries for help, he had callously thrown her into the adjacent river, and, with her, the bucket she had carried.

Calmly, unemotionally, he had gone his way. The people of the black tents, searching for the missing girl, had found only her bucket caught among the rocks. Its presence there gave sufficient explanation: an accident had occurred—the girl while getting water had leant too far forward and, losing her balance, had fallen into the river and been borne away by the current. Over one of her dresses, in his quality of chaplain of the tribe to which his victim belonged, Chös Tags, impressive and solemn, had celebrated, on her behalf, the office for the dead: the *powa* that sends the " spirit " of the departed to the paradise of the " Great Beatitude ": *Nub Dewachan.*

Years passed. Chös Tags had become rich and celebrated. He had delved deeply into the most secret of magic sciences. As inscrutable as the redoubtable

---

[1] *Dokpas* (hgrogpas), " people of the solitudes ", are herdsmen who live in tents in the great grass solitudes of Tibet.

deities with whom he had intercourse, Chös Tags was the object of mingled respect and terror. Nevertheless, success brought him no happiness; internally the canker of despair was torturing him; he knew himself to be old, and the thought of his approaching death filled him with anguish.

To live! . . . the aged magician had but this one desire; his past triumphs, his riches, his glory, all these things he held as naught. He wanted to continue to live for years and years. Yet he, who was capable of working so many wonders, remained in ignorance of an effective means by which to prolong his life for centuries.

Nevertheless, a means of the kind existed. An ancient manuscript that he had discovered in the dusty library of a *ngagspa* who had recently died gave an account of a treatise on this subject that had been buried by Padma Sambhava, in a cave near the summit of Mount Kangs Tise.[1]

He must have this treatise, but how to get possession of it?

Difficult as such an undertaking would be at his age, he might succeed in accomplishing the long journey from Ga (in Eastern Tibet) to the Kangs Tise, but, it would be impossible for him to climb it. Still Chös Tags thirsted to know the secret of immortality in our present flesh.

Reflecting deeply he remembered the maxim of the master who had initiated him into the mysteries of esoteric methods: "There always exists a means by which to obtain one's object. The question is to find it."

What matter that his body was devoid of strength, that his limbs had become stiff; if the fleshly envelope of Chös Tags could not be an efficient instrument for Chös Tags' will, this will was capable of creating another instrument that would be better fitted to serve its purpose.

[1] A mountain in Western Tibet that is sacred to both Tibetans and Indians. The latter call it Kailasa.

The magician understood the art of producing *tulpas* endowed with all the physical faculties of real beings, but animated by the thought of their creator and acting according to his intentions. More than once he had made use of these ephemeral creatures. He would do so again. A *tulpa*, having in it Chös Tags' ardent desire to live and rendered robust by the energy poured upon it from his mind, would go in his stead to the mountain and, obeying the impulses communicated to it, would, at the spot indicated, dig up Padma Sambhava's precious treatise and return with it.

Chös Tags went into strict seclusion in the darkness and set to work. The *tulpa* took form. As was the magician's wish its appearance was that of a young monk: the character that was the least likely to attract attention on a pilgrimage to the sacred mountain.

The phantom was kept for several months shut up with its creator, who gradually gave it life by pronouncing appropriate magic formulas and transfusing a part of his subtle substance into it. When Chös Tags thought it capable of moving into the world as a natural being, he sent it forth upon its journey. Although away from the magician, the traveller was bound to him by an occult tie and continued to be actuated by the will of its creator, who, through his clairvoyance, could follow it in all its movements.

The *tulpa* walked unceasingly, day and night. It had no need of food, drink, or rest. The force of the *mantram* (magic formula) pronounced over it together with the energy generated by the magician's concentration of thought sustained it.

Thus the pseudo-pilgrim crossed Lhasa, Shigatse, and followed the course of the Yesru Tsangpo. Then, having passed by many villages, it came to solitudes similar to those of Ga: where only herdsmen live.

One day, it reached a camp. The dogs did not bark at its approach. Always walking straight before it, it stumbled against a tent peg and stopped abruptly. In the tent was a girl.

At the other extremity of Tibet's vast territory, Chös Tags felt the shock that had just checked his *tulpa* in its walk. He saw the girl in the tent and recognized her: it was she whom he had violated and killed sixty years before.

The aged magician was well aware that all our acts, whether good or bad, produce effects that will overtake us sooner or later; but his crime of long ago had never interfered with his success and he had almost ceased to dread its consequences. By his great knowledge, he was able to penetrate the secret, hidden from the ignorant, of the past existences of all beings. He sank into deep meditation, and the ineffaceable images of past events appeared to him.

He saw his victim carried away by the current and heard her commend herself to the Lord of Compassion, the powerful Chenrezigs. "*Aum mani padme hum!*" she said, "*Nub Dewachan gyi shingkhams la kieswar shog.*"[1] And as she had during her short life assiduously recited "*mani*"[2] and practised charity, Chenrezigs received her in his blissful kingdom. Nevertheless, her merits were not great enough to allow of her making a long sojourn there. Barely forty years had elapsed—which time corresponds to scarcely one hour of *Nub Dewachan*—, when the young girl was reborn in our world and in a condition of life similar to the one that had been hers during her previous earthly existence. Once again, she was the daughter of a herdsman.

Chös Tags who had never known fear, trembled. The hour of retribution had come. He did not however give way to his alarm, but resolved to fight, believing himself capable of surmounting the obstacle that apparently opposed his purpose. First of all, it was necessary that

---

[1] "May I be reborn in the Paradise of the Great Beatitude."
[2] "*Mani*" is the current term for the formula "*Aum mani padme hum.*"

his *tulpa* should go away from the tent and resume its journey.

With powerful concentration of thought, he strove to impart to his phantom his will to continue its journey; and, for the first time, the *tulpa* did not respond.

The young girl, seeing a pilgrim monk standing outside the tent, came out to beg him to come in and drink tea. The *tulpa*, obeying a force more potent than that of its creator, entered.

Formed of the subtle substance of Chös Tags and impregnated therefore with the same sentiments that animated the magician when he made it, his creature carried latent in it the passionate desire to live, and, suddenly, upon contact with influences that proceeded from Chös Tags' criminal act, this desire became active. Simultaneously, Chös Tags' sensuality awoke in the *tulpa*. The magician and his creature were but one mind in two material forms.

At least, that is what they had been up till then, but other influences now came into operation. As a magnet, the desire to live and the sensual tendencies attached to the form of the *tulpa* attracted foreign elements that were to interfere with the magician's work. His creature was becoming vaguely conscious of itself.

The phantom-monk sat down: it seemed tired, a condition most natural in a pilgrim. It closed its eyes, and appeared to sleep. The parents of the young girl, a pious couple, deemed themselves fortunate to harbour a monk on his way to the sacred mountain. Days passed, and then weeks. The *tulpa* resisted the pressure brought to bear on it by the magician. It did not want to go to Kangs Tise; the herdsman's daughter pleased it. Fed from sources independent of the will of the magician, possessed by other minds than the mind of the magician, a separate intelligence was developing in it. The subtle tie that united the phantom-man to Chös Tags no longer served solely as a medium for the transmission of the

Master's will to the *tulpa*; along this conducting thread, the *tulpa's* rudimentary consciousness now ran and, coming into contact with its creator's mind, penetrated his designs. In this way it came to understand that the period of its existence was limited and that, once it had accomplished its task, it would be destroyed. This it did not want. It wished to live.

Chös Tags perceived its revolt. The old magician shut himself up again in the darkness. He made use of the most powerful *mantrams*, the most powerful of mind concentrations, those during which the whole of the vital energy flows out in a single stream. He summoned his tutelary deities to his aid. Nothing could make the *tulpa* continue its journey to the cave where the treatise containing the secret of immortality was buried.

Quite the reverse happened, Chös Tags felt that his phantom, strengthened by the occult forces it had incorporated, had itself begun to draw life and energy from him.

The thought of the danger he ran maddened him. It was now no longer a question of securing a treatise on the art of becoming immortal, but one of defending himself from imminent destruction, of dissolving the rebellious *tulpa*.

Chös Tags tried to bring it back to Ga, believing that he could achieve his object more easily if he had the *tulpa* at hand. His efforts were of no avail. Growing more and more conscious, become almost a man, the phantom perceived what the magician was plotting against it and defended itself with all the force that its hunger for life gave it.

To this craving was added another feeling. The *tulpa*, which by reason of its limited mental faculties was incapable of love, had nevertheless inherent in it the effects of Chös Tags' criminal passion. An irresistible sensual attraction, of which it was only partly conscious, drove it towards the herdsman's daughter. Often its thoughts would be occupied by the desire it felt for her, and during those hours of reverie its concentration upon the preservation of its own life was relaxed. The distant magician then took advantage of those periods of inattention in his occult struggle with his *tulpa*; but he, too, became poisoned by the evil emanations of his former passion, which he lived again in his memory.

A day came when the scene of the by-gone drama appeared before him as actually happening. His supernormal vision showed him the *dokpa's* daughter carrying a bucket, on her way to fetch water at the river, and the *tulpa* following her. Then, the same blaze of passion that had flamed in him sixty years before, once more burnt him with its infernal fire. Afar off, the *tulpa* felt its stinging bite and threw itself on the young girl.

But, to the magician trained for many years in the acute observation of facts, there yet remained sufficient clear-sightedness to seize the opportunity offered by his adversary. The latter, overcome by passion, surrendering itself to it, was no longer on its " guard ". Chös Tags controlled himself. By a powerful effort, he " retook "[1] within himself the vital *mantram* upon which the *tulpa's* existence depended, and, the terrified *dokpa* maiden saw the man who had her in his embrace dissolve as a cloud.

This supreme effort drained the aged magician of his remaining strength. He survived it only by a few months. Soon after having dictated his biography to a disciple, he was found dead upon his meditation seat.

It is doubtful whether, in a foreign language, I have been able to render the truly hallucinatory character of this Tibetan story. It is also impossible for those who will read it in Western cities to understand the impression it produces when told, in the evening, round a camp fire

---

[1] The rite of " retaking " *mantrams* has for object the undoing of a magic work that has been produced by the help of *mantrams*, or of counteracting or destroying an adversary's, which has likewise been based on *mantrams*. In the latter case, it is necessary to know exactly those that have been used.

in the desert *chang thangs*, while the moon, the clouds, and the blue flames of the blazing *chiwa*[1] are peopling the wilderness with dancing shadows. More impossible still is it to imagine the thoughts that it wakens in the one who, without accepting all its fantastic details, yet knows that the story hides a truth.

[1] *Chiwa*: dried yak's dung; the only combustible in Central and Northern Tibet.

VIII

THE KHAM COUNTRY

A JOURNEY through the Kham country naturally
included a visit to Kanze, the chief town of the Horpa
tribes.   According to information given us at Romi-
changku, the path I intended to follow was under water
in several places, and since the region it crossed was
practically uninhabited, it was pretty certain that the
damage done by the river would not be quickly repaired.

Ought I to attempt to travel on such a road with only
a few servants?   It seemed to me that it would be imprudent.   I therefore proposed to engage a muleteer at
whose house I was staying.   He would bring his servant
and four beasts.   Their co-operation would lighten my
own mules' loads and at the same time give my three
noodles less work, more company, and a pleasanter
journey.   However, I had reckoned without my host.   The
muleteer absolutely refused his services.   Two other
owners of mules also refused to hire us their animals.

My difficulty having been explained to the Chinese
magistrate, the latter, very graciously, signed a paper that
gave me the right to requisition carriers, men or beasts,
for the transport of my luggage, just as the officials have
when travelling.   He also added that, in two days' time,
he would have mules sent to me, for use on the first stage
of the journey, and that I should also be provided with
an escort of soldiers for crossing the mountains, where unpleasant encounters frequently occurred.

The morning of my departure, porters arrived in place

of the expected mules. Later, I was to congratulate myself upon this fortunate change. Loaded beasts could
never have negotiated the obstacles that the floods placed
in our path; my mules, which had only their saddles to
carry, found it difficult enough to reach Tao.

The magistrate had me informed that in place of the
armed "braves", he would send two men of the local
militia (a kind of unarmed police force). The men, however, were not ready to start with us, and it was
"officially" intimated that we should not wait for them,
assurance being given that they would soon overtake us.

The first day's march proves agreeable and the condition of the road much better than we anticipated. Without stopping, we pass close to a Bönpo monastery, then
we halt in a village where we obtain a relay of porters.
As the people of the place have not been warned of our
passage, it takes more than an hour to assemble the necessary number of men. During this time, I am able to
examine the village at my leisure. It is inhabited by
Gyarongpas, and, in its appearance, differs as greatly from
the ordinary Chinese villages as from those of Tibet
proper. The forest mountaineers of this frontier region
build wooden houses many stories high, encircled with
balconies, and surmounted with high, very sloping roofs.
The stables occupy the whole of the ground floor as they
do in the majority of Tibetan farm-houses. Here, the
buildings are particularly high. Seen from the narrow
streets, they look like "sky-scrapers".

At sunset, having deposited their loads in the place
that we have chosen, the porters return to their homes.
Only one of them goes on to tell the people of the next
hamlet that they have to send us men in the morning.

We remain by ourselves on a grassy hillock, not far
from the river, but on dry ground. I have just dropped
off to sleep, when I am awakened by shouts. People are
approaching. My boys, who are still up, drinking tea,

challenge them with the greeting in usage in this part of the world: "Halt, friends, or I fire." It is customary for the persons thus accosted, if their intentions be honest, to answer by shouting who they are and what they want. Otherwise they take to their heels, or else, if they can discern the challenger, shoot him before he has time to carry out his threat.

This time, the arrivals make themselves known: they are the two militiamen who were to join us. In order to satisfy myself that no mistake has been made, I leave my tent, and, standing in my night-gown, receive the two men's ceremonious genuflexions.

Next day, we reach Wadjo. My requisition order works marvels there; it gets us provisions. The villagers assure me that I shall not be able to obtain any more along my route. I take as much flour, butter, and grain as I think is needed for the journey, and, in addition, some milk, which, with care, may keep fresh for a day or two.

The peasants, who would have absolutely refused to *sell* me even an egg, seem quite content to have been forced to *give* me all these provisions. Knowing very well that I could have taken everything without payment, they appear delighted with the gratuities that Yongden distributes among them. This strange way of looking at things prevails nearly everywhere in Tibet.

Rain falls in torrents all the night. The next day the river has risen considerably. The villagers urge me to remain at Wadjo, while a gang of corvée workers will go and inspect the road and repair it where necessary.

The men return at sunset and tell us that we will be able to pass. The next day's march is very tiring; the path is still under water in places, although the flood has abated appreciably since the night before.

Towards the end of the afternoon we arrive in sight of the Bönpo monastery of Tesmon. To reach it, we have to cross a bridge. Like so many of the Chinese bridges this one is arch-shaped, and, for the moment, the only part of it that emerges from the water is in the centre of the river, which has risen to three times its normal height. The way on to the bridge from either side is by a primitive stairway, made of unhewn slabs of rock. This stairway has now disappeared under the water and the current beats violently against it. Between the first step and the place where we have stopped is about fifteen yards; this distance will have to be crossed in the rushing river.

Carrying their loads on their heads, the porters go over one by one, each of them supported on either side by a man who is not loaded. Other villagers form a chain, evidently with the purpose of catching their comrades should they fall and of preventing them from being carried away by the river. With their arms stretched out sideways, they all stand above those who walk in the water, instead of below them, facing up-stream. I wonder what their idea is. It is quite certain that if a man or his load were to fall, this chain of arms, placed where it is, would not prevent either of them from being swept away. But I must be the only one who thinks so. The imperturbable seriousness of all those around me plainly shows that they have no doubt as to the efficacy of the living dam.

In order not to stand in the mud during the time that it takes for the luggage to be carried over, I remain seated on my big black mule, watching the operation. When it is finished, Sönam and Tobgyal lead my beast to the stairway. This kind of bridge is never crossed on horseback, and now less than ever is it the moment for making the attempt. I therefore dismount on to the submerged steps. The mule will be taken over after I have passed across. The bank is higher on the other side, consequently the water has not spread so far inland. When I reach the other end of the bridge a man picks me up, puts me like a sack over his shoulder, and carries me to safety.

We are going to stay at the monastery. One of the monks gives up his quarters to me: two little rooms, one of which is a kitchen, the other a bedroom. I settle myself in the latter, and Yongden will sleep in the kitchen. My boys and the militiamen will be housed by another monk.

It has been a tiring day for the porters. I urge them not to return at once to their homes, where they would only arrive late in the night, but to rest first. In addition to their tip, I offer them a good supper; they can then leave at daybreak. The thought of a "good supper" instantly settles the question. They decide to remain. After giving orders for them to be provided with flour and meat for making soup, I go back "home".

The owner of the room that I have been given must be an ascetic, or else a poor man—unless he be simply a sage. His household goods consist of a low table, before which he sits on the floor; a brazier; a set of unpolished wooden shelves, which serves for a book-case; two blankets for a couch; and a long stick, suspended from the ceiling beams by cords, for hanging clothes on. To these must be added the "torma (ritual cakes) cupboard", a kind of tabernacle in which, by means of magical processes, the Lamaists, as well as their Bönpo colleagues, imprison a being of demon race or a wrathful deity.

My host carries away his blankets and some books, then leaves me alone. I hang my wet clothes on the stick and make my bed. While waiting for my meal to be cooked, I shall visit the temple, where an office must be in progress, for I hear the dull sound of a drum that is being rhythmically beaten. But before going there, I want to see what is in the tabernacle.

This wish is not idle curiosity on my part, but a desire for knowledge. Does a Bönpo stock it in the same way as a Lamaist? As a rule these cupboards are kept padlocked; for the uninitiated must not gaze upon their contents. The ordinary reason given for this prohibition is that the being who is held captive there may then escape or become irritated. However, the Tibetan occultists explain things differently. According to them, that which resides in the mysterious tabernacle is a force created by magical processes. They say that the *tormas* that are found in the tabernacle have been " animated " by the one who has placed them there and that an " energy " of a different order has been incorporated in each of them. Exoterically each *torma* is said to represent a different personality, divine or demoniac. Shut up in the tabernacle after having been thus " animated " and each of them provided with suitable " food ",[1] these *tormas* form a group of active energies, of " living entities ", among which various secret exchanges and mysterious combinations take place. It naturally follows that an inopportune opening of this occult laboratory may disturb the work that is going on within it and unseasonably liberate the force that should remain captive. This force, through not being controlled and directed by a competent initiate, can cause harm and take for its first victim its imprudent liberator.

At least, this is what I have been told, but my informants themselves have been careful only to apply these explanations to the tabernacles that belong to initiates in secret sciences. Those that are found in the rooms of the ordinary monks are of little or no importance, for their owners have neither the necessary power for " animating " the various *tormas*, nor the knowledge required for grouping them in the correct way.

My host's little cupboard must have belonged to

---

[1] This food consists of offerings of rice, meat, wine, tea, etc., or of other *tormas* that represent nourishment.

this last category. Made of roughly carved wood, blackened by smoke, it had nothing impressive about it. There was no padlock on the door. Inside I saw ten *tsa-tsas*,[1] which probably represented the ten Bönpo Sages, and a triangular *torma*, in front of which, by way of offering, lay a heap of dusty cutlet bones. All this was not of great interest. However when you are curious by nature, there is always some question that requires answering. Why were these bones, without exception, all cutlet bones? Did my host only eat this part of the animal, the remains of which he passed on to his favourite demon; or was it the demon himself who demanded these particular bones? Here was a mystery to be solved.

In the temple, on the other side of the court, someone continued to beat a drum rhythmically. Perhaps I could find somebody over there who, without my having to confess my indiscretion, would enlighten me as to the particular part that cutlet bones play in Bönpo rites.

So I go down into the court, mount the temple steps and enter the building. The interior is very gloomy, almost in darkness. A single lamp burns before the altar. Not far from it two people are seated; the man who is beating the drum and another man who is chanting in a low voice what he reads in a book that is lying on a narrow table in front of him. A lamp, placed close to the book, casts a curious light on the faces of the two monks.

My eyes becoming accustomed to the darkness, I am also able to distinguish some *tormas*, four tiny lamps, and the various other objects forming a *kyilkhor* (magic diagram)[2] that is set up on another table in front of the celebrants.

---

[1] Imitations, modelled in clay, of the monuments called *chörtens* (the *stupas* of India).
[2] Magic diagram on the different parts of which various objects are sometimes placed.

While I am watching them, some of my porters enter the temple. Doubtless, like me, they are strolling about until supper is ready.

They remain motionless for a time, then one of them takes a few steps forward. Something, a table or a bench, which he does not see in the shadow, lies in his path; he knocks against it and it overturns. The noise the thing makes in falling resounds through the empty hall. Under his breath, the man snaps out a low oath. The reader lifts his head.

"Go away," he orders, using the most authoritative and the least polite expression in the Tibetan language.

There are sceptics in the Kham country, and they exist in greater numbers than one would have thought possible. There, coming from the lips of a woman, I have heard the most terrible blasphemy of which a Tibetan can conceive: "I don't care a rap for religion, I like money better."

At the base of the intellectual ladder the sceptics of Kham remain usually in the state of mind illustrated by this impious woman, although, as a rule, they are more discreet as regards the voicing of their unbelief. On the upper rungs of the ladder, sceptics are occultists, or, sometimes, profound thinkers.

The man who had just sworn so rudely was an "unbeliever" of the lowest rung. As I learnt some hours later, he had lived at Tachienlu and at Chengtu, and had probably broadened his mind there after his own fashion.

He violently resented being ordered about in so rude a manner.

"I am not a dog," he said. "I didn't see the bench . . . it isn't broken. . . . I'll pick it up. There is no reason for you to speak to me in this way."

Whereupon he stoops, lifts something up, which scrapes the floor noisily.

"Go away!" repeats the celebrant.

"I won't go," retorts the man obstinately, making a movement in the direction of the lama.

181

"Do not come near the *kyilkhor*! " imperiously orders the monk.

This interdiction only irritates the aggressor the more. "Oh! your *kyilkhor*!, your *tormas*! " he shouts. "The *ta ren* (distinguished people) foreigners, who are very learned, say that it is *momo* (bread) dough and that all that is chanted in the *gompas* is only nonsense. . . . Speaking to me as if I were a dog! "

The rustic was wound up. His companions had seized him and were trying to drag him outside, but he was a hefty fellow and his anger only increased his strength. He freed himself, cursing, and again shouted.

"Your *kyilkhor*! . . . Your *momos*! . . . I will break them to pieces. . . . Speaking to me as if I were a dog! "

Then, as he rushed forward, the Bönpo, at the other end of the temple, seized the *shang*[1] that was beside him and shook it. An extraordinary sound, made up of a thousand unloosed cries, filled the hall with a surge of tumultuous vibrations and pierced through my brain. The scoffing peasant gave a cry. I saw him recoil violently, with his arms outstretched before him, as if to thrust back some terrifying apparition.

"Go away," the lama repeated again.

The other men hastened to their comrade's aid, and they all left the temple in a great state of agitation.

Dung! Dung! continued the placid drum, quietly marking time for the soft chanting of the Bönpo, who once more sat in front of the *kyilkhor*.

What had happened?—I had not remarked anything peculiar beyond that strange sound. I went out to question the porters. The braggart who had disturbed the office boasted no longer.

---

[1] The *shang* (written gshang) is a musical instrument that is special to the Bönpos. In shape it faintly resembles a cymbal with a turned-in edge, and has a clapper attached to it. When shaken the clapper is held on top, as in an inverted bell.

"I tell you it was a serpent," he was declaring to the others who stood round him in the court. "A serpent of fire, which came out of the *shang*."

"What, you saw a serpent of fire?" I asked him. "Is that why you shrieked?"

"Did you not see it? It came out of the *shang* when the lama shook it."

"You dreamt it," I replied. "I saw nothing at all."

"We did not see the serpent; but lights flashed from the *shang*," interposed his companions.

In short, they had all seen some marvel. Only I, unworthy foreigner, had been blind. However it might be, it was only fitting, since I was receiving hospitality in the monastery, that I should apologize for the rudeness of one of the men I had brought with me.

I re-entered the temple and remained standing near the door, waiting for the office to end. The acolyte who was beating the drum stopped at last, put the instrument back into its cover, and the celebrant wrapped his book in a piece of silk.

I went forward and expressed my regrets for my porter's behaviour. The lama courteously received my apologies. "It was not your fault, it had nothing to do with you," he said. "The thing is of no importance, do not think any more about it."

I had fulfilled that which politeness demanded from me. The Bönpo remained silent; there was nothing left for me to do but to go. Yet the strange sound I had heard and the villagers' visions continued to puzzle me. Unconsciously, I looked at the *shang*, the tangible cause of all this phantasmagoria.

It was not difficult for the lama to guess my thoughts.

"You would like to hear it sound again?" he said to me, with a vaguely mocking smile.

"Yes, *Kushog*, if it will not trouble you too much. That instrument has a curious sound. Will you please shake it again?"

"You can do it yourself," he answered, handing me the *shang*.

"I am not an expert at handling it," I made him observe.

For indeed the sound that I produced in no way resembled the one I had heard.

"I have not your skill, *Kushog*," I said, returning him his instrument. "No serpent has come out of your *shang*."

The Bönpo looked at me inquiringly. Was he pretending not to understand, or did he really not understand?

"Yes," I resumed, "the vulgar man who spoke to you so rudely declares he saw a serpent of fire come out of the *shang* and rush at him. The others saw flashes of light."

"Such is the power of the *zungs* (magic word) that I uttered," declared the lama, with a slight emphasis. And he continued in a low voice:

"Sound produces forms and beings, sound animates them."

I thought he was quoting a text.

"The *chirolpas* (Hindus) say that too," I retorted. And in the hope of inducing the Bönpo to express his opinion, and to speak of the doctrine he professed, I added:

"Some, however, believe the power of thought to be superior to that of sound."

"There are some lamas who think so too," answered the Bönpo. "Each has his path. Methods differ. As to me I am master of sound. By sound, I can kill that which lives and restore to life that which is dead."

"*Kushog*, these two things: life and death, do they really exist as absolutely distinct opposites?"

"Do you belong to the *Dzogschen* sect?" asked the lama.

184

"One of my masters was a *Dzogschenpa*," I answered evasively.

The Bönpo remains silent. I would like to bring the conversation back to the subject of life and death and to hear his theories concerning it, but his silence is not very encouraging. Must I interpret it as a polite hint that it was time I went away?

Suddenly, however, the lama mutters to himself, seizes the *shang*, and gives it several shakes.

Wonder of wonders! Instead of the terrifying sound that it has given out before and the anything but harmonious one I myself have produced, I hear a soft peal of silver bells. How can this be? Is that Bönpo simply a skilful artist, and can anyone, with the necessary practice, obtain such vastly different effects from so primitive an instrument as the *shang*, or else, must I believe, as he has proudly declared, that he is really "master of sound"?

The desire I felt to talk with the lama had greatly increased. Was I going to succeed in getting him to explain the mystery of the *shang*? . . .

A commonplace incident put an end to the interview. Yongden entered the temple to tell me that our supper was ready. The lama quickly took advantage of the interruption to escape from me, pretending, with a great show of politeness, that he did not wish to detain me.

Rain fell in torrents during the night, and it became again necessary to send a gang of mountaineers to examine the path I had to follow, before attempting to go along it myself with the beasts and luggage. This circumstance forced me to remain for a whole day in Tesmon. I determined to profit by the delay to try and see the "master of sound" again. Unfortunately it continued to rain, and the inmates of the monastery remained shut in their homes. I could not go and indiscriminately knock at their doors in order to find the one who interested me. Such behaviour would have given offence. However,

Yongden, as a young man, had greater liberty of action. He discovered the master of sound's house, and, thinking himself extremely diplomatic, invited him to come to tea with me.

The Bönpo accepted. An hour later, accompanied by a young *trapa*, he came to the cell I occupied.

Our conversation began with the usual polite enquiries. After which the lama wanted me to tell him about my travels in India. He questioned me concerning the customs of that country, then regarding its religious world: the Buddhists and Hindus, their practices, the supernormal powers they attributed to their *dubthobs* (sages who possess supernormal powers). I endeavoured to satisfy his curiosity, hoping to find a favourable moment in which to question him myself. He gave me the opportunity when speaking of the powers of the Indian *dubthobs*.

"There is no necessity to go to India to meet men who possess these powers," I said to him. "You, yourself, I think, made that clear last evening. And, moreover, the Hindus, who look upon Tibet with veneration, as the home of great sages, also believe that magicians exist here who are much more powerful than theirs."

"That is possible," answered the Bönpo. "I have never been to India. It is about the *shang* that you are thinking, is it not? Why do you attach so much importance to this trifle. Sound has many other mysteries.

"All beings, all things, even those things that appear to be inanimate, emit sounds. Every being, every thing gives out a sound peculiar to itself; but this sound, itself, becomes modified, according to the different states through which the being or thing that emits it passes. How is this?—It is because these beings and things are aggregates of atoms (rdul phra) that dance and by their movements produce sounds. When the rhythm of the dance changes, the sound it produces also changes.

"It is said that, in the beginning, the wind, in whirl-

186

ing, formed the *gyatams*, the base of our world.[1] This whirling wind was sonorous and it was sound that aggregated matter (*rgyu*) in the form of *gyatams*. The primordial *gyatams* sang and forms arose, which, in their turn, generated other forms by the power of the sounds that they gave out. All this does not only relate to a past time, it is always thus. Each atom (rdul phra) perpetually sings its song, and the sound, at every moment, creates dense or subtle forms. Just as there exist creative sounds, which construct, there exist destructive sounds, which separate, which disintegrate. He who is capable of producing both can, at will, construct or destroy. There is one sound that is called by our masters: 'the sound that destroys the base'. This sound is itself the foundation of all destructive sounds. The *dubthob* who could cause it to sound would be capable of annihilating this world and all the worlds of the gods up to that of the great 'Thirty-three', of which the Buddhists speak."

After this long speech, the Bönpo took his leave, wishing me to a happy journey and fine weather for the next day.

The rather abstruse theories he had propounded were not lacking in interest, but they brought me no light on that which remained, for me, the "mystery of the *shang*".

The rain having ceased, we start early next morning. The poor mountaineers have taken a lot of trouble to make the passing of my little caravan possible: notwithstanding their efforts, the path is in a terrible state.

The valley we are ascending forks just above Tesmon: one branch leads to the territory belonging to the Geshitas

---

[1] An allusion to the Tibetan cosmogony. According to it, the wind—explained as being movement—produced the first forms. These forms, the Lamaists conceive as *gyatam*, that is to say, the shape of two *dorjees* (ritual sceptre) placed crosswise. As a rule, the Böns imagine them under the shape of swastika—the symbol of movement. My informant belonged to the White Böns who have adopted many lamaist theories.

and the other to the hamlet of Tanli, where we are going.
Our path zigzags among rocks, between which the flood
has dug big holes that have remained full of sticky black
mud. I try to stay in the saddle, but I am soon forced to
give up the attempt. My mule finds it difficult enough,
even without a rider, to make its way among the obstacles.
It is extremely tiring to walk between these sharp-edged
rocks, against which you knock at every moment. In
some places, they form a kind of stairway, the steps of
which are so high that I am obliged to pull myself up
them by my hands.

Farther on, the path is under water. The roadgang
have had to cut a rough track, higher up, through the
woods. There, we stumble over roots, scratch ourselves
with the thorns of hastily severed brambles, sink into the
saturated earth, and, finally, after much effort, meet the
path again. Will we be able to continue along it until
we get to our destination? No. After having walked
painfully for about another two hours, we are once more
stopped by the flood. We shall have to do the same
gymnastics through the woods, as we did before. The
porters and mules begin to climb the slope. I lack the
courage to follow them. Yongden and I remain behind,
sadly contemplating the eddying river.

" Would you like to try and wade across? " my son
asks me.

" I was not going to propose it, but I feel very much
inclined to do so."

" Wait, I will see how deep the water is."

The lama takes off his robe and waistcoat and gives
them into my care, then, testing the depth of the river
with a stick, he goes part of the way. The water does
not reach much above his waist. He and I are about
the same height; we can go over. I undress, only
keeping on my underclothes. We each make a bundle
of our things, which we carry on our heads. The temperature of the water is cool, but not cold. It is an agreeable

and refreshing bath. On reaching the further bank, we wring the lower edges of our wet clothes, redress, and continue our way. The heat generated in us by walking will soon dry our underclothing.

It is nearly dark when we get to Tanli. There we come to the end of our aquatic ordeals. One more pass to cross, then we enter a region of immense tablelands and valleys, which generously offer to rivers as well as to travellers all the space they can desire for wandering about in at leisure.

Tanli, enveloped in evening shadows, reminds me of Switzerland. The scene is quite alpine: tall pines, tiny streams that wind through short grass or moss, and a few chalets. The air has the peculiar savour that is only found at high altitudes. This hamlet must be situated at a height of nearly 13,000 feet above sea level; for the map gives the neighbouring pass, which is reached without much of a climb, at 15,000 feet.

We are given two rooms in one of the chalets, and we prepare supper in our host's kitchen. The beasts are stabled at another farm, and have two villagers to guard them.

We have returned to the country where brigandage is both sport and chivalry. My host and his neighbours are certainly oftener on the high roads than in their fields. Here, as in Amdo, farming is commonly considered to be woman's work, merely an accessory source of income in a family budget, the chief revenue of which comes from more heroic labours.

However, this does not prevent the farmers from being very friendly people. So long as our goods and our persons are under their care, we have nothing to fear from them. They know full well that if we could point them out as the thieves who had stolen our beasts and our luggage, the Chinese magistrate would make them pay dearly for their temerity. They explain to me that it is not their turn to furnish the corvée of

porterage and therefore they have already sent a messenger to the tribe that must supply it.

Quite early, they bolt all the doors and close all the
shutters. While we are having supper by the hearth,
footsteps and voices resound from the road. Everyone
listens, then a man from inside the house hails the
nocturnal prowlers: "Who goes there? . . ." No
answer. "They are robbers who come from the North
valley," explains our host. Whereupon he begins to
relate many tales of brigandage, one more terrifying
than the other.

"Why don't you stop them on their way, these robbers
from the North valley?" asks Yongden.

The answer comes hesitatingly.

"We cannot. . . ."

The next day one of the militiamen, referring to
this conversation says to me: "Of course they cannot
stop them, they are engaged in the same business and
are often associates."

It happens that just those whose lot it is to be sent
to me as porters are natives of the North valley and
belong to the Shabrugpa tribe. Some men and two
chiefs arrive late next morning, having come from far.
The state of the paths from here on permits the use of
beasts of burden. The Shabrugpas are going to hire
yaks from the people of Tanli to carry my things to Tao
in two stages. They doubtless find it more profitable to
go to this expense than to bring their own beasts; a
proceeding, moreover, that would take a long time.

One of the chiefs has a remarkably fine Spanish head.
On looking at him, one immediately thinks of an Estrama-
dura hidalgo, who has become a brigand, owing to unfortunate circumstances. The typical hero of fiction:
dark, taciturn, with thin tightly closed lips, long slightly
hooked nose, big silver ring hanging from his right ear,
and a haughty bearing. What foreign blood runs in
this Khampa's veins?—In him, there is nothing of the

Tibetan, nor of the Chinaman, nor, even, of the Mohammedan, who, although rare enough in this region, could
have been one of his ancestors. He is altogether a fine
Spaniard with a touch of the Moor: an enigma in his
present surroundings.

The Shabrugpas pass the day in procuring beasts
and people to lead them, and the next morning we set
off into the forest, in the rain. The men with the yaks
are noisy and gay, they are being paid for their trouble.
The Shabrugpas, who pay, are not so happy, and the
hidalgo, always as romantic, his gun slung over his
shoulder and riding a black horse, is loftily grave.

At the intersection of the two valleys, I am shown
the shrub covered track that the brigands follow when
going to the Tachienlu road to lie in wait for the caravans
that are going to Lhasa.. And then, a little farther on,
we no longer see either the Spanish grandee or his companions. They have left us, thinking it needless to tire
themselves further, now that the dangerous place where
their presence might be of service to us is passed. Perhaps they are on their way in the valley that joins the
road to Tachienlu, having comrades and business in that
direction. One of the militiamen goes in search of them,
but they remain undiscovered. Happy journey! It is
not likely they will attack us. We know too well who
they are, and it would be easy for us to describe them
to the magistrate. We therefore tranquilly continue our
way through the forest.

Sprinkled by occasional showers, we slowly ascend
the gentle slope. Just above the tree line we stop and
make tea. Tobgyal is feverish and has neuralgia. I
hope that a hot drink and an hour's rest will do him
good. The yak drivers, anxious not to delay, go straight
on, escorted by the militiamen; they know this stage of
the journey to be a long one. We are to realize it for
ourselves before night.

The pass we presently go over has not the savage

grandeur of that of the Dza. The people of the country consider it to be higher than the latter, and on my map it is given an altitude of 4,613 metres (a little more than 15,000 feet), that is about 300 feet higher than the Dza pass. But the various maps of the Tibetan frontier-regions differ in many of their indications. We are now in July, the pass is free from snow, but at less than 300 feet above it there are fields of deep snow, which, probably, will never melt completely.

It must not be deduced from this that in Tibet and the surrounding regions the perpetual snow line begins at about 14,000 feet. Many passes of more than 16,000 feet high are perfectly free from snow in summer, and in many places the perpetual snow line is not lower than about 19,500 feet.

We descend the stony slope on foot, then enter a forest again. Evening comes, we have great difficulty in following a badly marked path, muddy and narrow. The rain falls in torrents. The invalid no longer complains; flushed and trembling with fever, he has scarcely strength enough to keep in saddle. We see no signs that indicate the proximity to a village, and we begin to fear we have lost our way. At last, the path leads out of the forest and continues through pasture-land, and, a little farther on, skirts fields under cultivation. We are at Lumbo.

We find shelter in a miserable hovel. Yongden and I have to put up with a tiny little room, in which a quantity of sheep and bullock skins are piled. Our host no doubt trades in them. They are at every degree of dryness: some still soft, others hard. The smell they give out is terrible. I insist on the window remaining open. My son makes objections.

"By means of a ladder, someone may enter the window while we are asleep," he says. This is quite true, only it is not possible to breathe in this stench. The window must therefore remain open, but, as a precaution-ary measure, Yongden will lie down under it, rolled in his blankets. If in the darkness a thief enters, he will step on his body and wake him. This is all we require. With his cry of surprise, Yongden will wake me, and once awake, we believe ourselves capable of dealing with any one rascal . . . even several.

An unrestful night, like many others that we have passed in wet clothes. We get up at dawn. The sun is shining; it will soon dry us. As is my habit I go on ahead, alone, for my morning walk of about two hours.

The valley continues to widen, the forests are left behind, and then, coming out on to the slopes that edge another large valley, we perceive in the distance, far below us, a road that cuts ours at right angles: it is the main road to Kanze.

Very soon we distinguish black masses creeping on the great road. Farther on, our path turns westward and continues along the mountain side, parallel to the highway, which it overlooks from a height. The indistinct black masses gradually become definite in outlines; they are yaks carrying bricks of compressed tea to Lhasa via Kanze.

It is an imposing spectacle, this dark slow moving host of big, thick-fleeced animals, with their mounted and armed leaders, and the big long-haired dogs that run in among the beasts committed to their care. The yaks are divided into groups, each of which is preceded by a man on horseback. Group follows group; there are perhaps two thousand animals. They will take three months to reach their destination.

The surrounding landscape presents the most perfect contrast imaginable to the one in which we have lived for the last months: no more narrow gorges and thunderous torrents; no more picturesque Chinese mountains with jagged rocks and sharp-pointed ridges. The adjacent grass-covered summits spread their rounded forms in comfortable abandon. The whole scene broadens, and lies bathed in an imperturbable calm, a kind of self-assurance, a settled placidity, which imposes itself on the spectator.

An air of mystery also envelops this straight white road, which disappears in the distance, among the blue tinged mountains. We know it to be long, surpassingly long, and, in thought, we see it crossing the grassy solitudes of the *chang thangs*, running along the immense blue lakes, and finally reaching, far beyond Lhasa, the most majestic of the world's sacred places: snow-capped Mount Kailas, the dwelling place of Shiva and his spouse Parvati.

Once more, we enter the fascinating land of Tibet, to which both Yongden and I are linked by different ties. Feelings of joy and reverent admiration overwhelm us as we continue our way.

Our path gradually descends towards the bottom of the valley, and, just before reaching it, passes through Tao, one of the important places of the region, although in reality nothing but a very dirty village.

Since I was escorted, it was just as well to enjoy whatever advantages this escort could procure me. I had therefore sent one of the militiamen on ahead to find lodgings for me. The man thought he was doing the right thing by addressing himself to the owner of the finest house in the locality, who at once placed an immense room at my disposal. I could have been very comfortable there, had it not been that another room opened into it, which was occupied by a Chinese officer and his family. This arrangement meant that every time husband, wife, and children wished to enter their room or to come out of it, they would have to pass through mine. As I expected to stay some days in Tao such promiscuity was impossible. There were no other rooms available in the house; nevertheless I quickly found a place where to establish myself.

The roof terrace of the house was very large. Along

the wall of one side of it ran a gallery, the roof of which
was supported by brightly coloured wooden pillars. The
gallery served as hay loft, but at that season it was
almost empty. There could be no pleasanter place in
which to set up my tent. Sheltered by the wall and
the roof, I had a large space in front of me to stroll
about in.

There was a magnificent view from that observation
post. Right and left, as far as the eye could reach,
stretched the great valley. Opposite Tao, deeply buried
in between the mountains, opened another valley, dark,
tortuous, mysterious, where two rivers met and rushed,
the one descending from the Kanze road and the other
from that of Tachienlu, both of them on their way to
join the Yalung. Penetrating with them into the shadow
ran the path that led to Litang. Brigands were said to
infest the region it traversed. Sometimes the idea would
come to me of leaving Tao before daybreak and going
away by that path, in order to escape from the benevolent
but annoying supervision to which I was subjected.

I then thought that if I went direct to Litang I should
not see Kanze, the capital of the region of Hor. I also
thought of the highwaymen who ranged the country on
that side, and who might very well steal my beasts and
luggage. But above all I thought of the river that flowed
between Tao and the valley that led to Litang. I could
not swim across it, and from the moment I needed a
boat, I also needed to warn the ferrymen; thus my plan
of a flight under the stars fell to pieces. Meanwhile,
after camping for many weeks on flooded ground, the
roof-terrace appeared to me to be a veritable paradise.

Tao is the seat of a Roman Catholic mission connected with the "Société des Missions étrangères de
Paris". The day after my arrival, I made the acquaintance of the resident French priest, Father D——. I need
hardly say he gave me a cordial welcome. I must repeat
the same thing of all the missionaries—except one—

whom I met in China, whatever their creed and whatever their nationality. But Father D—— was more than
a kind man, he was the hero of a dramatic adventure.

Some years before, the Tibetans of this region had
risen against the Chinese, and the Tibetans of Tao had
taken Father D—— and the Chinese magistrate of the
place prisoners. Then, having led the captives to the
Lamasery, they had stripped them and tied them by
their wrists, with their arms above their heads, to a pillar
in the great assembly hall. In this agonizing position
the unfortunate men had remained for several days, without either being able to sit or lie down. As food, their
gaolers held a dish of dog's mess in front of them. There
was never any question of religious persecution. Not at
any time did the insurrectionists ask the missionary to
abjure his faith.

They only required of both him and the Chinese
magistrate that they should recognize Tibetan political
authority. The Chinaman gave in and was freed. The
Frenchman persisted in his attitude, doubtless from self-
respect he would not let himself be mastered. Finally a
Chinese officer arrived at the head of some troops, forced
the Tibetans into submission, and liberated the missionary. Later I was to meet this officer.

I have never known what indemnity was officially
paid to Father D—— for the vile treatment he had been
subjected to, but the people of Tao, who nevertheless
admired his strength of character, said that in his
revenge he showed the same inflexible determination as
he had exhibited while setting his torturers at defiance.
They told me that the actual mission and its outhouses
had been built by villagers compelled to provide corvées
and that, every day still, the missionary, authorized by
the Chinese authorities, requisitioned a certain number
of non-salaried workers for his service.

As to whether or no these details were quite correct,
I would not like to say. Father D——, who had the

modesty not to relate the story of his heroic tenacity to me, did not either make me his confidant as regards his private feelings concerning vengeance, forgiveness, and the way in which he put them into practice. Some people think that the claims of charity are not the same for the man who lives in the world, as for the hermit philosopher. They say that although it is only right that the sages and anchorite saints should renounce all at the hands of others, the members of a social group must take into account the fact that immunity from punishment may incite some persons or nations to seek fresh victims.

The very day after our arrival, kind Father D—— sends me a present of provisions: live chickens and a bottle of good wine. He imagines that I have been long deprived of our national drink and is most astonished to learn that I do not drink any intoxicating beverage. More astonished still is he to hear that I absolutely refuse to have the birds killed for my consumption. It is already bad enough, I tell him, to buy butcher's meat, on which to feed my servants and . . . myself occasionally, when vegetables and flour are lacking and I am hungry.

The missionary is a hunter, like many of his colleagues, both Protestants and Roman Catholics. I always wonder how it is possible that these religious people do not come to see the terrible nature of suffering and how horrible it is to inflict it on any being, merely for personal pleasure.

From their point of view, since they deny that an animal has a soul, it should be much worse for them to kill an animal than a human being. The murdered man is not, according to their belief, really dead, for his soul —his real " self "—is immortal. His murderer therefore has only brutally removed him from one dwelling place and forced him to go to another. This change of locality may even be to the victim's advantage, if, by his virtues,

197

he deserves to be received in heaven.[1] But since, according to these theories, the animal that has been killed perishes absolutely, in depriving it of its present life, it is for ever despoiled of all that it has and all that it is.

The Chinese magistrate is also very obliging. He places three villagers who are on compulsory service, at my disposal. Two of these guard the mules as they graze on the mountain slopes and bring the beasts back to their stables in the evening, the third fetches water, tends to the fire in the kitchen, and helps my boys. Tao is in Tibetan territory, and the system of *ulags*—that is, compulsory corvée of porterage and service to travellers who are provided with requisition papers—is in force. It is usual for the traveller to remunerate the *ulags*, but the amount of the gratuity depends upon his generosity; besides it is not obligatory to give them anything. For my part I have nearly always made a point of rewarding the villagers for their services; nevertheless, the curious mental attitude of some of the natives has sometimes forced me to refrain from doing so. I have come across Tibetans who loudly proclaimed that those who paid them were common vulgar people, who deserved no consideration. The distinguished people, on the contrary, very far from paying them, exacted presents, provisions, and their servants beat those who did not hasten to supply these things. "It is only by such conduct," they said, "that one recognizes the people who are worthy of respect."

When confronted with an argument of that sort, which no amount of reasoning would have induced them to modify, I confess that, occasionally, I have shown myself "worthy of respect".

[1] It is in this way that the Hindus justify the sacrifice of animals to the gods. The victims are said to be reborn in a superior condition, above that of the animal kingdom, or else in the very paradise of the god to whom they have been sacrificed.

I have left Kum-Bum on the 5th of February, and now it is the beginning of August. Six months of travel along difficult tracks is perhaps sufficient excuse for wanting a little rest. I take that rest on the roof I am camping on. When I leave it, it is to walk with Yongden in the country. We talk with the people we meet. These conversations give us insight into the customs and ideas of the natives and, at the same time, provide a pleasant distraction, which relieves the nervous tension that has been caused by our worries.

One day, we come upon a man crouching on the bank of a stream. He is taking some twigs from a bag at his side and carefully placing them in the water. The watchful and serious air with which he works arouses our curiosity. What is he up to?

Hearing us approach, the strange individual looks round and, with a quick movement, hides the bag under his robe.

"What are you doing, friend?" Yongden asks him.

The answer is long in coming. The peasant looks fixedly at us, for some moments, then apparently satisfied with our appearance, he decides to speak.

"I have a *dibshing*,"[1] he says in a confidential tone.

There is not a Tibetan who does not know what is meant by a *dibshing*. Countless legends tell of exploits that have been accomplished by the aid of the piece of wood or the bunch of feathers that gives invisibility; but, as to anyone having seen a specimen of this wonderful talisman, the occurrence is much more rare, if indeed, it has even taken place.

"You have a *dibshing*!" said Yongden to the owner of the mysterious bag. "Where did you get it from? If you have one on you, how is it that I can see you?"

---

[1] The talisman that renders invisible the one who has it on him or the thing near to which it is placed. Some people imagine it to be a kind of twig which the crow can recognize. Others think that it consists in particular feathers in the plumage of crows and magpies.

"*Kushog*," politely answered the Tibetan, "when I say I have a *dibshing*, that means that I have one here in this bag. I have not yet been able to distinguish it from the other twigs with which it is mixed. I am busy putting them one by one to a decisive proof. The *dibshing* will travel up the current instead of being carried down by it. When the *dibshing* will have touched the water, its virtue, which is not yet active, will manifest itself, then when I shall take hold of it, you will no longer see me."

"Oh!" I ejaculated, "I long to see you become invisible. But when you will be invisible, what will you do when you go home? Your people will not be able to see you? And if you put the *dibshing* in a box, this also will become invisible. Perhaps the whole house, with all your family who live there, will become invisible? What will your neighbours think?"

It is not becoming to subject miracles to a too critical and minute examination.

The Tibetan threw a scornful and unfriendly glance at me.

"Do you think that I have forgotten to bring the *khablendo* box with me? When the *dibshing* is placed in it, it is without effect."

The *khablendo*, "the stone that seizes needles", is the natural magnet, which is used in Tibetan medicines. The peasant had put a fragment of it in the box in which he meant to keep his talisman, when he had discovered it from among the ordinary twigs.

Seeing the peasant's displeasure and fearing that in consequence of it he will not let us assist at the discovery of the *dibshing*, Yongden hastened to obliterate the bad impression my words had produced.

"She did not know about the *khablendo* box," he said. Then, sighing, he added: "Women are ignorant of so many things."

My astute companion hit the mark, the thought

that I had spoken thus from ignorance restored the offended man to serenity.

"Sit down, elder sister," he said to me, condescendingly.

Yongden and I sat ourselves down on the grass.

"Here is the box," he declared, showing us a small object, which he immediately replaced in his *amphag*.[1]

"Come, continue your work," suggested Yongden, who was eager to see what was going to happen.

The Tibetan plunged his hand into his bag, brought out a tiny piece of branch, and placed it on the water, which rapidly bore it away. A second, then a third piece had the same fate. The fourth, pushed by the wind, or for quite another reason, turned round, was caught in an eddy, and seemed, for the moment, to go up-stream. The would-be possessor of the *dibshing* gave a triumphant cry. Alas! His joy was premature, the twig reached the edge of the miniature whirlpool, was seized by the current and soon swept by it out of sight. One by one the rest of them followed in the same direction. The man looked with dismay at his empty bag.

The thing itself was comic, but what is never so, is sadness, however ridiculous may be the reason that causes it. Yongden tried to console his guileless compatriot.

"*Dibshings* are not easily found," he says. "Attempts at finding them have to be made again and again. You will be more fortunate another time. Besides do you really need a *dibshing*? Of what benefit will it be to you? No merit useful for this life or for those that follow it is attached to the possession of a *dibshing*. If your heart is not wholly pure, it could even be harmful to you, for, protected by your invisibility, you might be induced to commit bad actions

[1] The pocket that the voluminous Tibetan robe, which is held in by a waistband, forms over the chest.

201

that would lead you astray from the path of happy rebirths."

"You speak well, Lama," answered the Tibetan. "You are learned. What you say is true. . . . And also . . . I can always try again next year. . . . This is the fourth year that I search for a *dibshing*. . . . At Gartog, there is a *ngagspa* who knows words of power and who prepares charms. I shall consult him. Perhaps I have not gone to work in the right way."

"What is it that you do?" enquired Yongden.

"I do what it is said you should. If a crow's eggs are not hatching properly, the bird has need of a *dibshing* to enable its little ones to emerge from the eggs. Therefore you must force the crow to go and search for one, for that particular bird alone is capable of discovering it. In order to do so, you wait until the parents are away from the nest, then you take the eggs and boil them, quickly replacing them afterwards. If the crow does not notice anything wrong, it will continue to sit. Since the eggs have been cooked it is not possible for the brood to hatch. The male bird then goes to find a *dibshing* and, when it has found one, it places it near the eggs. As soon as you see the male bird has returned, you steal the nest and, just as I have done, you examine one by one all the twigs of which it is made. Such a method is infallible . . . all the same, this is the fourth time I have been unsuccessful with it. A demon or an enemy must have seen me while I was watching the crows, or when I was cooking the eggs, or else, when I took the nest. He will have placed some impure object in my path to dim my sight and prevent me from distinguishing the twig that ascended the current. . . . Or else he seized it himself without my knowledge. Oh! I am unlucky. . . . I must consult a *mopa*,[1] who will be able to see what beings are putting obstacles in my path."

---

[1] A diviner.

"Perhaps it would be as well," conceded Yongden, in order not to contradict the obstinate peasant. "But, now, since we have met, come with us and have something to eat and drink. A little distraction is good when you are worried."

"You are very good *Kushog*," answered the villager, "Yes I will come with you. I shall surely be successful next year."

"Without doubt," averred the Lama, imperturbably.

The *dibshing* seeker was well treated, and freely partook of each of the courses that were offered him. He ate an enormous portion of vermicelli soup, the whole of a boiled leg of mutton, and drank quantities of buttered tea. A bowl or two of spirits would have seemed to him a fitting ending to such a meal. I saw him look round for the one who would serve him with them. But as all alcohol is prohibited at my table, the Taopa had to resign himself to the absence of it, just as he had had to do with regard to the *dibshing*. His good humour did not appear to suffer appreciably in consequence. Only towards the end of the meal did he show signs of uneasiness, and he begged Yongden and me not to divulge to anyone what we knew about his search.

"I am certain to find *dibshing* next year," he said, confidently. "But the lamas at the monastery must not get word of my intentions."

"Why?"

"They say it is not good to possess a *dibshing*; that it brings bad luck to its owner. Also a *dibshing* often loses its virtue if a lama looks at it. And, perhaps, those at the monastery might try to take it from me. Researches of this kind should be kept quite secret. I don't know why I have spoken to you about them. The young lama (Yongden) must possess the power of making people speak when they wish to hold their tongues. . . . Yes, that must be it. . . . If only it does not bring me bad luck."

The Tibetan was beginning to eye us askance.

"Do not worry," Yongden said to him. "We shall not give you away. We wish you nothing but good. Further, in a few days, we shall go from here, never to return."

Upon these reassuring words, the seeker after a *dib-shing* left us.

In the house where we lodged at Tao, I noticed a ragged and apparently under-fed boy of about twelve, who, from morning to night, carried a baby in his arms. He was an orphan, and, out of charity my servants gave him food. His brother and brother-in-law worked for my host, who, in return for their services, provided them with some provisions, a few clothes, and the use of a wretched room close to the stables. The urchin's sister managed the primitive home for her husband and two brothers. The younger of these two, who was then a "nurse-maid", had some years before been placed at the monastery, in the hope that he would become a *trapa* and get his living there. His head had been shaved in sign of his admission among the clergy, but the child's con-nexion with the Religious Order had stopped at this simple ceremony. He had found no teacher from among the members of the *gompa* and had remained quite illiter-ate. Not being fathered by any of the monks, he had not been presented for reception among the little novices who assisted at the offices, consequently he had not enjoyed the benefit of the morning tea and the occasional meals served to the *trapas* in the assembly hall nor had he received a share of the monastic revenues. He had there-fore come back to live with his sister; and it was in this way that his brother's masters, seeing him without work, had made him their "nurse-maid", giving him some bowls of tea and soup in lieu of wages.

Sönam had one day jokingly said to him: "Will you come with us when we leave Tao?" The boy did not reply. But the next day, to the great astonishment of my servants, he came to them without his baby and solemnly announced: "Very well, I will go away with you." Whereupon he installed himself in the kitchen, cleaned the pots and pans, and saw to the fire, displaying an activity that, up to then, no one would have imagined him capable of. He then informed his family of his intended departure.

The little fellow seemed so determined that the idea came to Yongden to turn the joke into a reality and to take him away with us. He spoke to me on the subject. Once the boy was washed, suitably dressed, and properly nourished, he might become a good servant, grow attached to us, and, as he was an orphan, be taken to Europe. Naturally, we did not tell him of that vague and far-distant project. I merely let him know that, since he wished it, I would take him with us when we left.

When his sister, to whom the boy was only a burden, saw I had decided to take him with me, she declared that she could not bear to part with him and that, in depriving her of him, we would be doing her an injury. All these demonstrations had for sole object the obtaining of money from us. Yongden settled the matter by giving her four Szechwan rupees, and, for this paltry sum, the affectionate sister relinquished all claim to her dear little brother.

Before leaving Tao I visited the local monastery. It has a certain standing, but without, however, in any way approaching the grandeur and beauty of the lamaseries of Sera and Depung, at Lhasa, of Tashilhunpo at Shigaze, or even of those of Kum-Bum or Labrang Tashikyil.

It was said that there were learned lamas at Tao, but I did not meet any. I had intended to pay a visit to the Shalngo (elected head of the *gompa*) and, using the forms that Tibetan etiquette prescribes, to ask to be presented to some of the scholarly monks of the place. Father D——, who was a little too presumptuous on this occasion, thought to render me a service by announcing my visit

to the monastic authorities and by "recommending" me
to them. The effect of his intervention was the exact
opposite of what he expected; the learned lamas or those
of high rank suddenly found themselves suffering from
various ailments that prevented them from receiving me,
and the most distinguished among them immediately
remembered he was due to go on a tour of inspection in
the neighbourhood.

I had, consequently, to content myself with visiting
the temples, walking through the dirty streets—the
monastery at Tao is very badly kept—, and talking to any
trapa. In spite of everything I did not regret having gone
there. Instead of conversations on matters of deep
philosophy, the good people of the place recounted to me
some interesting facts concerning the frontier war that
had been waging between the Tibetans and Chinese. I
was struck by one particularly odd thing: these Tibetans
of Kham, little as they liked the Chinese domination,
frankly abhorred that of the Lhasa government.

IX

INTO THE HEIGHTS

ONCE more we are on the road. It is the beginning of a long period of fine weather in this region: a hot and dry ending of the summer, a luminous autumn, then an incomparable winter of snowy summits, great frozen rivers and vast lakes, glistening beneath a resplendent blue sky.

The Chinese magistrate has provided me with *ulags* for the transport of my luggage and graciously "imposed" two soldiers as escort.

Late in the evening, we reach a large farm where we are well received. Here, while we are having supper, I learn that a *dubthob* lives in the neighbourhood. There is no lack of hermits on whom the uneducated people bestow this title, ascribing to them a number of miracles, which are often very absurd. I have met many of these impostors, but my curiosity remains always alert concerning them. From among a dozen charlatan *dubthobs*, it is sometimes possible to discover one interesting individual, whom the good villagers artlessly liken to the frauds who exploit their credulity. Besides, these frauds, themselves, are often picturesque enough both in conduct and thought, for it to be worth taking the trouble to visit them.

I therefore prick up my ears when I find that my hosts hold him in great veneration. He lives in a cave in the mountain that faces Sharatang, on the other side of the river, and, as regards clothing, he shares the view of those ascetics of whom the Indians speak of as being "clothed in space", or "in sky", or again as being "draped in the cardinal points", which is an elegant way of saying that they go about stark naked.

I ask for further information: "Over and above his nakedness, what is this *dubthob's* most striking practice?"

"He does not accept money."

This is something that is certainly rare. I feel inclined to respect this disinterested sage.

"He only accepts spirits."

This pleases me less, in fact, not at all. This trait is not unusual; all Tibetans like strong drink. The *dubthob* has fallen back to the common level of his countrymen.

Nevertheless, there exist sects where intoxication is ritualistic and the excitement caused by alcohol is considered good for inducing certain intuitive perceptions. These methods furnish a number of drunkards with excellent pretexts for giving way to their vice, under cover of spiritual or superior psychic training.

Ritual intoxication was known in India long before the time of the Buddha, and this Master must have had opportunities, in his own country, of observing the disastrous effects of the search after transcendental intuition through alcohol and drugs; for he explicitly forbade their use to his disciples, who were all required to be total abstainers.

In Tibet, one of the principal features of Tsong Khapa's reform is that of having again brought into force this prohibition of fermented drinks; but, the Reformer was only able to impose it on the clergy of his own sect. Laymen and monks of the *ñingma* sects have continued to drink beer and spirits. However, it should not be inferred from their infringement of the Buddhic precept of total abstinence that the members of the *ñingma* sects are all of them inveterate drunkards. This is very far from being the case.

A hermit, belonging to the *Dzogschenpa* sect, whom

I questioned concerning the value of the stimulation produced by. alcohol as a means of inducing intuition, replied
that the man who is clever at dividing himself into two
parts, that is, at preserving intact his faculty of observation and examination when, at the same time, his thoughts
and senses are wandering, can gain instruction from a
state of semi-intoxication brought about by alcohol or
drugs.   But he added that the knowledge obtained under
these conditions relates almost entirely to the mental state
of him who attempts this experience.   Freed from the
shackles of reason, morality, habits, etc., which usually
control them, the tendencies that exist in his subconscious
manifest themselves, and some among these, which are
little active and nearly indiscernible in a state of sober-
ness, acquire, under the stimulus of alcohol, a force that
he who carries them in him does not suspect.   Such an
examination of the hidden elements in him can be very
useful for his spiritual development, as can be also all
other investigations undertaken while giving free play to
certain passions, such as lust, ambition, greed, etc.[1]

As to the worth of ecstasies, intuitions, or whatsoever
raptures that can be produced by a state of intoxication,
the hermit declared it to be non-existent.

I wondered what opinion the naked *dubthob* would
hold on this subject.   To stay a day longer for the purpose
of speaking with him on the subject might not be waste of
time.

I expressed my desire to my hosts, saying, that, if it
did not inconvenience them, I would like to spend a
second night at their place.

Their reply was most courteous; I was to act as if I
were in my own home.   Those farmers were very engag-
ing people, especially the master of the house, a sculptural
specimen of the fine race of Khampas.   In addition to the

---

[1] And, in the same way of thinking, the investigation and analysis of
the feelings that are experienced during dreams, at a time when the
contents of the subconscious has also free play.   For further details on the
subject see *Initiations and Initiates in Tibet*, page 121.

pleasure I anticipated to derive from my visit to the *dub-thob*, I looked forward to passing another evening talking with those friendly villagers.

Next morning, Yongden and I started for the *dub-thob's* cave. The two men of my escort insisted upon accompanying me. The Chinese magistrate's orders forced them to do so: I must be protected . . . and no doubt spied upon too.

It was a long way. We had to do half the distance that we had done the evening before over again, only on the other side of the river.

The *dubthob's* prehistoric dwelling was on a very steep grassy slope, at the end of a tiny valley. At the moment of my arrival he was seated outside. As soon as he saw me, he leapt to his feet, seized a stick, and began dancing and gesticulating, probably intentionally imitating the poses that the Tibetan painters give to the ghouls that are feasting in the cemeteries.

The man was thin, bony, and naked, just as I had been told. From the distance he looked like a moving skeleton: a sort of gruesome puppet, with angular and mechanical gestures. His dance ended, he rushed into his cave, where he started furiously ringing a bell.

I had already seen so many mountebank clericals of this kind that the pretentious gambols of this one did not impress me in the least. On the contrary, I doubted whether a conversation with such an individual would offer much interest, and I regretted having made the long journey in the heat for so poor a result. I was also angry with my two soldiers, who, going on in front, had heralded me as a person of importance to the *dubthob*, a proceeding that had led to his exhibition of feigned eccentricities, just when I wanted to take him unawares, in order to see what he did when he was not playing a part. In short, I was in a bad temper. My mood inspired me with the mischievous idea of revenging myself on the *dubthob* for my disappointment. I would leave him to his demonstrations and walk quietly away, without going up to the cave where he awaited me, and where, probably, he counted on astonishing me by further extravagant acts or words. The small humiliation I should thus inflict on him would be the penalty of his charlatanism.

Tolerably satisfied with my resolution, I turned my back on the cave.

Yongden, who thoroughly understands the minds of his compatriots did not let me long enjoy my malice.

"Do not rejoice over your mischievous trick," he said. "That cunning *dubthob* will find a way of transforming the humiliation you wish to inflict on him into glory. He will declare that, by his magic power, he has prevented a foreigner from reaching his dwelling. This fresh miracle will increase the veneration that his faithful pay him and be the means of bringing him an additional supply of spirits."

My perspicacious son was right. In the eyes of the villagers it would be I who would come defeated out of this comedy, and this thought made us both laugh.

This time, my escort consented to return to the farm alone, taking with them my mule and the lama's horse. We wanted to walk back slowly.

The handsome farmer is at first astonished at the slight appreciation we show for the local *dubthob*, and the women of the family are perhaps just a little shocked. After supper, I endeavour to dissipate this bad impression by sketching a portrait of the real contemplative hermit, such as I know him to be. Then I relate the history of the Buddha. Like the majority of Tibetan laymen, my hosts are only very imperfectly acquainted with it. I think my explanations will not be understood, but it is quite the reverse. They all grasp them, and the ideal of which these make them catch a glimpse deeply moves my humble audience.

"Ah yes!" murmurs the farmer, "if we could follow

that path. . . . But we cannot. . . . Perhaps later, in another life. . . ." And he ends his sentence with a sigh.

The next day, greatly to my surprise, I find him at the head of the *ulags* who are carrying my luggage. He certainly could have exempted himself from this corvée, by sending one of his servants in his stead.

"I wish to see for myself that all goes well," he says to me. "I want you to be satisfied and keep a pleasing recollection of us."

Wearing the new robe and the round hat in red silk that I have given him, the once little ragged urchin of Tao, exuding pride at every pore, heads the caravan, mounted on one of my mules. Amused at his triumphant air, my servants have nicknamed him Sezang Thales, the name of a rich merchant at Tao. A few hours have sufficed to turn the timid " nurse-maid " into a bold little rogue. True brigand blood runs through the veins of this young Khampa. Perhaps the gods have destined him for a "heroic" end on one of his country's highways; in the meantime, he is making himself exceedingly useful.

So great is his desire to please me and so spirited his daring, that on the third day after our departure from Tao, he already brings us an adventure.

In the afternoon we pass in sight of a herd of pigs. Among them some baby pigs are playing round their mother. Sönam, who is fond of joking and is amused at our young recruit's ways, says to him:

"The reverend lady, our mistress, would certainly like one of those sucking pigs to eat."

Without waiting to hear more, the little rascal, who does not yet know my tastes, digs his heels into his mule and gallops off in the direction of the herd. Arrived near it, he jumps to the ground, gives the bridle to a young peasant who is guarding the animals, and, rushing among the fleeing pigs, catches hold of a baby one.

From the distance I watch the scene, without understanding the reason for it. I hastily rejoin my servants and soldiers, who are roaring with laughter. Everything is explained to me. I have the enterprising youngster called back and order him to release his capture. He obeys reluctantly, unable to understand why his zeal and dexterity have called forth no congratulations.

Tobgyal wishing to prolong the joke says:

"Jetsun Kushog does not eat pork."

"Why did you tell me she did?" the boy demands of Sönam, giving him an evil look.

Sezang Thales does not allow people to make fun of him. He has not an easy character. I pretend not to hear anything.

This incident has put everyone in high spirits. It has also touched a cord that vibrates easily with the people of this country: the joy of conquest. And, suddenly, my *ulags*, quite simply, quite frankly, begin recounting to one another their exploits as knights of the highway.

They know that I am riding behind them and can hear all they say, but they trust me. I am touched by their confidence; they have, in truth, adopted me. Their talk is full of colour. Each one of these simple souls is a hero at heart.

They are not insensible to the lust for gain, but it appears that, for them, the act of getting possession of something by force, by combat, and by facing danger is joy in itself.

But what is far more surprising is that I have met among their kind some who are strict vegetarians. "Why?" I asked one of them. "Because an animal is weaker than a man, and to attack a being when certain of victory is cowardly," was the answer.

There even exist, among Tibetan brigands, men who have a singularly high conception of spiritual life. Naturally, this understanding remains, for them, pure theory, and he who has attained it generally defers the practice until one of his future lives.

A lama of Amdo became a hermit after a lesson received from one of these non-practising idealists. He was travelling with his servants and with mules that were laden with luggage and money, when he was stopped by a band of robbers and ordered to surrender his beasts, luggage, and money. He attempted to resist his assailants, but, in the struggle, he was thrown from his horse. Realizing his defeat, he begged for mercy, by taking advantage of his standing as lama. "It is not right to rob or to maltreat a monk," he pleaded.

"A monk!" retorted the chief of the brigands. "You say you are a monk. How could I know that? What is the meaning of this beautiful robe lined with astrakhan that you are wearing? Is it then permitted to a lama to clothe himself in the spoil of animals that are killed for their fur?—If so, what becomes of the compassion that he must practise. Has a monk also need of all the things that you drag about after you? I thought you were a rich merchant."

The lama took this lesson to heart. He prostrated himself before the brigand.

"You are my spiritual guide (guru)," he said; "you have put me on the true path. Take all that you require. I will end my days in a hermitage."

The one who related me this story knew the lama in question. He told me the brigand had refused to appropriate the possessions of a member of the Religious Order, and the lama, on reaching home, had given the greater part of his wealth to pious and charitable works, only keeping what was strictly necessary for his subsistence; after which, he had become an anchorite.

In the company of these picturesque *ulags* we arrive at Tangu, a dirty village, where we pass the night.

The next day we halt at Chao, and I find lodgings in the ancient palace of the chiefs of the country. Palace is, perhaps, rather a pretentious name for a number of commonplace buildings that the Chinese had set fire to at the time of the Tibetan revolt and that still show the traces of fire and pillage. My apartment is the one in which the "king" and "queen" formerly lived. The wainscots, which, once upon a time, were painted in red and decorated with inscriptions and gold flowers, have been blackened by the smoke. The rooms are extremely dark and open on to a gallery that is supported by large wooden pillars. It scarcely seems possible that anyone could have lived there continually. The present sovereign is a widow, and resides in another house, which she has built close to the ancient palace. This new five-storied building is of stone. Tibetans are fond of high houses, and, in them, the master's private rooms are always on the top floor, giving on to the roof-terrace, which is a place used for strolling about in and often ornamented with flowers growing in pots or tubs.

My hostess is very gracious and makes me a generous present of provisions. The special delicacy among them is a quarter of dried mutton, three years old. It has lost its colour and all its appearance of meat. It looks like a piece of whitish-grey wood. The meat comes away from the bone in fibres, or, as it appears, in splinters, which become powder under the pressure of the fingers. This old meat is, nevertheless, quite sound, without the slightest trace of maggots. Tibetans greatly appreciate it; for them, it is rich man's food. The queen has thought to give me a valuable gift. Dried up as it is, the mutton has not lost its flavour; on the contrary, its taste seems to have become accentuated, and I can well understand why the Tibetans consider it such a delicacy.

By pounding this extra-dry beef or mutton in a mortar, the Tibetans produce a meat powder, concentrated food, which those who are fortune's favourites take on their journeys. In Tibet, it is commonly said that in this way it is possible to put the flesh of a whole yak in a bag the length of a forearm.

The practice is to put a few pinches of the powder into a cupful of cold water, then to mix some *tsampa* with this uncooked "broth". There cannot be the least doubt but that this food is very nourishing and it makes it possible to carry in a very small compass sufficient nourishment to sustain a traveller for a long time. But I must confess that, personally, I find this Tibetan meat-powder, excellent as it is in its dry state, very nauseating when it is wet.

From Chao we ascend a low pass, which leads us into the valley of the Yalung that the natives call Dza chu. During our journey, our valorous little urchin astonishes us with fresh deeds of dexterity. One of our mules, which was walking free, takes it into its head to go wandering from the path on to the pasture-land, where it sees horses. The boy immediately runs after it, and, as Sönam's sword, which he proudly wears passed under his belt, bothers him when he runs, he places it on the ground.

Having caught the beast at some distance from there, he shouts to the two boys who are guarding the horses to bring him his weapon.

"Eat my excrements!" graciously answers one of them.

This phrase, current among the low class Tibetans, is regarded as a very grave insult.

Furious at the indignity that has been offered to him, the irascible Sezang Thales rushes at the herdsman boys. In spite of his childish stature he must look very terrible, for they run away. Then, having picked up his sword, he catches sight of one of those long ropes made of yak's hair that are used for tethering beasts, and, seizing it as compensation for the insult he has received, brings it to me with the air of a man who knows how to manage his affairs and does not let himself be put upon.

A little farther on, Sezang Thales, who has again taken

216

his place at the head of our caravan, is confronted by some of the enemy's friends, who want to beat him. They have the appearance of vagabonds and are armed with native rifles. The youngster does not falter, but draws his sword. One of the yak drivers rushes in front of him and explains to the aggressors that the lad is a servant of the distinguished personages who are coming along the road. Whereupon the men apologize and blame their comrades for having insulted the servant of such distinguished people.

I whisper to Yongden to tell my people to give back the rope, and I continue my way. However, two days' later I see it hanging from one of the bags. Why has it not been given back? " Ah! " answers Sönam, " the *ulags* begged us not to. They said that, if we did not keep it, the herdsmen would think we were of no importance and, perhaps, would fire on us from behind when we had gone on." He had not been able to argue the point, for those people knew the habits of their compatriots. Justice and prudence differ according to the country in which they are exercised. I have learnt some difficult lessons on the subject, during the course of my travels.

It would be easy for us to reach Kanze this very day, but we should have to wait in the street, surrounded by a staring crowd, until lodgings were found. In China, there are inns in almost every town that is situated on a frequented route. This is not the case in the region through which we are now passing. The only travellers, here, are a few officials, merchants, and pilgrims. The first enjoy the right of lodging in whatsoever house they fancy. The second either stay with friends or associates who reside along the routes they travel over, or, if the merchants are leading a caravan, they camp with it. As to the pilgrims, the poor ones sleep in the open air, in stables, in sheds, or anywhere where they are allowed to, and the richer ones, who travel on horseback, ask for hospitality, for which they pay, from private people.

Sometimes they have to knock at a number of doors before finding shelter. It is quite the customary thing to do, and, when I travel incognito, I do not mind doing likewise; but, as a foreigner, I am afraid of being an object of curiosity in Kanze. Therefore, it will be as well to make certain of lodgings before my arrival. Taking this fact into consideration, I stop at a place called Poyul, where a large house is placed at the disposal of passing officials and people of note. From there, I send Yongden with my card to the resident Chinese colonel at Kanze, to beg him, as it is the custom, to find us accommodation for a few days.

I do not fail to inform my soldiers that the Lama is going to Kanze. I also thank them for their services. suitably remunerate them, and urge them to return to Tao. Having expressed their gratitude, they disappear. I breathe again. Perhaps the authorities at Kanze will show themselves less thoughtful concerning my safety than those at Tao have done and I will, once more, be my own mistress.

Vain hope! Yongden has not yet returned from his mission when two other soldiers—in uniform this time— arrive, salute me, and announce that they are at my service. What is to be done? I can only smile and appear delighted at their chief's kind attention.

In the evening, I also notice the other two men. They have not returned to Tao. They doubtless wish to be able to report that I am duly on my way to Kanze, accompanied by the colonel's soldiers. Ah! I am well guarded.

The next morning I leave for Kanze.

The feeling of rapture that I had experienced when, from above Tao, I had first seen the wide and smiling valley below me was, in great part, due to the contrast it presented to those very narrow valleys in which the flood seemed to be so evilly disposed towards me. Little by little, the peaceful landscape, the fields, the rounded

218

summits bordering this "happy valley" had begun to
appear monotonous and I expected to find Kanze very
commonplace. It was nothing of the kind.

The site on which the town rises is really very
beautiful, even imposing. Like all Tibetan towns, Kanze
has been built without a plan. Most of its houses are
ranged in disordered rows on the slope of a hill, and the
rest of them lie scattered in an immense valley, where
flows the Yalung river, which is bordered on the opposite
side by high sombre mountains of fierce and savage
aspect.

The *gompa* at Kanze, if it were situated in Europe,
would appear a very large monastery, but in Tibet a
monastic settlement of less than two thousand monks is
considered of little importance. This one occupies the
top of the hill, above the town. Its numerous buildings,
for lack of space or for other reasons, are huddled together, leaving room for only narrow alleys between them.
Far from there, in the plain, rises the palace of the native
prince: a massive edifice, a veritable fortress, one that is
fitted to stand long sieges or to serve as a retreat for
gentlemen robbers, who are on the watch for passing
caravans. Such may very well have been the use it was
put to in olden times.

By favour of the Chinese authorities, a very agreeable
set of rooms is given me in a house standing in the
upper part of the town, from where I enjoy an extensive
view. These "authorities" consist of a magistrate and
a colonel. It is the latter that, some years before, had
delivered Father D——, when he was a prisoner at Tao,
at the time of the Tibetan rebellion. I am courteously
received by both colonel and magistrate. I make the
acquaintance of their families, I photograph them, and
dine with them several times during my stay. In short,
our relations are of the most cordial, but in spite of this
cordiality, the magistrate, in his capacity of governor, is
absolutely opposed to my going to Bathang by way of the

territory that has remained under Chinese control. He insists, nay demands, that I make a detour, and pass by Derge and Chiamdo, which are now in the hands of the Lhasa government. It is most strange. Why is this Chinaman so eager to have me go through a country that he knows is closed to foreigners. He says that the direct road from Kanze to Bathang crosses a region that is not safe and that he has not a sufficient number of soldiers at his disposal to furnish me with an adequate escort. Of course, the region is not safe, but the neighbouring regions are no safer. The Chinaman may prefer that, in the event of my being murdered, this should happen elsewhere than in the territory under his jurisdiction. All this is possible, but I suspect him of having other reasons.

All argument on my part is in vain, I cannot succeed in altering his decision; and I am given to understand that, were I to attempt to act contrary to his wishes, he would, if necessary, forcibly oppose my journey. Moreover, I am being watched at Kanze, and to go to Bathang I must cross the Yalung. No sooner should I have the mules loaded with my luggage, than the magistrate would be informed of it and the ferrymen would receive orders to withdraw their little boats from the river.

Unfortunately, a special circumstance helped the magistrate to give prudence as reason for his opposition. The fact that two brigands were in the local prison awaiting the day of their execution was put forward as proof positive of the unsafe condition of the country.

After repeated exploits, the band to which these two robbers belonged had been overtaken by Chinese soldiers. A fight had ensued: the brigands, on being worsted, had got away with their wounded, but two of them had been taken prisoners.

The law is rigorous, a captured brigand must be put to death. Of the two captives, one was quite young and the other a man of mature age. The latter informed the

THE CHINESE COLONEL COMMANDER IN KANZ
WITH HIS WIFE AND THEIR CHILD

THE GOVERNOR OF KANZE

governor that, as regards himself, he did not dispute the sentence imposed on him. He had played and lost, he would pay the penalty, but he begged that mercy might be shown his companion. The young fellow had never before either robbed alone or in concert with a band. It was his first expedition; had it to cost him his life at twenty. . . ?

I learn that the hardened brigand, who accepted his fate with such lofty pride, went on his knees to the governor in his endeavour to obtain pardon for his young friend. His plea must have been impassioned, for the magistrate was touched. He postponed the execution and sent a message to his chief, the commissioner for frontier defence, who resided in Tachienlu, asking him if he might spare the culprits, or at any rate the younger one of the two.

The answer came during my stay at Kanze. It was peremptory, the two men were to be shot.

One morning, when I was still in bed, I heard firing. What was happening? I got up and looked out of the window. I had missed the first act of the drama. It was related to me afterwards. The soldiers were leading the condemned men to the bank of a stream where the execution was to take place, when suddenly the elder man threw himself against the soldier at his side, dealt a fierce blow on the head of the one who was leading his young comrade, and, shouting " save yourself " to the lad, took advantage of the general confusion to try and escape himself.

From my window, I saw the men running in zigzags in their endeavour to elude the fusilade that was directed to them.

The plain on which they found themselves afforded no shelter. It was vast, treeless, practically level, and without buildings. The soldiers had every facility for shooting down the human game that were trying to save their lives.

I followed the heart-breaking spectacle through my field glasses. A jerky movement on the part of one or other of the fugitives would show that a bullet had reached its mark. Nevertheless the men continued to run in the direction of the river, where perhaps some hidden friends lay in wait to help them. If they could cross it, they would be safe. But it was too far. One of the men fell, struggled for a moment on the ground, then lay motionless. It was the younger one. A few moments later the other fell on his knees, regained his feet and continued his course, then fell again and once more got up, only he ran less fast. Another bullet hit him, he staggered, but went on. His pursuers drew nearer, a volley brought him to the ground, not far from the little temple at the edge of the plain. Just at that place began a series of hummocks. Probably if he could have reached them, the fugitive would have escaped. That, at least, was what the natives thought. But destiny had decided otherwise. When the soldiers came upon him the brigand was dead.

The same afternoon, one of the soldiers who had been in my service since Poyul begged leave to see me. Brought to my room, he saluted with the usual genuflexions and asked me if I had not some remedy with which to dress the wound he had in his arm.

It was he whom the brigand had struck that morning and thrown down among the ruins of a little wall.

While I attended to his wound, he began to recount the whole story of the brigands and the vicissitudes of their flight. I ended by silencing him; I had already heard too many details concerning the drama. . . . And, above all, I had *seen* too much.

Every day, on the roof of the royal palace at Kanze, at dawn and at sunset, the musician monks of the Prince's private temple gave an aubade and serenade to the gods. The monks of the *gompa* belonged to the State clergy, the *gelugpas* (commonly called Yellow Hats), but the native sovereign was a follower of the Karmapa sect, and the airs his monks played were the same as those that I had listened to, day after day, for so long, in a rustic monastery in the Himālayas. What memories those poignant melodies awoke in me! When softened by the distance, they floated up to us from the plain, Yongden, who belongs to this same sect of *Karmapas*, also listened to them, attentive, motionless. Of what did he think?—Of his childhood, when, as a little novice, he was rocked by this same tragic music; or of Europe where he was to go?—I did not ask him.

My visit to the Kanze monastery was very different from the one I had paid to the *gompa* at Tao. After visiting the temples, I was conducted to a large room in the college of the *Gyudpas* (the college of rites). There, a little private reception was held: several lamas, graduates, and professors were present, and tea was served. As all those present were experts in Lamaic rites the conversation naturally turned to that subject. Are rites useful?—What is their use?—Has not the Buddha explicitly declared that belief in the efficacy of religious ceremonies is an obstacle to enlightenment? Those were the questions that I put to my learned hosts.

The majority of them averred that the sole object of a great number of the rites was to keep the religious teachings present in the minds of the common mass of faithful and to incline them to live honestly by practising the simple virtues that were suitable to their condition. They, also, added that there were other rites: the *dubthabs*,[1] the purpose of which was to bring about a definite result by calling on certain " forces "—symbolized as beings (deities or others)—for their co-operation. These " forces " supplementing the force that was generated by the celebrant's concentration of thought gave it

[1] On the subject of *dubthabs* see *Initiates and Initiations in Tibet*, page 91.

the necessary additional strength by which to bring about the desired effect.

Basing their arguments on the statements found in apocryphal writings, which they held to be authentic, nearly all the monks denied that the Buddha had condemned the practice of rites.

However, among those who surrounded me, there was one lama who, more enlightened than the rest of his colleagues, admitted that the Buddha had really condemned the belief in the efficacy of religious rites, as a means of spiritual enlightenment. Having recognized this fact, he then proceeded ingeniously to comment upon it.

"At the time of the Buddha," he said, "the *Chirolpas* (Hindu-Brahmanists) believed the worship paid to the gods and the sacrifices offered them procured for the devotees a happy rebirth in the dwelling places of these gods. It was this cult of adoration and sacrifice that the Buddha condemned as useless and even harmful. It is certain that none of these things can ensure a man a blissful rebirth; for this depends upon the acts that the man has done during his previous lives. He who is cruel and full of hate, prepares a place for himself among demon beings, because he resembles them. He who wishes to go to the gods must practise goodness. It is not a question of offerings and prostrations.

"If rites are already powerless to ensure a happy rebirth, how much more powerless are they to produce Deliverance (*tharpa*).[1] This 'Deliverance' can only be obtained by the knowledge that is the result of the 'penetrating vision' (*lhag thong*) that is acquired by meditation and investigation.

---

[1] Salvation according to the Buddhists does not consist in entering a Paradise. The rebirth in a Paradise is merely the consequence of a virtuous life, and is considered to be a mediocre result. Salvation is the "Deliverance from the round of births and deaths" and is brought about by dispelling the false views concerning the nature of the "I" and of the external world. This state is definitely superior to that of the gods and is one that can be attained to in this present life.

"Have you ever heard a learned lama say that we practise *dubthabs* in order to gain *tharpa*?"

No, I had never heard any lama say so.

"The *dubthabs*," he continued, "are directed towards ends that are more or less material and foreign to this greatest of purposes: Supreme Liberation (*tharpa*). To obtain these inferior ends, which are often useful to those who have not yet 'entered the stream',[1] some rites and specially the *dubthabs* can be practised with advantage. To use them in this way is not to contravene the command of the Buddha."

This subject is one of those that lead to interminable discussions. As I was not remaining long at Kanze, I was obliged to content myself with what the lama had expounded to me. Moreover, his opinion was not new to me. I had heard it expressed before. It is fairly common among the well-educated clergy.

If there were some learned philosophers at the Kanze monastery, the commercial spirit seemed also particularly alive there. Many Lamaist monks engage in trade, but usually they show some discretion in their exercise of it. Never before had I seen them in a shop, behind a counter. Such a thing appeared quite customary in Kanze, and some of those fat and substantial merchant-ecclesiastics were visibly very well off.

In picturesque but rather painful contrast to this opulence, I saw, standing at the door of one of those prosperous clerical shops, the poorest, sorriest little monk that it had ever been my lot to come across. He was an urchin of about seven, and was quite naked, except for a strip of dark red serge, the size of a little napkin, which, placed on his tiny shoulders, served him for monastic toga and quaintly designated him as a member of the clergy.

---

[1] The traditional Buddhic expression that indicates those who have begun to perceive certain truths, after which they will not retrograde spiritually and will attain enlightenment sooner or later.

Since the magistrate of Kanze persisted in preventing me from going to Bathang through Chinese territory, there was nothing left for me to do—unless I retraced my steps and went to Tachienlu—but to obey him and to try and reach Bathang by travelling across the regions that had been conquered by the Lhasa troops and afterwards closed to foreigners.

After several rather unpleasant days spent in journeying through the rain, I arrived with my men in front of Zacco. The people of the place, having been previously informed of our coming, had pitched a reception tent in which to give us tea, as it is the habit in Tibet to do, when distinguished travellers pass through a village.

As soon as we had entered it, many villagers came into the tent. Among them was a Lhasa woman, fat, good-natured, and garrulous, whom, I thought, had had a little too much to drink. On hearing me speak the Lhasa dialect, she questioned me about the U province, which she had left twenty years before. The good woman, having ascertained that Tibet was really well known to me, pointed to our group—Yongden, my servants and me—and declared:

"They are Tibetans like ourselves!"

The people, who were already astonished at hearing us speak their language, then became convinced that we were sham foreigners, impostors, who wished to appear important. As we no longer had any interest for them, they departed disappointed.

I went myself to the officer who was in command at the frontier. He lived in a miserable house, badly kept, but ornamented with pots of flowers. He had, indeed, one really beautiful flower; a woman, who wore the costume and headdress of U (hair exaggeratedly full and surmounted by a sort of crown of large coral balls). She was the officer's wife.

He was not particularly polite to me; nevertheless,

he offered me some excellent tea and some Chinese biscuits. He said that he would not take it upon himself to bar my passage, but that on the other hand he would not give me either an escort or *ulags*, and he would have to send a message to his chief, the *depön* of Derge, to inform him of our presence in his district.

Since no one had stopped them, the *ulags* had gone on and were by then some distance ahead. We had lost much time at Zacco and it was necessary to push on: for we did not know how far it was to the place where they would leave our luggage.

Without being in any way striking, the landscape became interesting. At sunset, we entered a wooded gorge, the savage and mysterious aspect of which was specially suitable for an entrance into forbidden land. The path was narrow and bristled with rocks. We thought it wise to dismount and continue on foot; a proceeding that delayed us still more.

Night had come by the time we reached the place where we had to cross the Yalung. There was a monastery and village close by, but the darkness prevented our seeing them.

The river, the course of which we had never ceased to ascend, was much less wide there than it was near Kanze, and the current appeared less strong. This was most fortunate, for our mules had to swim across. Yongden suggested we should camp before crossing, but I insisted on going at once to the other side, while no one barred our passage. In this way we could start again as early as we liked in the morning.

Travellers and their luggage are taken over in little round boats, made of yakskin. Soon after we had crossed a *gyapön* (officer who commands a hundred soldiers) sent us a tent and, with it, some firewood, milk, and forage. We were also informed that the *gyapön* had given orders that, next day, *ulags* with their

227

beasts were to be placed at our disposal for transporting our luggage.

Seeing us arrive from Zacco with *ulags*, this officer thought we had a requisition order that gave us the right to them and to the other things he had sent us. This service becomes automatic as soon as it has once begun and, except when the traveller is passing districts where there is a governor, it is very unusual for anyone to ask to see the official paper that authorizes the requisition. And when it is merely the case of supplying a few beasts of burden, it is even extremely rare for the high officials to interest themselves sufficiently in the matter to verify the traveller's claim. The important thing is to have obtained the *ulags* for the first time.

I knew what the *gyapön* did not. His chief at Zacco had not wished to grant me free transport for my luggage. If he sent orders to this effect, the *ulags* would be taken away. This would be very annoying and would create a bad impression. It were far better for me to pretend to do without them, to give them up of my own accord. I therefore told the villagers that, having mules of my own, I did not require *ulags*.

They reported my decision to the village chiefs, and in about an hour, these men came and offered me a scarf in token of politeness and seven Szechwan rupees, which are current coin in this region.

The same automatism that controls the relays of *ulags* also rules the number of beasts of burden or mounts with which the traveller is to be furnished. I had arrived with seven requisitioned yaks, therefore these would have to be replaced by seven others.

If the traveller, who has a right to requisition a certain number of beasts, asks for fewer or completely exempts the villagers from their obligation, he is entitled to an indemnity that, in that region, is generally rated at one Szechwan rupee for each animal. Therefore, because

CHIEFS OF THE LAND OF HOR
Eastern Tibet

I exempted the Tibetans from supplying me with seven beasts, they brought me seven rupees.

In this blessed country, officials, travellers who stand well with these last, and even ordinary soldiers on their rounds, can, thanks to this system, make quite appreciable sums of money. He who is authorized to requisition twenty beasts, if he travels with his own animals, reaps a profit of twenty rupees at each stage of the journey. These relay stations are sometimes close to one another, especially in some relatively well populated parts of the country, where transport is done by the slow travelling yaks. Good mules can, in one day, very often do the distance of three yak relays, and in each one of these relays the happy possessor of a requisition order for twenty beasts can pocket twenty rupees, that is, a total of sixty rupees a day. Such a harvest is perhaps exceptional, but even with a smaller profit to which must be added all the forage, fuel, and provisions that are given with the service of the *ulags*, the traveller is often able to pay his travelling expenses or even to amass a pretty round sum, if his journey lasts long enough.

It can be understood how such a system causes the peasants to dread the passing of people in possession of rights that fall so heavily on them.

During another journey, I remember asking some riverside inhabitants of the upper reaches of the Salwen why they did not learn to build bridges instead of being content to cross rivers hanging on to a single rope that is stretched from one bank to the other.

"We are quite capable of building bridges," they answered, "but we prefer that there should be none in our country. Their absence makes travelling more difficult for the officials of the Lhasa government and for other notables. It does not please them to be obliged to cross rivers hanging on our ropes; they take other routes in order to avoid having to do so, and in this way we escape their visits and the consequences that follow in their train."

I have mentioned the least of these consequences; there are many others that greatly tax the resources of the poor peasants.

So here I am with seven rupees in front of me, which Prudence would have me accept so as not to go counter to local customs. By refusing them, I shall make myself conspicuous and, perhaps, an object of suspicion; but, I still retain some scruples on the subject, and, probably, always shall. I commission Yongden to surround my refusal with all the reasons that are most likely to diminish its strangeness. Shut up in my tent, I hear him acquitting himself of this ticklish task.

He gives me back my character of *Khadoma*. He tells them that the lady traveller, who, in the darkness, they were not able to distinguish clearly, is an incarnated *Khadoma*. Gifted with superior intelligence, she has foreseen that the seven rupees would be useful to them (in saying this he runs little risk of making a mistake) and in her beneficence she returns them. The moment a gift comes from a religious personage one's dignity is safe. This explanation apparently satisfies the villagers for they give thanks, prostrate themselves before the closed curtains of my tent, and go away.

The night is cold. On waking, we find the tents and the grass round them covered with hoar-frost. Yet, it is still August. The winters must be very severe in this part of the country.

Very early, before we have struck camp, the *gyapön's* messenger passes by. As the officer has warned us, the man goes to the *depön* of Derge to inform him that we are on our way there.

During the whole of the day we proceed very slowly. My servants, who do not understand the reasons that prompted my action, feel injured by my having refused the *ulags*. They have become accustomed to be served

230

rather than to serve, and to travel in the saddle. To-day all our beasts are loaded. While at Kanze, knowing we were about to cross a sparsely inhabited region, we had provided ourselves with a large stock of provisions; this has to be carried, therefore the men are obliged to walk. A proceeding that is little to their liking and they advance at a snail's pace.

At night-fall, we reach Ape. The travellers' halt and the *ulags'* relay is marked by a black tent. The village itself is farther on, away from the road. A young man is in the tent, and we think he is in charge of it, for it is the hour when travellers are most likely to arrive. He says, however, that he is a stranger and not in any way connected with the people of Ape.

The *gopas* (village chiefs) do not show themselves. We shall not be able to get anything: the beasts will consequently have no fodder, and will have to content themselves by nibbling the short, scanty grass that is around us.

It is quite dark when several men come up. Questioned by my servants, they declare they are neither the *gopas* of Ape nor the men in charge of the halt. They are simply sheltering there for the night. Sönam seizes hold of one of them and forcibly drags him before my tent. I myself ask him who he is. He pretends to be a traveller. I feel that he is lying. Travellers, even wandering beggars, have always some luggage, little though it be: a rag of a blanket and a little food; but, like the young fellow we found there on our arrival, the newcomers have also nothing with them. Their attitude seems suspicious to me. Yongden thinks they are robbers, who intend to steal our beasts and are merely waiting before doing so until there is no longer any fear of people passing by.

Little Sezang Thales, who has been sent out as spy, reports that there are seven of them in the tent. They have each a sword, but no gun. This is good news. If things turn out badly we can hope to keep them at a distance with our weapons. However, it will be better to avoid a fight, and for this reason we must try and give them a wholesome fright, then to go and inform the people of the village and ask them for watchers.

We therefore load our guns and revolvers. The glow from the little fire that we have made with the fuel we brought with us lights up our preparations. Yongden makes me load our rifle twice over, having rapidly unloaded it in the shadow and again passed it to me near the fire. This manœuvre is to induce those who are observing us to think there will still remain two guns in our tent when Sönam and Sezang Thales have taken the other two with them into the village.

It is rather imprudent for us to divide our forces in this way. If the men in the black tent are really thieves, they may take advantage of our weakness to attack us separately. I rather think, however, they will hesitate to do so, knowing that we have fire-arms.

All the luggage is piled into the middle of my tent. Sönam and the young boy each jump astride a mule and go off to find the village; Yongden and Tobgyal sit outside and guard the beasts. Then, as I have nothing to do, I eat some *tsampa* and butter, seated on a bag at the entrance of the tent, the curtains of which I leave open so as to keep careful watch on the surroundings, to whatever extent it is possible to do so in the darkness.

Some time passes, then I see shadows advancing cautiously, which, on coming nearer, stop in front of me. They are the unknown suspects. Is it that, taking advantage of the absence of my two boys, they are beginning the attack?

As they remain silent, I call out:

" Who is there? "

Whereupon the shadows stoop and kneel, pushing towards me something black in the middle of which is something white, and I hear murmurs of: " Long life!

232

Long life!" It is the polite phrase used in Tibet when apologizing, imploring, thanking, and so forth.

"What do you want?"

"We bring milk."

Ah! this is the something white in a black pot.

"We are going to bring fodder and wood."

"Who are you?"

"We are the men in charge of the halt and the village chiefs."

Finding that I do not try to kill them, they take courage and all begin speaking at once.

"You are bad people," I say to the liars. "You did not want to provide us with what we have a right to. It was for this reason that you pretended to be travellers. Be thankful that I am a religious person, otherwise I should already have had you fired on, and several of you would now be dead."

The murmurs of "Long life! Long life!" are resumed with even greater fervour. I have an idea that these wishes are chiefly addressed to themselves.

I call Yongden. On learning what is happening, he severely harangues the villagers and sends two of them to fetch Sönam and Sezang Thales.

I rather admire the quiet bravery of the little fellow, who, young as he is, goes into the night with a single companion, knowing he may have seven bandits at his heels. There are no cowards in the beautiful country of Kham.

It is fortunate for us that the seven strange-mannered individuals have not proved to be thieves; for we could not have counted on receiving any help from the people of Ape. Sönam, on his return, tells me what took place in the village.

"All the windows and doors were shut," he said. "When I knocked, the dogs in the yard barked, but no one appeared or answered. In two of the houses, some women shrieked with terror on hearing the noise I was making at their door. In vain I explained that we were travellers asking for help, but it was of no avail. At the last house I went to, no one replied at first, then a man shouted from behind a shutter that, if we did not go away instantly, he would fire. He thought we were thieves who were trying to get in by ruse.

" Seeing that no one would come to our aid, I was just coming back when I met the men you had sent to fetch me. In spite of all they say, they probably did have the intention of robbing us. They have given up the idea of doing so and are now showing themselves as friends because they saw we were well armed and thought the risk they ran too great."

What he says is quite possible. In any case, the attitude of the Ape people promises little for the safety of the country.

However, we are safe for that night, and as I feel tired I am glad to be able to sleep instead of having to keep watch.

On our way, next day, we meet some travellers. They advise us to be on our guard : the previous evening, a caravan of merchants has been attacked on the road. They have spoken with the victims.

We cross uninhabited alpine pasture-land, through which flows the Yalung river. A chain of mountains borders its left bank. The gentle outlines of the landscape produce an impression of great calm.

Later, we descry a group of hermitages crouching in a wooded recess of the mountain—white-washed huts dotted here and there among the fir-trees. Solitude, detachment, peace, and all the divine bliss that exists over and above and beyond what these words represent! I, too, have been a hermit on a lonely mountain, and I have tasted the intense voluptuousness of that peculiar life. No doubt I was not yet worthy to remain at that height, and it was for that reason I had to come down from there to wander again in the world. Will the day come, when

234

I shall once more plunge into such solitude and silence?
Towards the end of the afternoon we pass by some
sulphur springs, the temperature of which is fairly high,
but the water soon cools as it flows into the open. We
must be at an altitude of about 10,000 feet; for since quitting Kanze[1] we have continued to ascend the course of
the river, and after leaving the river, our path has still
steadily mounted.

Before arriving at the monastery of Dzogschen, we
rejoin the caravan route we diverged from a few miles this
side of Kanze. It now passes through an immense
valley edged by sombre mountains. The soil of both
valley and mountain is covered with short thick grass,
which the premature frosts have already withered and
turned brown. The track, stamped by the feet of millions
of yaks that during centuries have carried Chinese silk and
tea to Lhasa, is at the moment deserted. Not a herdsman's tent nor a herd relieves the impressive and almost
tragic emptiness of the scene.

We hope to obtain shelter in the hamlet that is
dependent on the monastery, but we have some difficulty
in discovering it. Feebly lighted by the last rays of a setting sun, the low squalid huts are scarcely distinguishable
among the rocks of the hill. On the slopes the temples
and monastic houses rise in rows, but it is already too
dark for us to see them.

The miserable inhabitants of the hamlet live in close
intimacy with their animals. Their dwellings consist of
a single room, one side of which serves as stable and the
other as kitchen. The owners, their family, and their
guests sleep where they can between the hearth and the
beasts. However, the house where I am lodged is a little
more comfortable. Between the place reserved for the
horses and the wall, a sort of cubicle has been made by
a curtain that hangs across the room. It is the best
accommodation the inhabitants have to offer me.

[1] On the maps it is given as situated at an altitude of 9,850 feet.

I suggest camping, but the villagers energetically dissuade me from doing so. It would be most imprudent; robbers roam through the whole country. A few days before a fight between some travellers and brigands had taken place in the neighbourhood. Such incidents are frequent. I must therefore remain content with this minimum of comfort. I shall sleep behind the curtain, my son will lie at my feet, and we will both try, while asleep, to remain pressed against the wall, and not to stretch either an arm or a leg out under the curtain, for were we to do so, we would run the risk of receiving a kick from one of the horses.

The next day, accompanied by Yongden and Tobgyal, I go up to the monastery. Dzogschen *gompa* is not at all imposing. Its buildings, scattered in confusion over a wide expanse, instead of being enclosed within an encircling wall, are quite ordinary. Nevertheless the monastery is celebrated throughout the whole of Tibet. It is the seat of one of the heads[1] of the " Great Accomplishment" (*dzogs-chen*) sect, Lama Padma Rigdzin, whose successive incarnations occupy the abbatial throne of the monastery. Dzogschen *gompa* is also held to possess amongst its members an elite of masters. Some of them are deeply versed in occult sciences and others in the methods of the " Short Path",[2] which enable those who follow them to attain Supreme Liberation (tharpa) in this life.

The site on which the monastery is built is more in keeping with its reputation that the monastery itself. On looking at the wild desolation of the surrounding solitudes, a Westerner would easily conclude that only men who were pursuing extraordinary ends could remain for long

---

[1] Another of the heads resides at Mindoling, in southern Tibet, near the bank of the Yesru tsangpo (the upper course of the Brahmaputra). I visited this place on my way back from Lhasa.

[2] On the subject of the philosophical and mystical doctrines of the so-called " Short Path " *Lam chung*, see *Initiations and Initiates in Tibet* also *With Mystics and Magicians in Tibet*, page 243.

DZOGSCHEN GOMPA : THE MONASTERY OF THE
'GREAT ACCOMPLISHMENT' : EASTERN TIBET

in such a spot. But it must be remembered that Tibetans are accustomed to live amid grand and often terrifying scenery, consequently they are less likely to be impressionable on this score than either Europeans or Americans. Some very ordinary monks, sons of the neighbouring herdsmen, can pass the whole of their lives at Dzogschen and be perfectly happy.

On reaching the monastery, I visited some temples and the great assembly hall. Then I went on to see another *gompa*, which is situated close to that of the Dzogschen, but quite separate from it, although the Grand Lama Padma Rigdzin considers himself its suzerain. Finally, I asked to be shown the printing-house. I thought there would be, just as there was at Kum-Bum, a library attached to it, where it would be possible to buy some works written by members of the " Great Accomplishment " sect.

I was mistaken. At Dzogschen *gompa*, they only printed to order. That is to say, anyone who wanted a book had to bring the necessary paper and ink for the printing of it, feed the printers during the time they spent on the job, and in addition, as gift, pay a sum of money into the common fund of the printing-house.

The ecclesiastical heads of the monastery would have gladly allowed me to stay there during the time necessary for printing a few works, but I had reason to think that both the *depön* of Derge and the Kalön Lama of Chiamdo would not allow me to do so.

If I wished to reach Bathang, it was essential for me to hasten across that part of the country now closed to foreigners. I therefore contented myself with writing down the titles of a number of philosophical and mystical treatises as well as of those dealing exclusively with the occult sciences. Arranged on shelves, the engraved blocks[1] of these works and others filled many rooms. I

---

[1] The Tibetans print from engraved blocks.

intended to get the books later, and I succeeded in doing so the following winter.

I had been so absorbed in my inspection of the printing-house that I was surprised to find that Yongden was no longer with me. Tobgyal had also not noticed his going. Some *trapas* said they had seen him leave with some of their friends, so, thinking the monks had probably invited him to take tea with them, I resumed my walk.

A little later, two *trapas* came up and asked me if I would follow them. I thought they wished to show me a temple I had not yet visited. They led the way to a large building. After entering it, we had to climb one of those uncomfortable Tibetan flights of stairs: a trap-ladder, with high steps, fitted in between two partitions. The stairs gave on to a landing or an antechamber, which was so narrow that I could touch the walls on either side at the same time. I stood in complete darkness, for a door had been closed behind me, and I heard several men whispering, but could see no one.

Suddenly I had the idea that they had brought me to this dark place in order to kill me. Several times before it had happened that I had only just escaped a fatal accident and, although well aware of the danger I was running, I had never been frightened. My first and only experience of terror was there, in that dark and airless corridor. It scarcely lasted a second, the duration of a shiver, then I began to reason again. Why should these *trapas* wish to kill me? The Tibetans have a horror of killing, except in fair fight, when each adversary runs equal risks. A few murders are committed in Tibet for political reasons, but these are of rare occurrence, and I could not be classed among those who need fear such a fate. And then, after all, death is not an extraordinary thing. At Dzogschen or elsewhere I should have to meet it one day. . . .

A few seconds later a door opened in front of me,

lighting up the tragic antechamber and the faces of a few smiling monks, and I entered the apartment of the Grand Lama Padma Rigdzin. Seated on a pile of cushions, near some young monks who were dressed in rich Lamaistic costumes, I saw Yongden looking mischievously at me.

I was invited to dinner.

"When I heard that a foreign lady who spoke our language had arrived and was visiting the monastery, I thought it might be you," the Grand Lama said to me. "I have known of you for a long time."

Several old students of the Dzogschen monastery, whom I had known in Amdo, also lama Gurong Tsang, with whom I had travelled when going from Pekin to Kansu, and the unfortunate Tibetan secretary of the Amban General of Sining, Aka Mela, who was assassinated at Lhasa, both pupils, also of Dzogschen *gompa*, had spoken of me during their visits to their professors or friends. What they had said must have been complimentary, for the reception I received from Padma Rigdzin was cordial and flattering.

As I have already mentioned elsewhere, preoccupations of a commercial order seemed to hold a great place in the Grand Lama's mind. He questioned me at great length about Burma and French Indo-China, wanting to know the kind of merchandise that could be exported and imported to and from these places.

Whether those very material preoccupations were in keeping or not with the transcendental doctrines of the sect of which he was the head, no one seemed to care. These *tulku* lamas, supposed reincarnations of eminent personages of past centuries, are not positively required to give proof of exceptional merits. They are venerable as being the present forms of men who, in olden times, were remarkable in some way, and their words and acts, however common and eccentric they may be, are considered to be dictated by superior motives.

The Lama's apartment was very luxurious. Along

the walls of the principal room were glass cases filled with antique works of art: magnificent porcelain or cloisonné vases from China, statuettes in jade, ivory, or coral, beautiful specimens of Kham gold and silver work. There were also rare ritualistic instruments, among others a *phurpa* (magic dagger) made of "iron fallen from the sky", that is, made from an aerolite. Was it really "iron fallen from the sky"? I would not like to guarantee it, but everyone had held it to be so, during several centuries it had formed part of the treasure of the Dzogschen *gompa tulku* Lamas.

Among all these precious things, a special case was set apart for some very miserable samples of Western work, which the lama and those about him appeared to prize as much and even more than the beautiful things in his Chinese collection. They were articles made of inferior glass, such as hawkers have for sale: goblets, glasses with stem or feet, vases of different shapes, candlesticks. I was shown some dreadful green, blue, and pink rubbish, of which they seemed to be very proud and concerning which Padma Rigdzin asked my opinion.

An excellent dinner was served, and then, just as I was taking my leave, they brought me the gift the Lama wished to offer me. It was very bulky: eighteen big bricks[1] of compressed tea packed in leather, just as they are sent from China to Lhasa.

I expressed my thanks but refused this cumbersome present, merely taking the silk scarf that accompanied it.

After my visit to the Lama, while I was strolling about the monastery, a young *trapa* came up to me.

"My Master would like to see you," he said politely. "As he is in retreat and cannot go out, he begs that you will come to him."

Neither Yongden nor I were in a hurry to return to the dirty hovel where we would have again to pass the

---

[1] Each brick weighs several pounds.

night. The invitation was welcome; we followed the *trapa*.

He led us some distance, nearly to the top of the hill on which the monastic buildings rose one above the other. At this spot the houses were far apart and had the appearance of *tsams khangs*.[1] Because of this appearance and of what my guide had said, I expected to find only one monk. I was therefore rather surprised to see four of them seated on cushions in the tiny room.

The customary compliments having been exchanged, tea was offered us, then, all ceremonial at an end, one of the lamas came to the point.

"We have heard of you," he said to me, "from some lamas and *trapas*, and also from some merchants who have seen you at Kum-Bum, where, I believe, you have stayed for some years. It appears, too, that you have been in the south of Tibet, that you know Tsang Penchen Rinpoche,[2] and that you have lived as *ritöpa* (hermit) for a long time. All this has greatly astonished us. We have never known of any foreign lady who shares our beliefs or who practises our religious discipline. Is it true what we have heard concerning you? As you have come to us, we want to ask you about it."

"It is all perfectly correct, *Kushog*."

"Why do you live in this way? There are foreigners at Tachienlu and at Bathang. They say that our religion is bad, that we are ignorant and dirty. I have heard it. Our way of preparing tea disgusts them. . . ."

"It is not in the least disgusting to me," I hastened to answer. "If I may be allowed to do so, I would like to ask you for another bowl." And saying this I emptied mine.

My rejoinder made the lamas laugh. A young *trapa*

[1] Small houses in which the monks shut themselves up to meditate. For explanations on this subject see *With Mystics and Magicians in Tibet*, page 249 and following pages.
[2] The Grand Lama of Tashilhunpo, the one whom foreigners call the Tashi Lama.

poured me out some more tea. With truth, I could say it was excellent. So close to Tachienlu, the tea is not yet subjected to heavy transport charges and the best is obtainable at a reasonable price, even for people with light purses.

My interrogators returned to the point that had roused their curiosity:

"Why do you live differently from the people of your country. What did you hope to gain by living in a hermitage?"

"I did not seek to gain anything. Life in the solitude is, in itself, blessedness."

"If you really think in this way, why do you travel?" said one of my listeners.

The question was not lacking in logic. More than once I had asked myself the same thing.

"Doubtless it is the effect of past acts and old thoughts," I answered. "The wheel, because of the impulsion that has been given it, continues to turn for some time after the potter has ceased to move it."

This comparison, which is repeated in a number of Eastern philosophical treatises, is current among Buddhists as well as Hindus. The lamas nodded their heads in agreement.

"Have you carefully pondered over this simile of the wheel that continues to turn as the result of a past impulsion?" asked another of them.

"I have reflected upon it," I said, "but I have certainly not yet grasped all that there is to be understood on the subject.

"It is possible the belief in an 'impulsion that has been given' may in itself be one of the causes that push the wheel and keep it in movement. Perhaps it is the principal cause of the movement, or, who knows, it may be the only cause."

The lama who appeared to be the master of the house smiled:

"What is your opinion," he asked me: "if a man had lost all memory of his past acts, of his native land, of his family ties, of every kind of relation that he has or has had with other people, of the thoughts that have come to him, which he has held secret or professed publicly; in short, if he had completely lost all recollection of what he *is* and what he *has done*, do you believe he would act in the same way as if all those things were present in his memory?"

"He would most likely behave very differently," I replied.

I thought I knew what he was leading up to, so I continued:

"If a man, without losing the memory of his past, regards this past as being a dream or as concerning another person than himself, it will also probably happen that he will act in a different way from the one in which he would have acted had he firmly believed he himself had really accomplished all the physical and mental acts he remembers. So, too, the effect of the recollections that he keeps of his family ties, of his nationality, of his relations with other people, and of all his associations with the outside world will differ according as he considers them to be the result of real facts or of pure imaginings."

The theory I outlined resembled those held by some Dzogschenpa authors, whose writings I had read. I hoped that the lamas would enlarge upon it, but they had become like sphinxes and looked curiously at me without speaking.

Finally, the one who had questioned me last spoke:

"Truly," he said, "all that exists is the product of causes.[1] Beings are what they have made themselves by their works. Nevertheless, these works cease from fettering when it is perceived that no non-compounded and

---

[1] "All things proceed from a cause" is one of the fundamental declarations of Buddhism.

permanent 'self' exists, either in the person or in any-thing, and that the constituent parts of the aggregate, which appears as personality, alone go their course.

"This cannot be either taught or expressed in words; it must be *seen* in meditation."

"Do people meditate in your country?"

"Not often, and what they call meditation does not resemble what is understood by meditation in Tibet and India."

One of the other monks then changed the subject, by returning to what I had said in the beginning of our conversation.

"If you find such blessedness in a hermit's life," he said, "do not go farther. We can easily find you a hermitage in the neighbourhood."

I thought of the *depön* of Derge. He would not let me establish myself in that forbidden land, but I did not wish to discuss the question with the lamas.

"Reasons prevent me from doing so, *Kushog*," I merely replied.

"Reasons . . ." repeated the lama.

Then, either under the influence of the ideas that had just been expressed or by the occult force of the thoughts that had been fostered in that room by recluses who had given themselves up to long contemplations, I suddenly felt, nay, I *saw* all my reasonings, all my conceptions fray out as rags blown by the wind, dissolve, sink into nothing-ness. All that which had appeared to me to be solid obstacles no longer existed: the *depön* of Derge, my servants, my mules, my luggage, and my own self were "images seen in a dream"

The vision lasted, probably, less than a minute.

"Here or elsewhere, *Kushog*," I said, "I hope the day may come when I shall again find myself in a hermitage."

"I wish it may be so," said one of the monks.

"It must be," declared another.

Yongden and I then took leave of our hosts. The young *trapa* who had led us to them took us back to the hamlet, and, night having come while we talked, he lighted our way with a flaming branch.

On my return to the house where we lodged, I found a man had been waiting for me. He was a messenger from Padma Rigdzin and had brought me a letter and several books. The Grand Lama wrote that, as I had not been able to procure all the books I desired at the monastery, he sent me some as a present with his wishes for a good journey.

The next morning we left for Derge, accompanied by two merchants who were going there and who had asked to travel with us.

Yongden had insisted on our asking for *ulags*. We could no longer hide our identity, and he argued that it was necessary for us to keep our mules fresh in case some unforeseen circumstance should force us to demand a special effort of them.

The natives made some difficulties. The messenger sent by the *rupön* of Zacco had, in passing, told them that they were not to provide us with pack-yaks. I appealed on a point of grammar. Had the soldier said *mi chog*: "it is not permitted you", or *mi gös*: "you need not", meaning "you are not obliged to". He had said *mi gös*. I then argued that, if the village chiefs were allowed to refuse me beasts of burden, they were nevertheless not forbidden to provide me with them, and that, as it was my intention to pay for them, it was to the chiefs' interest to render me this service.

The prospect of receiving payment added greatly to the weight of the arguments I drew from the respective meanings of the verbs *chogpa* and *göpa*.[1] Besides the inhabitants of the place, poor illiterate herdsmen, began to doubt whether a person "so learned" in Tibetan grammar could really be a foreigner; for in these regions

[1] Written respectively: *chhog pa* and *dgos pa*.

245

everyone has the unshakable conviction that all foreigners are stupid. In short, three men with yaks were commissioned to transport our luggage to Derge.

And now we are travelling amid the grassy solitudes. On our way I am shown the spot where two days before a travellers' camp had been attacked. The brigands had stolen twenty-seven beasts, mules and horses, and killed two men in the fight that took place. This was adventure indeed!

Is it the excitement caused by the pictures that rise in my mind of this wild life or the effect of the intoxicating air of the high, empty regions, the *chang thangs*, that is turning my head? I am listening to a call, and something deep within me passionately answers it.

To go to Bathang is to turn my back on the enchanted solitudes of Upper Tibet, on that land which is the subject of so many heroic and mystic legends, where one is shown strange traces of the wonders performed by Gesar, the Chieftain-God of the Tibetan epic,[1] and where, according to the natives, an attentive seeker can discover the hidden portals that give access to mysterious worlds of genii and fairies. I remember the sojourns I have already made in this magic land, on the borders of the great blue lakes. An overpowering desire to live there again takes possession of me. . . . Yet, I am walking towards Bathang, from where the route leads across Chinese land to Yunnan and farther on to colonized Indo-China. How tame the prospect of such a journey in contrast to the majestic vision of the *chang thangs*.

Owing to the lengthy discussion concerning the *ulags* we had started late, so towards the middle of the afternoon, seeing that we cannot reach Derge the same day, the merchants, our travelling companions, propose that we camp close to a river, in a valley where the grass is plentiful and where the beasts will be able to graze to

[1] See *Superhuman Life of Gesar of Ling*.

246

their hearts content. The suggestion seems a good one. We pitch our tents. It is really a pleasant spot; the prairie is covered with alpine flowers, the sun shines, and the animals grazing round us give a pastoral note to the landscape. Then, while I am still dreaming of the fascinating solitudes that I am leaving behind me, I hear the sound of distant music.

A few minutes later a small procession comes into view from the opposite direction to the one from which we have come. At its head ride two troopers, blowing a pleasant flourish on Theban trumpets. They use their instruments well; the sound is true and clear. Behind them, another trooper carries an unfurled standard of crimson silk, on which is designed a yellow lion. Then comes a fat man wearing a very dark purple robe and mounted on a beautiful horse. Lastly, closing the procession, is a fourth trooper.

Instead of passing on its way, the procession stops. I see the fat man dismount and enter the merchants' tent. A few minutes later one of them comes to ask me if I will permit the newcomer to pay his respects to me. Permission being granted, the man arrives and offers me the traditional scarf, token of respect and friendliness, then sits down and talks to me.

He is a *gyapön* (captain commanding a hundred men). He is on his way to Dzogschen to open an enquiry regarding the murder of the two travellers and the theft of their twenty-seven beasts. Shigaze is his native town, and he speaks of that part of his country, where I have been. After which he leaves me.

A few minutes later up comes a *shalngo* (a kind of sergeant), whom I had met the evening before at the house where we slept. With an embarrassed air he asks me to return to Dzogschen, explaining that he cannot let a foreigner pass without having been authorized to do so by the *depön* of Derge. I must wait until he has received instructions concerning me.

247

I reply that his chief already knows I am on my way to Derge to see him and if my visit is displeasing to him he has had ten times the time required for stopping me. Moreover, the *rupön* who is in command at the frontier has seen me and let me pass, therefore I am in order.

Respect for those of superior military rank does not seem to be a strong point of the Tibetan army. This common sergeant, to whom the *gyapön* has just given instructions, calls the *rupön*, who is a colonel, an incapable fool. The two subordinates have resolved to bar me the road and oblige me to return to Dzogschen, to remain there, I don't doubt, until they inform me of my expulsion from the forbidden territory.

Night comes: we have supper and then go to sleep. Very early next morning the *gyapön* accompanied by the *shalngo* are before my tent and begin repeating all that which they have said the evening before: I must retrace my steps and leave the forbidden country at Zacco, the place where I have entered it, or I must remain at Dzogschen for the *depön's* decision. However, I need not fear to have to return to the dirty house at Dzogschen, where I have passed two nights. They will give me comfortable lodgings in the monastery and provide me with food for myself, servants, and mules.

All that they say is very characteristic of the Tibetan spirit. The Tibetans have for a long time wished to keep foreigners away, but those who have been found among them have not been molested, they have simply been conducted to the frontier, surrounded by all the comfort that the country had to offer. Nowadays, having acquired more worldly knowledge, the Tibetans would consent, without enthusiasm, but also without aversion, to receive foreign travellers who have a definite and legitimate purpose in view, especially that of trade; but they are no longer at liberty to do so.

I am as obstinate as these two soldiers. I refuse to

While the troops in Lhasa wear European
style uniforms, those staying in other
parts of Tibet keep the usual
Tibetan dress

return to either Zacco or Dzogschen, nevertheless I realize
it would be better not to insist on going to Bathang; to
do so might be imprudent. The region swarms with
brigands, and the Tibetan authorities sometimes find it
diplomatic to switch some of the knights of the highway
on to those whom they dare not get rid of by legal
means. Having carefully considered all these things, I
declare that, since I find myself in a lawless country,
where subordinates allow themselves to question the conduct of their superiors and to act against what these have
permitted, I have ceased to wish to remain in it, as I no
longer feel safe there. I shall consequently not go to
Bathang, but I shall go elsewhere, to a place of my own
choosing. And without further ado I break camp.

We do not go far; I want to think things over. What
shall I do? No matter what, so long as I do not retrace
my steps. Having once more set foot on the forbidden
ground, I wish to see all I can of it. The temptation is
all the greater, because I am again on the track I left the
morning when I turned towards Derge on my way to
Bathang, and I know it leads to a small isolated town
in the middle of the *chang thangs*. A Tibetan town
that remains under Chinese control and, consequently,
is still free territory. What if I listened to the call, and
instead of ending my journey in Yunnan or Indo-China,
I made for this town, which emerges as an island in
the middle of the grassy solitudes. What if I were to
visit the camping ground of the famous robber tribes
—the Ngologs? What if . . . if . . . . The name of
the town is Jakyendo, I do not know anything else
about it.

Meanwhile the *gyapön* and the *shalngo* had installed
themselves in a tent, in front of which their scarlet
standard floated in the breeze. Around them camped
their escort of soldiers: the two trumpeters, the standard-
bearer, the fourth trooper, those who had come from
Derge, and in addition several others who had joined

them, I do not know from where, making about a dozen in all.

My people and I occupied two tents pitched at some hundreds of yards away from those of the Tibetans. The unfortunate herdsman, whose unlucky star had led them to establish themselves at this spot, paid in sheep, butter, milk, and cheese for their part in the comedy that was being enacted. They fed the actors in it. Such is the custom in Tibet. Discussion followed discussion. When hoarse, enfeebled, and made desperate by my silence and imperturbability, the orators stopped talking, they ate. It would have been possible for me to have remained there a month and more.

However, I had come to a decision: I would go to Jakyendo.

Therefore, on the second day, I say to the boys: "To-morrow, we will get up before dawn and start away at once. We will breakfast on the road."

This programme is followed to the letter, but we have been probably watched all night. As soon as the servants' tent is struck, the *gyapön*, the *shalngo*, and the rest of them come along carrying a whole sheep, which has been killed and prepared the night before, also more butter and some *tsampa*. With an air of indifference, I order these provisions to be packed and remark:

"I am going away. I go to Jakyendo."

I am answered by exclamations of horror. The *gyapön* and the *shalngo* are doubtless asking themselves whether they have not made matters worse by barring me the road and whether their chief will not reproach them for having thus pushed me farther into the newly conquered area than I originally intended to go.

The greater part of the luggage is already on the mules. I prepare to walk on ahead.

"*Kale jugsden jag Kushogs lhengyai*,"[1] I say, using the most polite form of farewell salutation.

[1] "Sit down slowly, gentlemen."

But I have not gone two steps before they all surround me, holding on to the long sleeves of my Tibetan robe.

How shall I manage to free myself?

"It is useless to make such a fuss," I say. "You have your guns, you have only to kill me, then you will be quite certain that I shall go neither to Jakyendo nor elsewhere."

Whereupon there is a further chorus of protestations: Kill me! How awful! They only wish to serve me.

I know they are sincere. The Tibetans are a kind-hearted people. I have not only a friendly feeling for them, but also a real esteem. I am sorry for those who are in front of me, I would like to spare them the annoyance I am causing them. It would be so nice for us all to sit round the camp fire and talk amicably together. Why do there exist men who, for sordid interests, contrive to set other men against one another, and when will the latter poor innocents understand that they are merely dupes?

It is not the moment in which to give myself up to reflections of this kind. I have said: "I am going to Jakyendo," and I will go, unless I die on the spot. It is not discreditable to die in carrying out a purpose, even a futile one; what is so, is to let oneself be beaten and to accept one's defeat.

The excellent Tibetans who surround me have no desire to murder me; but they cling to my robe, a thing that worries me much more. Suddenly I become quite melodramatic. Raising my stick, I begin brandishing it about. These unexpected movements free me and I walk impressively towards my tent, which is still up, crying:

"Give me my revolver. I shall kill myself. Everyone will then believe that you have murdered me and you will suffer the consequences of this crime."

Yongden, who is in the tent, foresees the issue of the drama and calmly continues to cord the last bags;

but young Sezang Thales, becoming terrified, rushes past me, seizes all the weapons, and carries them out of my reach. 'Good-hearted little innocent!

The Tibetans are at the end of their tether.

"*Please go quietly away,*" the gyapön says, with a sigh, making use of the most polite form of farewell to one who is going away.

The poor man has tears in his eyes. I am really touched. I have a great wish to kiss him, as a sister kisses her little brother when he is unhappy.

I go off alone, stick in hand, towards the unknown. The excitement of this lively scene has given me a little fever and . . . I am still fasting. I am hungry, and, above all, thirsty. I kneel down to drink at the river's edge, and the words of the Psalmist come into my head. "He shall drink of the brook in the way: therefore shall he lift up the head."[1] I accept the prophecy of this verse, which seems to promise success to the new journey that I have just planned, but the absurdity of all that has happened amuses me. Still it is strange that my thoughts should turn to Biblical texts at such a time.

I have already gone some distance and my caravan is not yet in sight. Can it be that the gyapön has kept it back in order to force me to return? I sit down on a rock and wait for my people to show themselves. A moment later I descry a man coming towards me. He is alone. As he approaches, I recognize Sezang Thales. When he sees that I have noticed him, he starts running and ends by flinging himself down at my feet, with the exulting cry:

"You are the victor, Jetsun Kushog!"

Nothing counts with this young savage but the brutal fact of victory. He is proud of being in my service. If I had been worsted, he would probably have left me, and most certainly have despised me. Had

[1] Psalm cx: 7.

252

he been older, this contempt might have led him to
rob me in the desert. Such is the mentality of the
people of this country, and of elsewhere, too, for that
matter.

My caravan has not been detained. The *gyapön*
has given me three soldiers for escort and two other
men to act as guides. Sezang Thales says they are all
coming along. In fact, in the distance, I discern a
moving mass. Reassured, I continue my way with the
young boy.

We arrive at a place where the valley forks again.
I hesitate. Must I go to the right or to the left? On
the latter side the track is more clearly marked. This
must be the one to Jakyendo. Looking in this direction I see a troop of horsemen advancing towards me.
They are trotting quickly, and, notwithstanding the
distance between us, I can see they carry rifles. Who
can they be? Certainly not traders who are travelling
with mules laden with merchandise. Caravans advance
slowly. Then? . . .

Sezang Thales does not hesitate.

"*Jagpas!*" he says.

Brigands; that is what I think. Once having turned
the spur of the mountain that hides them, they may
fall suddenly on my people, who continue their way
quite unconscious of the danger that threatens them.
I must warn them. Backing out of sight of those who
are coming, I fasten my handkerchief to my stick and
wave it. My caravan is not far away, the men who
are with it have seen my signal; one of the soldiers
comes up at a gallop.

"Armed horsemen, who appear to be numerous,
are hastening in our direction," I tell him. "They will
be here in a minute. They are probably robbers; warn
your companions. I do not wish a fight. You must
not risk your life either in defence of what belongs to
me or of my person; but, as regards your own defence

and that of your horses, you will act as you think best. This being understood, we must nevertheless try to impose on these brigands so as to prevent their robbing us."

While I am speaking another soldier joins us. I cannot understand why the *jagpas*, whose horses were trotting quickly, have not already made their appearance. Keeping close to the mountain, one of the men goes forward to the end of the spur that hides from our view the other valley down which I have seen the horsemen, and, holding himself out of sight, scans it carefully. It is deserted.

Have my eyes deceived me? If I were alone, I should almost think so. But Sezang Thales has also seen the troop of men. Where have they disappeared to? However, on looking up, I see two horsemen with rifles gazing at us from a height.

I point them out to my companions. The soldiers examine them for a moment, then one of them says: "*Da*" (enemy).

Meanwhile our caravan has come up. It is a delicate situation. There cannot be the least doubt but that the brigands have left the track in order to conceal themselves in the mountain. Will they attack us? This we cannot tell, and, moreover, in these solitudes there exist no places of refuge. We must continue our way, we shall soon see what will happen.

At this point, the two guides intervene. Since I am acquainted with the Lama of Lop and wish to go to him, I should take the valley on the right, which will lead to his monastery. The way passes through country that is rich in grass, where my beasts will find good grazing; and the *gyapön's* written orders will enable me to obtain meat, milk, butter, and cheese from the herdsmen who are camped there.

At this moment one of the soldiers whispers in my ear:

"They want you to travel through a region where

254

there is nothing to see. There, you will not even find the herdsmen of whom they speak. Along the Jakyendo road, on the contrary, there are many villages and *gompas*. You will be able to sleep each night in a house."

His concern for my welfare is not entirely disinterested. The soldier has no tent and will be glad to have a sheltered resting place each night, and also, as I am soon to discover, a Tibetan soldier finds many profitable opportunities along a road that crosses inhabited areas.

I decide to follow the route by the villages.

"In that case, we will go back," say the guides.

"Good! A safe journey home."

They go off, and we move forward. The brigands do not attack us.

A few hours later we meet a big caravan coming from Lhasa. I begin to understand the robbers' attitude. They are not after us; we are too small game. They have concealed themselves in a cleverly chosen spot to await this caravan that they know to be on the road.

I hail those whom, by their richer costumes, I recognize as the master merchants, and I tell them that in all probability a band of robbers is lying in wait for them.

"Thank you for the information, we will be careful," they answer.

An order is sent to each of the men surrounding the mules, and the caravan continues its way.

I feel more troubled than when we ourselves passed under the eyes of the invisible brigands who were watching us.

It is quite true that the route I have chosen does pass through an inhabited region. Even the first night we put up at a monastery. The day's incidents have tried me a little and I intend to take advantage of the pleasant quarters I have found to rest the next day.

The monastery, though not a large one, is fairly

rich. The tombs of the Grand Lamas are magnificent.

The fact that I am accompanied by soldiers of the Lhasa army seems to react unfavourably upon the cordiality of my relations with my monastic hosts. They are polite, but reserved to the extreme, not to say, " shut in ". I only see subordinates. The principal lama says he is ill and, in this way, excuses himself from receiving me; others offer various pretexts for not seeing me. However, I am allowed to visit the big library. It appears forsaken. The large volumes wrapped in their " robes " are covered with a thick layer of dust, and some of them have been partially eaten by insects or even by rats. Were it not for the wooden boards and the material that keep the leaves bound together, they would fall to pieces. It is a sad sight!

If, as regards religious studies, my halt has lacked interest, on the other hand, it has afforded me the opportunity for observing from close to some curious local types.

Late in the evening, just as I am going to bed, I hear a whisper outside my door, as if I were being called by someone who dared not lift his voice. I open the door : a *trapa* is there with a woman. Both sign to me not to make a noise and come into the room.

The woman, after offering me a scarf and a piece of butter, makes a strange request. Her husband is ill, she wants me to go and see him immediately.

What! at this hour of the night. . . . . I will go to-morrow morning, if the sick man's house is not too far from the *gompa*.

No, I must go at once. The woman insists. It is a question of a wound, a bullet in the thigh. The wounded man has to be taken away to another place.

This all seems very confused.

I question her.

" How did the accident happen to your husband? "

" It was while gathering medicinal plants."

Good. I understand. I am familiar with this euphemism. The man has taken part in a brigand expedition. Was he by chance one of those I had caught sight of yesterday? Exactly, and it is because they had seen me pass by and had learnt that I was stopping at this monastery that the wounded man has now sent for me.

The woman tells me in a few words what happened. The caravan was attacked, the merchants, who were many and on their guard, had defended themselves vigorously. The brigands had had to flee; two of them had been killed and some wounded.

Several of the merchants had also been wounded. Their companions had tied them on to their horses and taken them away.

Now that I know all, the woman counts on me. She is convinced that I have foreign remedies that will make the wound heal quickly. She had not dared to come to me during the day, for fear of the soldiers who accompany me. They must not be told that her husband is hidden in the neighbourhood. They might arrest him. The people of the monastery must not know about it either; the *trapa* who is with her is a friend of her husband's family, he has been able to let her secretly into the monastery, and, in the same way, he will make it possible for me to go out and come in again. A man is waiting for me outside, with a horse; in less than two hours I will be back again; but we must make haste, for the wounded man must be taken to a safe place before morning.

I try to explain that I am not a surgeon and that I do not know how to extract a bullet. The woman will not listen. She cries and continues to beg me to go.

I finally yield to her persuasion, in order to console her, and, also, because I am curious to see at close quarters one of the *jagpas* of the band that I spied in the distance the day before and to know how he is taking his adventure.

By way of "wonderful" foreign medicines, I take some aspirin for deadening the pain; boric acid for washing the wound; a packet of antiseptic cotton-wool and a phial of olive oil for the dressing. Oil has been used for this purpose by all the ancient peoples, and it has always produced excellent results on the wounds of any native I have nursed. As to the bullet . . . Well! it will work its way out by itself or will remain where it is, I cannot help it.

I start out. The night is very dark. I cannot see where they are leading me, but in a very few minutes I am outside, on the road. What co-operation, friendly or due to the fear that brigands inspire, has helped me to leave the monastery? I wonder.

A little farther on, a man holds two horses by their bridles.

"He will lead you," says the woman. "Please mount."

"And you? Are you not coming with us?"

"No I must remain here," she answered, becoming rather embarrassed. Better not to enquire further; here is something that does not concern me.

I get into the saddle. The woman leads my horse slowly forward for a few moments, then takes her hand off the bridle.

"You have only to let your horse follow mine," says the man who is to accompany me, "it knows the way."

This is very fortunate, for I should find it very difficult to guide the beast in the darkness. We have left the road; I feel we are riding on grassy ground. My guide's horse begins to trot gently, mine does the same. Where am I being taken to? Perhaps the distance is not very great, but in the night, this strange ride seems endless.

We arrive at last. At the foot of a hill, I see a group of men, some tethered horses, and a little tent.

The men hail their companion with the words:

"It is all over. The bullet has been extracted."

They help me to dismount, greet me, and thank me for having come.

If "all is over", there is nothing for me to do but to go back.

Certainly not, they all insist that I should see the wounded man, who is lying in the tent. They light a little earthen lamp, the wick of which is stuck into butter, and hold its flickering flame close to the wound. It is enormous and bleeding freely. It seems to me impossible that a bullet received the day before could have caused such a wound. This bullet that has just been extracted. . . . In what way? . . .

"You must know how to go about it," says the would-be surgeon to me. "I have extracted many of them in my life. It is simply a question of knowing where the *tsas*[1] are and of not cutting them. This bullet, here, was right in a fleshy part; I had only to search for it."

He laughs, feeling very proud of himself.

"Thank you, you are very good," says the tortured man, and, looking at me, he repeats: "Thank you, too, Jetsun Kushog. Have you brought some medicines? They will complete my cure. I cannot remain here. They are taking me away."

"Yes, I have brought some," I reply.

The clever surgeon has used his ordinary knife: the one with which he cuts the meat he eats; the cords or leather straps, when he mends his bags or his beasts' harness; or again, the nails of his dirty feet, when they become too long. All talk about antiseptics would be useless.

I wash the wound in unboiled water, with a little boric powder in it. This water, coming straight from the stream, is less likely to be unclean than that which they would boil in the one greasy saucepan that is there, which has the dregs of buttered tea in it.

_____
[1] A word that means at the same time, veins, arteries, and nerves.

I administer a little aspirin, which may relieve the pain; then I leave a packet of cotton wool, another of boric powder, a piece of white cotton material, and the phial of oil. I tell them to keep the wound clean, protected from dust and flies, and free from any accumulation of pus, also to be careful to wash the wound with a very weak solution of boric acid, before dressing it.

The pure air of the country and the Tibetan's robust constitution will do the rest. Before a month has elapsed, he will once more be on horse-back and, probably, taking part in fresh adventures.

They all appear to be very grateful.

"Will you go on gathering medicinal plants?" I ask the wounded man. "You might have been killed, as your two companions have been."

"Oh! yes, that is very true. . . ."

"And your next life? Where do you think you will be reborn, if you do evil?"

"We do not evil," protests one of the other men. "The soldiers have done more of it in the country than we have. We only fire when we are fired on. The Chinese magistrates as well as those of Lhasa show no pity for the poor; these officials force the villagers and the herds-men to give them much more money and many other things than we take from the travelling merchants. We only ask of the rich. . . . We let your caravan pass by, Jetsun Kushog."

Undoubtedly, these gentlemen have shown themselves very courteous in my regard. I have nothing to say in reply. Perhaps I ought to thank them, but I feel I have sufficiently acquitted myself of my indebtedness by tending their friend.

My patient makes a sign to one of his companions, who pulls a scarf out of his *amphag* and offers it to me in token of their respect and gratitude. Something heavy is tied up in one of its corners. The *jagpas* have knotted that end after having placed some silver coins in it. This

INTO THE HEIGHTS

sort of thing is often done in Tibet; no one is offended at
receiving a present of money, and to place it in a scarf is
a polite way of offering it. I have accepted more than
one such gift so as not to displease kind people. But this
one . . . These few little rupees may have been taken,
with many others, out of a traveller's bag. Ought I to
take them? I incline towards a refusal, but just as I am
going to express it, my eyes meet those of the man who
has offered me the scarf. His face is lit up by the little
earthen lamp, which is held by one of his comrades. He
is serious, almost grave, with rather a haughty expression
that is not lacking in dignity . . . in truth, a grand
seigneur.

The refusal of an offering made under the present
circumstances would be in the nature of an insult, and if
the one who rejects it belongs to the Religious Order it
would amount to a curse. I have come to help a wounded
man, not to set myself up as judge. I therefore accept the
scarf and its contents; I shall soon find some poor devil
who will be happy at receiving the money in charity.

The wounded man is about to leave; his companions
have just folded the little tent that sheltered him and
put it on a horse. They now lift him and seat him on
another beast, which carries a thick pad made of many
blankets in place of a saddle. The unfortunate man's legs
rest on a bag. He must be suffering horribly. I ask him
if this be not so.

"Not too greatly," he replies.

One of the men leads his horse by the bridle, the
others get into saddle, and they all go away. The party
disappears almost immediately in the darkness.

The one who came to fetch me takes me back to the
monastery.

The *trapa* and the woman are waiting at the spot where
I left them. I reassure the latter concerning her husband's
condition. He will get well.

A few minutes later, I am in my room.

261

The peasants of this region are more intelligent, more shrewd than those of the other parts of Tibet. The difference of character is probably due to the proximity to China: to frequent intercourse and intermarriage with the Chinese.

At Dolma Lhakhang: a temple dedicated to the goddess Dolma, round which are grouped a few houses, we have to cross the Yangtse, which in this country is called the Dechu. Although, here, it is far from having the width it has near its mouth, in China, it is still very wide. We cross it in leather boats followed by our swimming beasts. The current is strong; the mules regain their feet on the other side at a spot that is far below the place where they have entered it, but nothing untoward happens.

From here the country becomes again desert; we return to the great alpine pasture-lands. On the opposite bank of the river we see a monastery, whose head lama passes for a performer of miracles. He has, we are told, stamped the imprint of his foot on a rock. This kind of miracle seems greatly to please the Tibetans. In many places there are to be seen similar impressions, more or less distinct, which are held to have been made on the rock or on separate stones, by the foot, the hand, or the head of a lama.

We are now on the last stage of our journey in forbidden country. Beyond the farm where we pass the night stretch the vast *chang thangs*, which are only inhabited in some parts, and then solely by the herdsmen of the black tents. Jakyendo is a Chinese outpost in Tibetan land. Between the town and the road I have followed, the frontier is not clearly marked; my escort do not dare to venture farther, for fear of any Mohammedan Chinese soldiers they may encounter. On the contrary, my hosts, who are natives of this region, circulate freely

JAKYENDO, WITH THE MONASTERY ON THE HILL ON THE RIGHT

both sides of this badly defined frontier. They load my luggage on their yaks and we go on.

We have exhausted our provision of butter, and now that we are in the land of herdsmen, the moment seems propitious for laying in a fresh supply. It is difficult for foreigners to imagine the place that butter occupies as food in Tibet. My servants cut themselves great chunks of it, which they hold in their hands and eat as we would a biscuit.

Twice, in passing close to the tents, I send Tobgyal to ask the occupants to sell us some pieces of butter. The herdsmen refuse to do so. The owners of the second tent to which he goes are even inclined to be arrogant: "We have no butter for you," they declare.

We continue our way over an immense grassy table-land. Towards the end of the morning, we again descry a herdsman's encampment, round which a great number of yaks are grazing.

Yongden, who is riding near Sönam and Sezang Thales, says jokingly to them:

"Shame on us, if when passing within sight of such big herds, we cannot procure butter and milk."

The two rascals put their own construction on his words. They gallop off and rejoin us an hour later. We expect to find that they have had the bottle that hangs from Sönam's saddle-bag filled with milk and have managed to buy one or two pieces of butter; instead they are laden with spoil. They have brought back more than twenty pounds of butter, in several big pieces, each sewn in skins; and from their sleeves, the ends of which they hold tightly together so as to form bags, they take out a large quantity of dry cheese. They have carried out a raid.

I question them.

"What did you say to the *dokpas*?"

"I said," Sönam answers triumphantly: "'My chief, who is going by there on the road, has no butter. Let a piece be brought to me from every tent.' And when they did not make haste I lifted my rifle."

I am dumbfounded and want to laugh. The others are delighted and quickly stow the butter and cheese away among the luggage. Then, before I have time to utter a word, the two madmen rush off again, having caught sight of some more tents in another direction.

Upon which, the sky darkens and an unexpected hail-storm breaks loose! My mule begins to rear, bewildered and bruised by the enormous hail-stones. I am blinded. All of a sudden it begins to freeze. My mackintosh, which Yongden has helped me to put on, stiffens on me.

Fortunately we are nearing an encampment. We point it out to the *ulags*, who are behind and who do not appear to have noticed it. They urge on their yaks and, as soon as they have joined us, put them with the mules in the shelter of the tents. All the beasts turn their tails to the wind and the men shelter behind the animals.

Tobgyal hurries me into a tent, demands milk, has it boiled, and gives it to me to drink. Yongden has entered the next tent.

The storm passes quickly, and the weather becomes immediately fine again. I leave my shelter. Where is the Lama?

Tobgyal, who went out before me to get my mule, answers. "He is collecting butter." What?—More butter.

I see Yongden sitting, surrounded by *dokpas*; they are bringing him pieces of butter. He anticipates any remark on my part by an imperative:

"It's serious. Don't say anything," spoken in English.

I say nothing. Having been respectfully saluted by the peasants, we remount our beasts and go on our way.

When out of earshot, I question Yongden.

"What about this butter?"

264

He laughs.

"When I entered the tent," he says, "I asked for some tea and also for a bowl from which to drink it, because mine was in my saddlebag and I could not go out into the rain to get it. The owners of the tent answered me rudely 'There is no cup.' They did not respect me. Their attitude was dangerous; this region is uninhabited, we have luggage, and we must camp to-night. You know the character of these people. Those whom they do not fear, they rob.

"Then I took a tone of command and, stamping my foot, I answered: 'Let a piece of butter be brought from each tent and without delay. Ah! you do not recognize me.'"

"They had never seen you before?"

"That does not matter. Their attitude immediately changed. They brought me their best silver-lined bowl and a piece of butter. Then as soon as it ceased to hail, they went and fetched other pieces from their neighbours. We can camp now, if necessary, they will not dream of attacking us."

Such are the country's customs, they are the same as those of the Koko Nor region.

Sönam and the young scamp do not come back. Have they lost their way in the storm, or have they been severely punished for their audacity? I am beginning to be anxious. Since they left us we have travelled some distance. Will they be able to find us again? We blow our whistles; the wind has dropped, perhaps the sound will reach them. No one answers. It is a long time before the two boys appear.

This time they have carried their effrontery too far. There is more butter and, as they did not know where to put it, they have brought away some good leather bags, and, in addition, a few goatskins, with which to make rugs. The loss of these things will not ruin the *dokpas*, but I think their conduct rather excessive.

265

Besides they have met with resistance. One of the women incited her neighbours to refuse to give them anything. My servants were assailed. They defended themselves, and then had the impudence to pretend to take everyone before the local chief, whose white tent was close to the encampment. After that the assailants began to excuse themselves and make propitiatory offerings to the two rogues, whom the natives took for soldiers. These apologies did not prevent my boys from continuing to play their parts and from going to the chief to levy a contribution. Their imperturbable audacity was completely successful, the chief authorized the levying of a piece of butter from each tent and those who had not already given it were forced to provide it.

Little Sezang Thales beams—a fine specimen of brigand is this young Khampa—and the *ulags* hold their heads high, proud of serving people as "powerful" and "respectable" as we are. As concerns me, thinking over the curious incidents that have marked this day, I am astonished to find that, if my travels have led me to a place to where I had never dreamed of going, it has had the even more unexpected result of making me become the head of a band of robbers. Fortunately my "victims" do not live far from Jakyendo and, since I must remain there for some time, I shall find a discreet way of compensating them for their loss, without lowering myself in their opinion or losing the esteem that my boys' prowess has won for me.

Close to the monastery of Benchin, we find a small house reserved for the use of travellers; instead of camping, we install ourselves there for the night.

Next morning the sun shines brightly, but the air is sharp. While waiting for the *ulags* to finish loading the mules, I stand in the doorway looking at the landscape. My glasses show me a wide stretch of alpine pasture-land, beyond which lie the openings of two immense desert-looking valleys. Touched by the intense light that envelops the whole scene, the grass in them, reddened by the early frosts, glistens as copper.

Another track passes in front of the small rest-house and, running close to a limpid river that sings over a pebbly bed, enters a third valley. This is the one that I am to follow. It, too, lies in sunshine, and the mountains that border it are wrapped in that peculiar atmosphere of mystery, of reticent welcome, of vague menace, which is so fascinating to the traveller in Tibet. What has fate in store for me in this direction?

With a slightly preoccupied mind I take the measures that are usually adopted by foreigners when travelling off the main routes in China. I send Sönam on ahead to present my card to the magistrate residing at Jakyendo, with the request that he will be kind enough to direct me to suitable lodgings.

Meanwhile I ride slowly behind the laden beasts; I am in no hurry to arrive. On our way, we pass before the Tangu monastery, with which, later, I am to become so well acquainted, then finally, Jakyendo emerges from the desert.

Its situation is not lacking in grandeur. The town is built on a rise at the foot of a chain of mountains. Above it, looking down on the laymen's dwellings from a rocky spur, stands a monastery, the buildings of which, decorated with red and white lines, show it as belonging to the Sakyapa sect, while dominating the crest on which the monastery rises, a magnificent background of massive summits bars the distant horizon.

Three *gompas* relatively close to one another: Benchin, Tangu, Jakyendo! Hope lies in the thought! There I shall be almost certain to find a few learned lamas, to be able to collect some valuable information, and to do some interesting work.

Sönam, who has returned to meet us, leads our caravan to the lodgings the Chinese magistrate has had prepared for us. It is a suite of rooms on the first floor of a house situated in the principal street. It should prove an excellent observation post from which to study the local population.

The lateness of the hour permits me to put off all official visits until the next day. I am glad. I long for rest. I need it after these seven months of arduous travel. Night comes, shadows invade my room, and, as I fall asleep, they move on the whitewashed walls, pointing at me with fantastic gestures.

"Sleep," they appear to say, "rest; it will not be for long. Jakyendo is but a halt on thy path. From here start tracks that pierce the distant horizon and lead to far-off regions. Soon, one or other of them will capture thy fancy and will carry thee to fresh adventures."

INDEX

INDEX